www.wadsworth.com

www.wadsworth.com is the World Wide Web site for
Thomson Wadsworth and is your direct source to dozens
of online resources.

At *www.wadsworth.com* you can find out about supple-
ments, demonstration software, and student resources.
You can also send email to many of our authors and pre-
view new publications and exciting new technologies.

www.wadsworth.com
Changing the way the world learns®

From the Wadsworth Series in Communication Studies

SECOND EDITION

Effective Small Group and Team Communication

JUDITH D. HOOVER

Western Kentucky University

THOMSON

WADSWORTH   Australia • Canada • Mexico • Singapore • Spain • United Kingdom • United States

THOMSON
★
™
WADSWORTH

Publisher: Holly J. Allen
Acquisitions Editor: Annie Mitchell
Assistant Editor: Aarti Jayaraman
Editorial Assistant: Trina Enriquez
Senior Technology Project Manager: Jeanette Wiseman
Senior Marketing Manager: Kimberly Russell
Marketing Assistant: Andrew Keay
Advertising Project Manager: Shemika Britt
Project Manager, Editorial Production: Jane Brundage
Art Director: Carolyn Deacy
Print/Media Buyer: Emma Claydon
Permissions Editor: Kiely Sexton
Production Service: Hockett Editorial Service
Text Designer: Adriane Bosworth
Photo Researcher: Linda Sykes

Copy Editor: Sarah Magill Mueller
Cover Designer: Bill Stanton
Cover Images: Images in ovals, top to bottom: Getty
    Images/Lisa Peardon; Getty Images/Ken Fisher; Getty
    Images/Pando Hall; Getty Images/Mark Andersen.
    Background image: Getty Images/Steve Richardson.
Compositor: International Typesetting and Composition
Printer: Webcom, Ltd.
Photo Credits: **1**, Corbis; **21**, **37**, Image provided by
    PhotoDisc © 2002; **54**, Jon Feingersh/Corbis; **71**, Image
    provided by PhotoDisc © 2002; **88**, **106**, Corbis; **126**,
    Image provided by PhotoDisc © 2002; **146**, JFK Library,
    Boston, MA; **163**, **180**, Superstock; **197**, Brownie
    Harris/Corbis.

Printed in Canada
2 3 4 5 6 7 08 07 06 05

For more information about our products, contact us at:
Thomson Learning Academic Resource Center
1-800-423-0563
For permission to use material from this text or product,
submit a request online at
http://www.thomsonrights.com.
Any additional questions about permissions can be
submitted by email to
thomsonrights@thomson.com.

Library of Congress Control Number: 2003117044

ISBN 0-534-63344-7

Thomson Wadsworth
10 Davis Drive
Belmont, CA 94002-3098
USA

Asia
Thomson Learning
5 Shenton Way #01-01
UIC Building
Singapore 068808

Australia/New Zealand
Thomson Learning
102 Dodds Street
Southbank, Victoria 3006
Australia

Canada
Nelson
1120 Birchmount Road
Toronto, Ontario M1K 5G4
Canada

Europe/Middle East/Africa
Thomson Learning
High Holborn House
50/51 Bedford Row
London WC1R 4LR
United Kingdom

Latin America
Thomson Learning
Seneca, 53
Colonia Polanco
11560 Mexico D.F.
Mexico

Spain/Portugal
Paraninfo
Calle Magallanes, 25
28015 Madrid, Spain

Contents

Preface

Small-group studies go back many years in the field of communication, as well as in sociology and psychology. However, the trend toward greater use of business teams with more significant managerial responsibilities has led to increased concern over the quality of these groups' communication practices. Recent calls to look at the messages people send and receive in small groups have resulted in studies of organizational teams as they struggle to work together under the pressures of performance appraisals and bottom lines. In response to these calls, much of the research for this text centered on observations and interviews with members of functioning organizational teams in manufacturing, health care, and the service sector. You will see examples and case studies related especially to an aluminum mill, a hospital consortium, and a number of service-sector organizations. Regardless of their specific roles as nurses, teachers, technical customer-service representatives, or crane operators, all of these employees carry the additional responsibility of communicating effectively with their teammates. Some even take on the tasks of hiring, evaluating, and terminating team members. These management functions require employees at all levels to be good decision makers and problem solvers.

Funding for these employees' activities often results from the presentation of competing team proposals; recognition and financial rewards may come from presentation of team achievements to upper management. These proposals and presentations require employees at all levels to be able to gather and organize data, to prepare visual and verbal messages both to illustrate their findings and persuade their audiences, and to use computer-generated or other technological enhancements in their presentations. As you move through this text, you will find activities designed for the practice of all of these skills.

This book places group communication in the context of teamwork and, therefore, encourages the development of a team spirit in the classroom. Examining the "best practices" of employees in manufacturing, health care, and the service sectors, *Effective Small Group and Team Communication* shows a variety of ways in which individuals communicate effectively within their groups. In this second edition, you will find an enhanced emphasis on virtual teamwork with added materials on leadership, idea-generation strategies, conflict, and ethical considerations in those environments. This edition also features a case study for each chapter accompanied by discussion questions or activities related to each case. Greater emphasis has also been placed on the global nature of teamwork by incorporation of more examples from other cultures besides that of the United States.

Plan for the Book

In Chapter 1 you will be introduced to the concept of teamwork by learning how real people in real organizations, including voluntary community organizations, function on a day-to-day basis. Group membership can provide not only career advancement, but also may satisfy basic human needs for self-esteem or inclusion.

Chapter 2 investigates the importance and complexity of the communication process through a number of useful theories developed over many years in efforts to improve human relationships.

Chapter 3 focuses on the value of diversity among team members, in whom differences need not divide but can strengthen groups. In this chapter we come to understand the ways culture, race, gender, age, status level, ethnicity, and organizational membership affect the ways we see the world and its possibilities.

Chapter 4 explores ways that groups carve out and establish their identities as effective teams within highly complex organizations. A group may choose to be associated because of the members' personal commitments to an issue, a cause, an interest, a need, or an idea.

Chapter 5 describes the internal cognitive processes that help members accomplish their goals. You will study ways of improving the team's level of creative thinking to generate ideas, setting criteria for evaluating ideas, and thinking critically in order to solve problems.

Chapter 6 explains the roles members play in completing tasks or in assuring the group's survival. You can explore a variety of perspectives on decision making and problem solving, as well as concrete planning and implementation strategies.

Chapter 7 explores traditional leadership and power theories and presents a useful "nonstandard" leadership model, created from the best features of effective theoretical leaders.

Chapter 8 takes us through a set of effective meeting practices designed to prevent such fiascoes as are portrayed in *Dilbert* cartoons. Comparison and contrast of face-to-face meetings with so-called virtual meetings reveal their complexities, pitfalls, and potentials.

Chapter 9 provides a realistic look at the obstacles, such as human and organizational barriers and communication failures, that can derail any group's efforts to use teamwork.

Chapter 10 presents methods of managing the conflicts that challenge team members. This chapter also describes some of the benefits of conflict in effective group and teamwork.

Chapter 11 guides you through processes of developing a presentation, whether written, oral, graphic, visual, computer generated, or a combination.

Chapter 12 emphasizes the need for evaluation and urges the use of self-assessment both for individuals and for teams. Several sets of criteria based on members, processes, skills, and communication factors as well as team goals and objectives are suggested.

Features

Career applications   appear at the beginning of each chapter. They are drawn from the literature on teamwork found in communication studies and other fields such as business, psychology, management, and leadership.

Key words and concepts,   useful in helping students focus on the specific vocabulary of small group and team communication, are listed and highlighted in bold in each chapter.

Figures and models   are incorporated to accommodate the differing learning styles of visual and verbal learners. Bulleted lists point out attributes sought in employees, qualities of effective oral team presentations, and effective group communication skills. Both classic and contemporary models of group communication tasks, processes, and skills are provided throughout.

Case studies   have been provided for all chapters and are accompanied by discussion questions or activities.

Collaborative learning activities   accompany each chapter to provide experiences working with others and opportunities to understand a variety of personalities. These activities (and additional activities found in the Instructor's Manual) may be used consecutively to build actual teams in the class, or they may be assigned in any order to accommodate a variety of teaching methods.

Uses for This Textbook

This text is designed primarily for use in undergraduate small group communication courses but also may be relevant in graduate courses in applied organizational communication or applied small group communication. It shows students how to function as group or team members while it provides sufficient theory to explain why groups behave as they do. The book incorporates both ethnographic research and more traditional theoretical underpinnings of small group communication.

Acknowledgments

I would like to thank Dennis Gouran for introducing me to the teaching of small group communication many years ago. His enthusiasm for the work of groups proved contagious. In addition, I must thank the employees I observed and interviewed during the research process for the book, as well as the organizations that let me come in. Thanks also to two graduate assistants, Zheyang Du and Wenli Yuan.

Chapter 1

Teamwork and Its Advantages

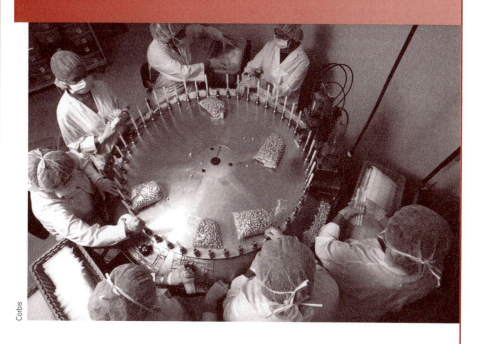

Corbis

The Potential to Satisfy Both Human and Organizational Needs

KEY WORDS AND CONCEPTS

affection needs

brownfield/greenfield teamwork locations

communication competencies

control needs

inclusion needs

kaisen

Maslow's Hierarchy of Needs

motivation

ownership of one's work

pay for skill development

productivity advantages

Schutz's Needs Theory

self-actualization

self-esteem or self-worth

sense of belonging

sense of control

sense of purpose

small group communication

team concept

teamwork

Theories X, Y, and Z

 To find out more about the Key Words and Concepts discussed in this chapter, use InfoTrac College Edition. Type in the keywords and subject terms. You can access InfoTrac College Edition from Wadsworth/Communication homepage: http://communication.wadsworth.com.

CAREER APPLICATION

Management literature suggests that teams succeed if they are well enough trained in these competencies:

GROUP-DYNAMICS SKILLS

- Effective listening: giving and receiving feedback
- Problem finding and problem solving
- Consensus building and decision making
- Conflict management and resolution
- Influencing and negotiating
- Planning and coordinating
- Running effective meetings
- Making informative and persuasive presentations
- Screening and hiring
- Training and coaching
- Performance review and assessment
- Disciplining
- Termination

Stokes, 1994, p. 44

THE TEAM CONCEPT

This is a book about **teamwork.** The concept itself, though far from new, has become increasingly important to business, industry, commerce, finance, banking, health care, education, voluntary associations, and every other organizational form in American society and around the globe. One writer for *Fortune* magazine has called companies that have converted to a teamwork model "adaptive" organizations. They've adapted by "aligning what the corporation wants—innovation, improvement—with what turns people on, namely a chance to use their heads and expand their skills" (Dumaine, 1991, p. 37). When Toyota opened a visitors' center in its first North American manufacturing facility in Georgetown, Kentucky, it featured teamwork as a defining characteristic of the Toyota Production System (Embry, 1994, p. E1).

This is also a book about **small group communication,** which is probably the name of the course in which you have enrolled. We will consider the communication process in greater depth in the next chapter, but for now think of small group communication as "communication in a particular setting among a limited number of people for the purpose of achieving a common objective, primarily directed toward the resolution of a common problem" (Samovar, Henman, and King, 1996, p. 8). Why differentiate between groups and teams? Generally, teams consist of small groups of people who work together, and thus communicate with each other, on a daily basis. However, for any set of people, actually becoming a team requires not just talk but effective use of both verbal and nonverbal communication links. In this text, you will learn the skills necessary to make those links.

A basic understanding of human nature teaches us that people make employment decisions on the basis of a number of factors, the most important of which, perhaps, is salary or wages. However, numerous studies have shown that once a basic level of compensation has been reached, other features of our work life become much more important. These include enjoying the work itself, feeling that the work matters, interacting with pleasant co-workers, being acknowledged as a worthwhile individual, and being treated with respect.

A basic understanding of the American economic system teaches us that business decisions are made on the basis of a number of factors, the most important of which is likely to be profitability. Even in public-service institutions, activities cannot be undertaken if they cost more than they are worth. So the question arises: Why have we turned to a teamwork model in the United States? What does this innovation accomplish for business, service, or manufacturing organizations that older management methods have failed to do? Our efforts in this chapter to understand the advantages of teamwork will be focused on the two basic ideas expressed above. Teamwork holds human benefits to the individuals taking part in the process while it simultaneously provides additional financial advantages for the organization itself.

Although we are all at least familiar with sports teams, either as participants or spectators, we may not all have taken part in business or professional teams. Even so, many college students have worked for companies that claim to advocate a team philosophy. Unfortunately, little teamwork may have occurred there because of the short-term or part-time nature of such jobs. In the same way a street or backyard game of pickup basketball lacks the style and finesse of the championship games among the Final Four, groups made up of uncommitted, "here today, gone tomorrow" employees lack the productivity and success potential of a genuine business team. Likewise, employees who work for companies that talk about teamwork but don't actually practice teamwork will lack the support needed for success. What makes certain volunteer organizations, such as Habitat for Humanity, succeed is that they practice their beliefs, not only by helping their fellow human beings but also in working together as a team with those for whom the homes are built.

What are the differences that matter between a group and a team? Returning to our sports example, think of the resources of money and time required to produce any championship team. Just as universities must devote scholarship funding, coaches' salaries, and physical facilities to their women's and men's athletic programs, so must business and industry provide time and resources for training and practice in the skills needed for teamwork. Although individual athletes must devote their time to practicing a variety of moves, they must also learn to communicate with each other on and off the court or the field in order to achieve excellence as a team. In the same way, individually talented accountants, nurses, teachers, and customer-service representatives must learn and practice the additional skills necessary to make decisions or solve problems. The differences that matter, then, between a mere group and a real team consist of time and resource commitment on the part of both organizations and individuals, communication skill building, and a **sense of belonging,** or being a part of something that works. "What Are the Differences between a Group and a Team?" puts these distinctions into a classroom perspective.

Groups and teams certainly permeate other areas of life besides sports and business. Community service organizations, universities, churches, and even members of Congress divide their tasks and distribute their work by forming into committees. The old adage that "a camel is a horse made by a committee" may be either a positive or a negative comment about the products of committees. Although the shaggy appearance of the camel cannot compare with the sleekness of a stallion, its potential for survival in a desert makes it a much more reliable beast in that environment. Through their combined efforts, groups and teams have taken people to the moon and back, have created constitutions and charters, have chosen Nobel prize and Academy Award winners, and have modified and combined automobile and truck designs to produce today's highly successful sport utility vehicle (Ward, 1994, p. E1).

As the great economic pendulum swings back and forth through time, business organizations seek competitive advantage in first one way and then another. The recent era of downsizing resulted in a variety of management functions being handed down to employees who had not previously done such work. Savings made as a consequence have, in some cases, even resulted in subsequent growth. Some threatened plant closures have been avoided through teamwork initiatives.

WHAT ARE THE DIFFERENCES BETWEEN A GROUP AND A TEAM?

Typical Classroom Group

First Week of Class: The teacher says, "Divide into random groups of five and for the next ten minutes share your experiences with working in groups."

Behavioral Characteristics: The groups probably consist of strangers who will join together for the common purpose of completing this class activity. The members may enjoy the interaction and benefit from learning at least a little about four other classmates. However, they will begin tentatively, wonder what they're supposed to do, and hesitate to say that they've finished the assignment.

A Functioning Classroom Team

Next to Last Week of Class: The teacher says, "Meet with your group for thirty minutes to make final preparations for your oral presentation, answering a question of policy, which will be due at the next class meeting."

Behavioral Characteristics: The members will greet their teammates, arrange their chairs in a circle or around a table, get out their notes, and polish up their agenda for the presentation. They will have worked together for a number of weeks and will have been taught the principles and processes necessary to answer this type of research question. They will have committed themselves to doing their best work for the good of themselves individually and for the good of the team. They will have struggled with their differences, discovered their strengths and weaknesses, and overcome or even benefited from conflict. They are ready for the final performance.

Even without downsizing, the current push toward flexible hours combined with a need to operate businesses and institutions twenty-four hours a day, every day of the year, has led to an urgent need for creative scheduling of hours cooperatively determined by those actually doing the work. Add a strong focus on quality products and services, and the need for employees to talk with each other about their work processes emerges as a high priority. One study of American culture following the terrorist attacks of September 11, 2001, even listed teamwork as a "character strength" alongside such attributes as gratitude, kindness, leadership, and love (Peterson and Seligman, 2003). Team skills are considered increasingly important, of course, in other parts of the world besides the United States. In Malaysia, for example, children between the ages of seven and thirteen are offered camp experiences in which teamwork, leadership, and especially "sharing, trusting and co-operation" are emphasized ("Children Learn. . . ", 2003).

The medical profession has long featured treatment teams, but it is now placing a new emphasis on improving both the work and the usefulness of teams. At a major university hospital in Chicago, team membership is not only expected, but nurses, for example, must be "excellent in teamwork as well as excellent in clinical practice" (Hospital Consortium Presentation, 1994). Mental health literature features examples of psychiatric treatment teams, often seeking the meaning of "teamness—the key set of intangible phenomena that allow a team to function synergistically as more than the sum of its parts, and with a sense of team identity" (Yank et al., 1992, p. 250). In northern Israel, efforts have even been under way to utilize the "coexistence" within joint Jewish and Arab medical teams to attempt to strengthen the "Jewish-Arab bond and commitment for peace in the region" (Desivilya, 1998, p. 429).

If employees are going to manage, to schedule, and to improve processes, if medical professionals are going to care for both patients and procedures, what additional skills will they need? They'll need those **competencies** typically found in a college course in small group communication: information gathering and processing, reasoning, agenda setting, discussion techniques that lead to sound decisions, problem solving, assessment of their own decisions and solutions, conflict management, and presentation of data to an audience. Indeed, George David, president and CEO of United Technologies, Inc., says that because we have traditionally learned as individuals, we have entered the workforce prepared only to work as individuals. However, from his perspective, employees will be expected to work in teams, and therefore students need to improve their "relationship" skills—"team building and team participation" (Stinson, 1995, p. 56). An article in *Computerworld* asserts that "[i]nformation systems (IS) managers with teamwork experience have a valuable job skill that should be emphasized

---

EMPLOYEE ATTRIBUTES WE'RE LOOKING FOR*

- Team Influence: Ability to persuade others and facilitate the group process
- Teamwork: Sensitivity to the needs of others and their levels of participation, listening
- Problem Solving: Quality of ideas, anticipated outcomes of alternatives, creativity
- Communication Abilities: Verbal and nonverbal skills, clarity, ability to have conversations with others and build their trust

*Employment criteria obtained from various research sites whose locations will remain unidentified here because of the proprietary nature of the information.

EMPLOYMENT SELECTION CRITERIA*

- General Aptitude
- Interpersonal Skills
- Flexibility
- Desire to Learn
- Problem Solving Skills
- Physical Ability

*Employment criteria obtained from various research sites whose locations will remain unidentified here because of the proprietary nature of the information.

---

when seeking new positions"; these skills include "interpersonal communication, leadership, and management of groups and projects" and "the ability to work closely with users and customers" (Panepinto, 1994, p. 119). Still further afield, recent agricultural engineering graduates are advised in three of the "nine keys to getting hired," to "be a team player," to "sharpen your communication skills," and to join "that uncommon but essential combination of independent thinkers and leaders who work well in a team setting" (Rider, 1999, pp. 23–24.)

A variety of trade and professional journals along with those published by academic disciplines describe the teamwork qualities needed by applicants in today's job market. In the service sector, for instance, one employer seeks those who "treat . . . others with respect—not just customers but fellow employees, too" (Hall, 2002, p. 10). In engineering, teamwork tops the list of "what companies want from graduating seniors," ahead of oral and written communication and even ahead of technical ability (Rorrer, 2003, p. 50). According to a recent article in the *Journal of Marketing Education*, employers "increasingly value general qualities, such as effective communication, presentation, and teamwork skills . . . rather than specific knowledge of the marketing function" (Taylor, 2003, p. 97). "Employee Attributes We're Looking For," "Employment Selection Criteria," and "Personal Characteristics Assessed for Employment" illustrate the personal skills required for employment in three typical teamwork environments. You will note a high level of agreement among these three companies about what they want in their employees. How do you fit into the scheme?

INDIVIDUAL ADVANTAGES OF TEAMWORK

What do employees gain from working in a team environment? They seem to be expected to know more and to do more, so there must be some sort of reward for that investment of time and energy. Personal advantages may be categorized

PERSONAL CHARACTERISTICS ASSESSED FOR EMPLOYMENT*

- Organization and Planning: Ability to determine what needs to be done by the group to coordinate the group's effort to accomplish a goal
- Problem Analysis: Ability to seek out important information about a problem and to figure out its causes and solutions
- Decision Making: Ability to make quality decisions for the group based on logical assumptions that reflect factual information, that is, sound judgment
- Decisiveness: Willingness to make decisions, render judgments, or take a stand
- Tolerance for Stress: Exhibits stability of performance under pressure, opposition, disappointments, and/or rejections
- Human Relations: Friendly, warm, and responsive to others; willingness to praise others for their positive efforts and ideas; willingness, when appropriate, to express one's agreement with and acceptance of the contributions of others
- Oral Communication: Ability to get one's ideas across to others so that they understand what is being said
- Persuasiveness: Ability to sell one's ideas to others
- Social Sensitivity: Ability to understand and react sensitively to the needs of others in a group
- Integrity: Playing according to the rules
- Leadership: Willingness and ability to direct a group's efforts in a participative, nondomineering manner
- Energy: Maintaining a steady and high activity level during group exercises
- Flexibility: Ability to change one's approach to problems or people when the situation requires it
- Tenacity: Ability to stick with one's position or plan of action until the desired objective is achieved or until it's no longer reasonable to do so

*Employment criteria obtained from various research sites whose locations will remain unidentified here because of the proprietary nature of the information.

into four groups: an increased sense of belonging, gains in **control** or **owner- ship of one's work,** improved **self-worth,** and tangible rewards.

Belonging

The sheer volume of information available and work to do sometimes seems to overwhelm us all. However, knowing that your team exists to share that work- load, that someone will "pitch in" when necessary, provides a measure of relief. A prime example of the importance of sharing both responsibility and expertise in decision making can certainly be understood in the health-care profession in which life-and-death decisions are daily occurrences. A unique type of team, composed of "a physician, nurse, social worker, occupational therapist, and physical therapist" that practices "arena assessment" of frail older adults, for instance, must confront not only ethical questions but also must make "place- ment decisions and end-of-life planning" decisions that are better handled "with the collective wisdom of the team." Making such decisions with other professionals may even be a "transformative experience" by allowing cross- disciplinary learning to take place (Coppola et al., 2002, pp. 14, 25).

Companies with dispirited or "alienated" employees sometimes imple- ment teamwork to solve morale problems ("High-Performance Workplace," 1994). Those that succeed in improving job satisfaction claim that the "fuel that makes [it] work is the team spirit" ("People Power. . .", 1987, p. 18; "Teamwork Enhances. . .", 1993; Stayer, 1990; Spiro, 1956). The "camaraderie" that comes with teamwork is often given credit for helping employees believe that their work is "fulfilling" and for making believable the concept of "one for all and all for one" ("Fueling Productivity. . . ", 2003, p. 12).

Control

Ownership of their work comes to team members in many forms, one of which typically relates to the removal of layers of organizational control between themselves and "the top." A recent publication from the Work in America Insti- tute put the issue this way: "When you make your own decisions, you come to work in a different type of attitude than when you don't. Nobody likes being told what to do—that's being a kid" (Friedman and Casner-Lotto, 2002). Re- moval of structure often leads to less formality and a more relaxed atmosphere. "An Example of Job Ownership" captures the essence of this sense of control.

An Example of Job Ownership

"You manage your own time. I like making my own decisions, working within the guidelines of the corporation and the budget, but still, you've got x amount of dollars to spend, and you decide how you are gonna spend them. It's nice to be able to look at the whole picture and make an informed decision rather than have someone hand you down a decision that you may not agree with." — Hospital Group Employee Interviews, 1994.

Self-Worth

In the management literature and among those I observed and interviewed for this book, the most frequently mentioned individual benefit of teamwork is the opportunity it affords for enhancement of personal self-worth. A union official spoke of the advantages to people who for years had been told to "leave their brains at home" while they worked because no one wanted to know what they thought. He also saw those same people grow from the opportunity to stand before a management group and take part in a presentation about their team's goals for the coming year. One of those formerly silent persons said, "I feel like they're using me for something besides my hands." "Teamwork's Multiple Advantages" illustrates a number of individual benefits derived from one person's perspective in the health-care field.

Teamwork's Multiple Advantages

"When we learned that it wasn't a competition, that somebody wouldn't be the boss and everybody else would be the followers, it was a team. It was a group effort; all decisions were made together. Everybody in the group was equal. You weren't looked down upon because you didn't have a certain degree. Each person brought her own expertise into the group." — Hospital Group Employee Interviews, 1994.

The teamwork environment also gives members opportunities for learning, which always enhances **self-esteem.** Through role rotation, through training in decision making and problem solving, through personal and team goal setting and accomplishment, through controlling a budget, people uncover their hidden sources of strength, their creative potential, and their previously unrecognized skills. In addition, in many places they are given tangible rewards by being **paid for skill development** needed to rotate management functions.

In terms of individual student benefits of learning to work in a team, advantages would include practice in the more daunting skills of "persistence when facing adversity [and] willingness to perform difficult tasks." Additionally, however, students gain the "ability to translate knowledge from one task to another, greater social skills, and intrinsic motivation." Fortunately, according to writers in the field of education, "cooperation is related to indicators of mental health, including high self-esteem" (Johnson, Johnson, and Smith, 1998).

Needs Theories

In these examples, we see practical implications of theoretical perspectives long thought to be useful in psychology, sociology, and communication studies. The universal question, of course, is "Why?" Why do people work? Why do they strive? Many studies of human motivation have found that beyond financial gain, people work to have a **sense of purpose** and to take pleasure from their activities. Several theorists have developed category systems based on human needs. We will look at two of these sets of categories and then at a very early teamwork application of needs theory.

Maslow's Hierarchy of Needs   Abraham Maslow (1954, pp. 80–92) conceived of human needs not as a simple or random list but as a hierarchy, that is, as a set of needs arranged from a lower to a higher order that could only be achieved in a particular sequence. Once our lower-level physiological needs for food, air, or water, for example, are met, Maslow argued, then we could move up to the next level of safety needs. Once we satisfy ourselves that we are, indeed, safe from harm, we can move up to the level of social needs for belonging or acceptance. After that need is met, we can seek esteem, or recognition and status. The highest level, **self-actualization,** or reaching one's potential, can only be sought and achieved, according to Maslow's theory, after all lower-level needs are satisfied. Figure 1.1 illustrates Maslow's hierarchy.

Although Maslow's theory was not inherently pessimistic, he predicted that few individuals would be found at the level of self-actualization. A little description of the time in which he wrote may give us some cause for hope. During most of the world's history, few of the many people alive were able to put aside their cares about survival long enough to learn enough to become self-actualized. Even in the United States in the 1950s, restrictions, both formally legal and informally social, prevented women and members of minority groups, as well as persons from lower economic levels, from achieving economic equality,

FIGURE 1.1   MASLOW'S HIERARCHY OF NEEDS

Self-Actualization
Full Utilization
of Your Potential

Esteem Needs Satisfaction
Recognition or
Status Achievement

Social Needs Satisfaction
Love, Belonging, Acceptance

Safety Needs Satisfaction
Freedom From Fear of Physical Harm

Physiological Needs Satisfaction
Enough Food, Water, Air, Etc. to Sustain Life

Maslow, 1954, pp. 80–92.

much less social prominence, with the middle-class establishment. Most aspects of life were hierarchically arranged, that is from a lower to a higher order, and regardless of the folklore about the "land of opportunity" and the ability to "pull yourself up by your own bootstraps," climbing the social pyramid was difficult.

Although we have not reached utopia yet, many more opportunities are available today for those who wish to strive for self-actualization. The lucky child born into a family that satisfies physiological, safety, belonging, and esteem needs can "go to the head of the hierarchy" by means of school success, creative genius, or sports talent. The lucky employee working for an organization that values and empowers its human resources can, as we have seen, satisfy some achievement needs in the workplace.

How does Maslow's needs hierarchy apply to college students? Although we might hope and expect that students have conquered the lower-level needs and are working toward self-actualization, everyday life interrupts progress sometimes. For instance, try as you might to listen to a lecture in the early

---

CASE STUDY   **PUTTING MASLOW'S THEORY TO WORK**

*R*obert Ardrey, who has written at length about the origin and progress of the "human animal," provides an early application of needs theory to the workplace. In his book *The Social Contract* (1970, 181–86), Ardrey tells the story of Willem James, operator of a refinery in the Netherlands, who decided to try out Maslow's theories on his employees. James intervened at the esteem needs level by giving the employees, either individually or in groups, work problems to solve. Authorizing them to solve real problems indicated a level of trust that they had not previously enjoyed. Not only did morale improve but productivity also increased. Management theorists have utilized this example, as well as others occurring since then, to justify the high costs of training employees in problem solving.

Discussion Questions for Case Study

1. How could schools (use your own experience in elementary/middle/high school) tap into students' esteem needs to make those schools more "humane"?

2. What sort of training might students need to accomplish such problem solving?

3. What individual benefits might students gain from this teamwork activity?

4. What organizational benefits might the schools gain?

5. What are the ethical considerations in such a project?

morning, lack of sleep (physiological need level) could cause your listening ability to suffer. Scheduling classes from early morning right through midafternoon similarly could allow hunger to interfere with the learning process. Weather anomalies such as snowstorms or hurricanes bring your safety into question. Belonging needs may also rise to the top of your priorities if you have left home and friends for the first time; you may spend a good deal of energy reestablishing connections. Esteem may decline for some who have been local success stories but now feel unable to compete academically with their college peers. Nontraditional students may find themselves wondering who they are in their new environments. The case study on page 12 illustrates one way Maslow's theory has been used in the business world.

Schutz's Needs Theory   William Schutz (1966, pp. 18–25) developed a classification of needs that are comparable to Maslow's social needs category. He offered three: **inclusion, affection,** and **control.** Inclusion needs certainly can be satisfied by membership in a team. Although team members might not call what they experience affection, they do sometimes "bond" into a cohesive group held together by esteem and respect. We have seen how teamwork in some instances offers a greater degree of control over one's work life. "Schutz's Needs Theory" illustrates his categories.

What advantages await students who work in a classroom team? Certainly students have had both good and bad group experiences throughout their years in school and in their part-time and summer jobs. Nontraditional students may even have worked in team environments as part of their careers. But students can still gain a great deal.

Much of what is called group work lacks the purpose and structure found in a communication class, not to mention the skill building sure to take place. Students have the chance to see where their strengths fit the group's needs best. They may also isolate the competencies they need to strengthen with the help of their teammates and instructor. The human needs for inclusion, self-esteem, and control of the learning process can be met by working in a classroom team.

SCHUTZ'S NEEDS THEORY

Inclusion: Satisfactory sense of belonging

Affection: Sense of being loved or satisfactorily in contact with others

Control: Able to determine one's own actions and exert influence over others

Adapted from Schutz, 1966, pp. 18–25.

ORGANIZATIONAL ADVANTAGES OF TEAMWORK

Although exceptions certainly exist, two general conditions characterize teamwork sites. So-called **greenfield** locations have been built from the ground up as team-managed organizations. **Brownfield** sites have existed since long before the corporate team concept developed and thus have been reorganized or "retro-fitted" for teamwork. Some have employed both unionized and nonunionized workforces, and others have never been unionized. Still others have a combination of such labor-management relationship types.

As one would assume, it is far easier to begin with teamwork than to impose it on an existing organization. Potential employees, whether for hourly, salaried, or management positions, can be screened, tested, and hired on the basis of their attitudes and communication skills needed in working with others. Management personnel will understand what is expected of team leaders or facilitators.

In traditional organizations, top-down structures and practices must be changed to enable teams to take on both authority and responsibility. Managers who are accustomed to being the boss and who have never actually sought the input of so-called lower-level employees will face problems of adjustment. Yet the very features of teamwork—widely distributed input, authority, and responsibility—are among the keys to the corporate advantages of teamwork. Actual advantages come in three forms: products, processes, and personnel.

Productivity Advantages

One of the benefits of teamwork most commonly mentioned in management literature is increased productivity, or the amount of output per hour of work. At a garment factory in California, for example, the change from pay by "individual piece rate" to pay by "group piece rate" increased "worker productivity by 14 percent on average" (Hamilton, Nickerson, and Owan, 2003, p. 465). Productivity can come in the form of cardiac rehabilitation instruction for hospital patients; the number of calls received, orders processed, or technical services provided to mail-order customers; or tons of aluminum produced. It can, of course, also include the number of hamburgers fried, fast-food customers served at the drive-up window, or swimming pools installed. Regardless of what we call the outcome of our work, all of it can be categorized as productivity.

Productivity is a component of profitability, as are cost saving, waste reduction, and quality improvement—also frequently mentioned as teamwork advantages. For example, a team of hourly workers at a General Electric plant in Alabama "met daily for three months and spent about $10,000. When they were done, 37 percent of the waste was gone" (Stewart, 1991, p. 41). In the accounts payable department of a hospital group in Kentucky, "teamwork saved $25,000 a year by cutting out overtime and temporary help. It also lowered the weekly number of unprocessed invoices by 68 percent" (Song, 1994, p. 10B).

The Japanese concept of continuous improvement, or *kaisen,* "can flourish [among] self-directed teams that harness and concentrate the energies of the individual members" (Stokes, 1994, p. 41).

Process Advantages

Profitability is also dependent on efficient and effective processes for getting work accomplished, and teamwork offers improvements there as well. Indeed, according to small group theory, "the more people participate in decision making through having influence, interacting, and sharing information, the more likely they are to invest in the outcomes of those decisions and to offer ideas for new and improved ways of working" (Burningham and West, 1995, p. 107). In such diverse settings as banking and high-tech information systems organizations, teams are encouraged to collaborate across departments and divisions in order to help improve their organizations' processes overall (Nelson, 2002; D'Antoni, 2002). Teams are "a powerful form of work design for solving work problems" (Pearson, 1991, p. 519). "Time Saving through Problem Ownership" provides an example of one such solution.

Time Saving Through Problem Ownership

"Learning about finances helped us understand. If we went back to the old way, we would fail. Problem solving took so much money. Instead of reporting a problem to the foreman, who reported it to the unit manager, who reported it to the manager of shop operations who reported it to the plant manager, we can meet as a team and solve it ourselves because it is our problem." — Interview with a team coordinator

Although business problems may not be as dramatic as NASA's problems depicted in films such as *Apollo 13,* corporations often send executives to NASA facilities to learn how "teamwork overcomes adversity and to take that back to their companies" ("Project Managers. . .", 1994). Teamwork also improves cooperation, coordination of efforts, and integration of processes typically by communicating needed information up, down, and across the organization ("People Power. . .", 1987, p. 20). Teams also help break down "institutional barriers" that hinder process improvement by "forcing [employees] to become knowledgeable about other areas" of the organization. Additionally, by "pooling . . . employees' knowledge, insights, and skills," organizations can succeed more effectively in "anticipating and adjusting to a . . . changing environment" (Webb, 1988, p. 50).

Personnel Advantages

Teamwork benefits the organization by enhancing its employees' motivation, responsibility, commitment, knowledge base, and morale.

THEORIES ABOUT HUMAN NATURE AND WORK

Theory X: People are not interested in work, do not want to work, and must be made to work by force or reward. They cannot be trusted with responsibility or authority without being carefully monitored.

Theory Y: People work as naturally as they play. If they are challenged by interesting and rewarding work, they will perform well without constant monitoring.

Theory Z: Also referred to as Japanese management, the theory assumes that work comes naturally to people who also want stability of employment and a harmonious community environment for their work life.

Theories X and Y adapted from McGregor, 1960; Theory Z adapted from Ouchi, 1981.

Motivation, Responsibility, and Commitment   Once we move away from the idea, represented by **Theory X** (McGregor, 1960), that people are not to be trusted, that they will not work unless they are forced to do so, and that they must be "motivated" by threats and fear, what do we have left? Teamwork provides **motivation** through its philosophy that people will be self-motivating if they are both valued and rewarded for their knowledge and skills. "Theories about Human Nature and Work" illustrates various ideas about what motivates people to labor.

In a team, motivation also comes from mutual responsibility, or interdependence. "Motivation through Interdependence" illustrates how this happens in a manufacturing environment.

Motivation Through Interdependence

When asked about changes he had seen in four years during which his place of employment replaced an old-style, top-down workplace with a teamwork environment, one team facilitator had this to say:

"When I started, the people on the line saw their jobs only in terms of completing a specific job, like putting this screw in this hole, whether there was a hole there, whether it was in the right place, whether they had the right screw, or not. At the end of the day, that's all they cared about. Now each person is responsible for the success of the line and sees the whole process necessary to accomplish that success." — Interview from research site

---

Among those who live in Israel's kibbutz system, such motivation becomes more than a work-related value; it becomes a philosophical way of life. "Interdependence as a Whole Way of Life" describes that culture of teamwork.

Interdependence as a Whole Way of Life

Although the desire of the average [member] to work in the kibbutz economy is explicable in terms of the security this economy offers him, this ego function does not suffice as an explanation for the devotion, zeal, and responsibility which he displays in his work. The latter can be explained only in terms of that superego function which the kibbutz terms, hakkara. *This term, literally, may be defined as "consciousness"; but* hakkara *connotes more than consciousness, as that term is generally understood. This is an ethical-ideological concept, connoting a conscious awareness of one's moral responsibilities to the kibbutz. . . . His work is not supervised by any supervisor, foreman, or overseer; he punches no clock when he comes to work or when he leaves, and there is no one to check on his punctuality or his efficiency. . . . He may work alone . . . , or he may work with a work-detail; but in either case he does not leave his task until the lunch hour. . . . His job, performed with* hakkara, *becomes more than a job and more than a way of making a living. It becomes a sacred task, a calling . . . dedicated . . . to the welfare of his group. . . . In the kibbutz, a mistake by one person will not only cause him to suffer, but will bring suffering to the entire group. The survival of a culture depends, ultimately, upon the motivational system of the members of its society.* — Spiro, 1956, pp. 88–89, 250.

At a hospital group in Kentucky, team members refer to a "shared sense of duty" whereby others will "pitch in" and help if needed "instead of 'looking busy' as they might have before" (Song, 1994, p. 10B). At Saturn, they speak of "commitment" that comes through consensus decision making whereby team members are "directly involved in the process" (Lewandowski and O'Toole, 1990). The sense of "community" fostered by teamwork in public schools is said to reduce absenteeism, promote greater enthusiasm among staff members, and result in less "class-cutting" and more "engage[ment] with academics" among students (Shields, 1999, p. 9).

Knowledge   In terms of the untapped knowledge potential of team members, we start with the basic premise that those performing tasks understand those tasks far better than those not performing them, even though those others might be "the boss." Thus in a teamwork environment, these so-called "front line employees" are encouraged to "question decisions or suggestions, even though they might originate with upper management" (Steel, 1994). Those completing organizational processes are best able to "find ways of operating more efficiently and effectively" ("People Power. . .", 1987, p. 20; "High-Performance. . .", 1994; "Employees Make Success Story. . .", 1994).

In the past these employees received very little business information, except for what they needed to do their individual jobs. At a manufacturing plant in Danville, Kentucky, the plant manager explained that the lack of information was perhaps a response to an "adversarial" relationship between union and management. Now that the team concept has brought a change in that relationship, he freely shares information once considered "proprietary" or secret because "now it's just information" (Plant Manager Interview, 1994). As a result of having access to more information, employees can gain a "better understanding of organizational objectives" and an increased "appreciation for the difficulties encountered in managing any complex organization" (Webb, 1988, p. 50). This increased sense of being a vital part of the organization improves morale and reduces turnover, "thus saving the immense time and expense involved in hiring and training new people" ("Teamwork Enhances. . .", 1993, p. 1).

ETHICS AND ADVANTAGES OF TEAMWORK

We shall consider ethics in a number of places throughout this book, but the issue of who or what benefits from a cultural practice such as teamwork requires an exploration here. The health-care field provides excellent examples of benefits not only to employees and organizations but potential benefits to clients or patients as well. Much time is spent today developing "holistic treatment plans for all patients," and these plans sometimes involve the ability to "think, problem-solve and understand key multi-professional issues within the scope of [one's] own professional practice." Without collaboration, "fragmented care can result," and "team members from different disciplines may actually work at odds with each other." Unfortunately, "dominance by any one profession" and "tribalism" that occurs when one group of practitioners becomes "over-protective of their roles and responsibilities" can destroy collaboration. Customary practices in medicine, and especially the elevation of the doctor role, "tend . . . to oppress other professional disciplines" (Webster, 2002, pp. 15–18). Still, because "no one person can think of everything" (Zinn, 2002, p. 57), as we mentioned earlier, a respect for others and their expertise, though different from your own, is essential to teamwork.

The arena assessment process described earlier is one method of avoiding these problems of hierarchy and status differences. Because each member of the team—doctor, nurse, physical and occupational therapists, and social worker—is present as the others interact with the patient, the analysis engaged in by the whole team can be more comprehensive than any analysis completed by one member alone. Each can see the patient through the perspectives of the others, and each can see how necessary those other perspectives are to the diagnosis and subsequent development of the patient's treatment plan. Indeed, as an assessment team at the University of North Carolina at Chapel Hill notes, "It is not unusual to find that the initial problem presented is not the underlying one." Instead, more important and often contradictory issues are often uncovered through the combined expertise of the team members as they work their way through the data they have gathered (Coppola et al., 2002, p. 22).

CONCLUSION

To say that you will gain from a course in proportion to whatever you put into it is, of course, a cliché. The overuse of this notion reveals its truth, however, and its truth is nowhere more apparent than in a course that teaches teamwork. As you saw earlier, the group that decides to play any sort of game with no training, no practice, no facilities, no rewards, and no commitment of time and effort beyond the moment will never become a team. Student groups may bond into fully functioning teams that any employer would benefit from hiring. However, groups may also fail to achieve because they let one or two members either do all of the work or do none of the work or because they do not arrive at a common vision or goal for themselves. Using the information found in this book, you will find effective ways to work around the scheduling conflicts, personality clashes, and working-style differences that may require more than simple perseverance. "Behavioral Necessities for Successful Teamwork" lists the team-member attributes necessary for teams to be successful.

The guiding philosophy of this textbook places the highest value on you, the student. The teamwork emphasis in American business and industry values individuals by handing over more power to nonexecutive level employees than ever before. In the same way, the teamwork emphasis in this text hands over more control of the learning process to students than is typically found in a lecture course. Research studies on stress in the workplace have shown that those with the greatest sense of control over their work lives enjoy the lowest levels of stress on the job. This same result can occur in an interactive classroom.

BEHAVIORAL NECESSITIES FOR SUCCESSFUL TEAMWORK

- Attendance and punctuality
- Agenda access and construction by all members
- Respect, equality, civility
- Shared responsibility for leadership and followership
- Adherence to time limits and requirements
- Good sense of humor
- Reasonableness

Indeed, the goal of this textbook is to pass on the wisdom of members of the American workforce who have experienced teamwork on good days and bad days and have learned how to work effectively in teams.

GETTING TO KNOW YOU ACTIVITY

First day   Find an unfamiliar person to talk with for ten minutes. Gather data about the person to present to the class. As people introduce their partners, the audience notes similarities and differences and makes informal charts of first names. After each two have been introduced, the class says their names aloud. By the end of the first class period, all have a little knowledge about each member and all the names listed.

Be sure to return to the same seat for the second class period. On that day go over your names and try to remember them without looking at your chart. (For classes larger than thirty members, break out into groups of twenty-five to thirty and adapt this exercise to your needs. The purpose of the exercise is to allow class members to start the process of getting to know a reasonable number of individuals.)

COLLABORATIVE LEARNING ACTIVITIES

1. Through a show of hands, determine who has been a member of a team, either a sports team, a work team, a project team, or any other example. Distribute those persons through a randomly assigned number of groups consisting of all class members. The groups then interview these individuals to gather data on their experiences in teams. The groups then decide how to present their data to the class and make those presentations. A volunteer can record the experiences on the board in terms of categories determined in advance by the class, such as types of team memberships, types of organizations exhibiting teamwork, and personally rewarding or detrimental experiences.

2. Divide into four randomly selected groups, each of which develops one scenario to illustrate the concept of motivation in environments representing Theory X, Y, or Z, or a teamwork model. Present your scenario to the class. Be sure each member of your group has a speaking part in this exercise.

Chapter 2

Teamwork and Communication

Image provided by PhotoDisc © 2002

Verbal and Nonverbal Speaking, Listening, and Responding

KEY WORDS AND CONCEPTS

communication

communication contexts

communicative competence

communicative performance

confirmation v. disconfirmation

creation of shared meanings

defensive v. supportive
communication climate

dialogue v. monologue

empathy

eye contact

feedback

ideal speech situation

listening skills

message purposes

message sequences

message variables

noise

nonverbal communication
systems

one-way v. two-way
communication

partial v. whole messages

responsive communication

silence

speech acts

systems perspective

 To find out more about the Key Words and Concepts discussed in this chapter, use InfoTrac College Edition. Type in the keywords and subject terms. You can access InfoTrac College Edition from Wadsworth/Communication homepage: http://communication.wadsworth.com.

CAREER APPLICATION

As a pre-employment test one company puts potential employees in a simulated team situation and looks for these communication skills. Could the person be understood?

- Did the person need to repeat what had been said?
- Did the person speak too quietly?
- Did the person speak too quickly?
- Did others indicate that they failed to grasp what the person said?

Data from research site.

THE COMMUNICATION PROCESS

In this chapter we explore ways **communication** can be employed on behalf of effective group work or teamwork. For our purposes here we define communication as a process of **creating shared meanings** in order to bring people and ideas together. If we look to the Latin roots of this word, we find that communication provides a way of making common that which was separate. You have come into this class as separate individuals. In due course, through communication theory and group discussion practice, you may try to build successful decision-making and problem-solving teams. Successful teams do not consist of interchangeable machine parts; rather, they consist of diverse individuals who develop common goals and work together to achieve them.

The word *communication* has taken on an enormous range of meanings over the course of human history. According to early speech models, it simply seemed to refer to an orator speaking in public to an audience. Even in later telecommunications or media communication models, it indicated a speaker, this time in the person of, say, Dan Rather delivering the news via the broadcast medium to an audience watching television. Such communication, though accompanied perhaps by jeers or applause, or by Nielson ratings, still focused on messages that flowed largely in one direction. Some forms of organizational communication still seem to be **one-way**, as shown in Figure 2.1. However, effective communication, regardless of its setting, is a highly complex **two-way** process.

Figure 2.2 illustrates communication's complexity as just two individuals talk together about their plans for a project. Note the differences in the fields of experience of the two persons. One may have participated in school fundraising activities for many years while the other may be quite new to the process. Thus, one can speak with **communicative competence** about the issues involved by drawing on a background of knowledge the other lacks. The person with little experience may also be fearful of revealing a lack of competence and may stumble, use inappropriate terminology, or otherwise exhibit poor **communicative performance** as a result. Both persons listen and watch for cues as to the other's meanings and use their observations as a basis for further communication. This process of building your own messages on those you receive from others is referred to as the feedback loop in this systems model of communication (Von Bertalanffy, 1968).

FIGURE 2.1	**ONE-WAY MODEL OF COMMUNICATION PROCESS**

Sender → Message → Channel → Receiver

Example:
CEO's memo transmitted by e-mail to middle managers

Adapted from Berlo, 1960.

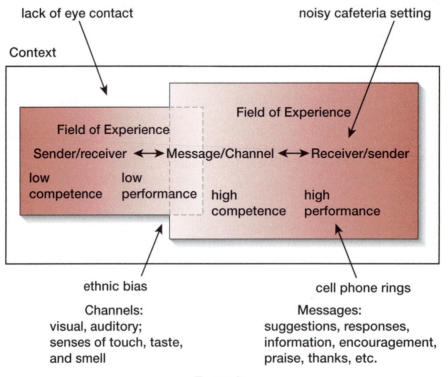

Adapted from Schramm, 1954; Berlo, 1960; Von Bertalanffy, 1968.

Two other features of Figure 2.2 bear explanation. **Context**, or the setting for the communication, may be thought of in many ways. The social context concerns status differences among the individuals; the psychological context, closely related sometimes to the social context, reflects the level of comfort each feels in the encounter. Physical context can certainly be controlled to match the communicative purposes; two people would not choose to meet for private conversation in a large room, for example, if they had access to a smaller, more intimate space. Temporal context, or timing of the event, could affect its outcome, depending on the topics under consideration and whether those involved consider themselves "night people" or "morning people." The arrows pointing inward, labeled **noise** in some models, represent any number of factors that can interfere with a communication event. These interfering features may be contextual, personal, or both, as you can see from the examples given in Figure 2.2.

FIGURE 2.3   **GROUP/TEAM MODEL OF COMMUNICATION PROCESS**

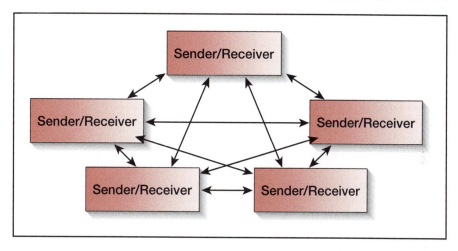

Example:
A work team decides to order in pizza while they discuss
how best to solve a work-related problem.
Messages flow among all members.

Adapted from Schramm, 1954; Berlo, 1960; Von Bertalanffy, 1968.

In a teamwork environment, communication necessarily flows in multiple directions with unforeseen and interwoven consequences. Figure 2.3 illustrates the enormous differences between simple one-way communication and group or team communication. If we can imagine adding in the interferences, related both to the context and to the five persons, all of whom function as senders and receivers, and if we add in the personal qualities of experience, competence, and performance levels of each, we see clearly the complex nature of the group communication process.

Communication today, even in speaker-audience contexts, is recognized as at least two-way in nature. As a process, then, what does it accomplish? When I first began my studies of communication, one of my teachers said that communication was the very center of life, that through communication we created everything else. Although I did not understand that broad claim at the time, subsequent experience has shown me that he was right. We create the cultures we live in, whether in the family, work organization, region, or nation, through talk. As we talk about our jobs or our schools, we shape them into the realities we describe. Communication is a constructive activity. Conversely, it may become a destructive process, as well.

THEORETICAL PERSPECTIVES

Thinkers ranging from philosophers to small group researchers have pondered the question of why some groups succeed while others fail. As we shall see, much depends on the quality of the communication practices of the group. We will consider the work of one philosopher, Martin Buber, and one critical theorist, Jurgen Habermas, as well as communication researchers, for our approach to team communication. Neither Buber's nor Habermas's concepts have been applied to small group studies, but they provide ideal perspectives that we may think of as benchmarks against which to measure our behaviors.

Dialogue

Martin Buber (1947) urged us to practice "dialogue" rather than "monologue" in our communication with those we care about. **Monologue** consists of impersonal and instrumental messages that are useful, perhaps, in everyday interactions with strangers but would be inappropriate in meaningful and genuine relationships with teammates. **Dialogue,** on the other hand, requires more difficult and complex behavioral choices. Challenging as it may be to achieve, dialogue is often used to set a standard for ethics in communication (Johannesen, 1996).

Team members practicing dialogue would speak openly and "authentically," that is, they would "be" who they are rather than "seeming" to be someone they are not, but they would temper their "being" with care for others. They would engage in "inclusion," in that they would try to understand the experiences of their teammates. They would confirm, or value, though not necessarily approve of or agree with, others. They would be "present" in their interactions with their teammates by listening and responding throughout rather than "tuning out" of the conversations. They would not seek power over their teammates but rather would insist on equality of all members. Finally, they would help foster a supportive communication climate (Buber, 1958, 1965).

Confirming versus Disconfirming Communication

A number of interpersonal communication theorists have defined **confirmation,** which generally means behavior that makes it possible for others to maintain their self-worth, as opposed to **disconfirmation,** which would threaten another's self-concept. "Confirmation/Disconfirmation" provides Dance and Larson's (1972) categories.

Although we all would prefer, of course, that others agree with and support our positions, we appreciate and value being simply recognized rather than ignored. The disconfirming behaviors range from the mildly disconcerting practice of changing the subject to the more disturbing event in which the person may deny being angry in an angry tone of voice accompanied by a scowling face. This so-called incongruous response only serves to provoke reciprocal anger and frustration.

CONFIRMATION/DISCONFIRMATION

Confirmation

Behavior that causes others to value themselves more.

1. Direct Acknowledgment: Recognizes you but may disagree
2. Positive Feeling: Expresses positive regard for your statement, but no need to agree or disagree
3. Clarifying Response: Asks you to explain or expand
4. Agreeing Response: Agrees and reinforces you
5. Supportive Response: Expresses understanding or empathy

Disconfirmation

Behavior that causes others to value themselves less.

1. Tangential Response: Answers with perhaps a "yes, but . . . " then quickly changes the subject, or moves the direction of the conversation off on a tangent
2. Impersonal Response: Avoidance of first person; uses "one" instead of "I"
3. Impervious Response: No recognition of your presence
4. Irrelevant Response: No response to your statement; talks about something else
5. Interrupting Response: Will not let you finish speaking
6. Incoherent Response: Not understandable, rambling, much retracing
7. Incongruous Response: Verbal and nonverbal do not match

Adapted from Dance and Larson, 1972.

Defensive versus Supportive Communication Climates

These confirmation and disconfirmation constructs relate closely with the issue of communication climate, which, according to Gibb (1961), may be either **supportive** or **defensive**. Table 2.1 provides Gibb's categories.

As you will note, these items are arranged as opposite pairs. An example illustrates how the categories can apply to group communication. Think of a time when you had a disagreement with a classmate over simple information, perhaps over the meaning of a term or concept. If both of you managed to speak

TABLE 2.1	SUPPORTIVE VERSUS DEFENSIVE COMMUNICATION CLIMATES

Supportiveness	Defensiveness
Description—just facts	Evaluation—judgment
Problem Orientation—deals with the problem only	Control—effort to change other person, not just the problem
Spontaneity—seems real	Strategy—hidden motives
Empathy—other "feels" our problem	Neutrality—unwilling to take sides
Equality—gives no sense of status difference	Superiority—seems to feel "better" than others
Provisionalism—open minded	Certainty—dogmatic

Adapted from Gibb, 1961.

only about possible definitions of the problematic concept rather than accusing each other of being "wrong," and if you refrained from trying to change each other, then you remained on the supportive side of the chart. If, on the other hand, you both stubbornly refused to see how the other could possibly have such a viewpoint (obviously inferior to your own), then you veered over to the other side and added to the defensive nature of the situation. Multiply such disagreements by the number of people in your group, and you see the potential for the creation of defensive group climates.

Ideal Speech Situation

Jurgen Habermas (1970), as a part of his **speech acts** theory, proposes a general symmetry requirement that facilitates an **ideal speech situation.** Habermas divides speech acts into three types: constatives, or claims of truth; regulatives, or statements that seek to control others or interactions; and avowals, or one's attitudes about issues of concern to the group. Simply stated, all parties to the situation, or in your case, all members of your team, will have equal rights to speak; to gain recognition by expression of their attitudes, feelings, intentions, and motives; and to oblige or command others according to your socially constructed and accepted behavioral norms. Think about how different such an ideal group would be from some typical work groups in which messages flow largely downward, from manager to employees or from leader to followers. In your learning groups all members can practice these ideals because you will all be equal in status. "General Symmetry Requirement" provides the principles necessary for groups to practice this equality among team members.

Theoretical Synthesis and the "Bottom Line"

So what really matters here? Effective team performance requires quality in two areas: the interpersonal relationships among members and the requirements of

GENERAL SYMMETRY REQUIREMENT

The Principle of Unrestrained Discussion

"All those involved in the speaking situation must have the same opportunity to speak."

The Principle of Unimpaired Self-Representation

"All participants in a speech situation have an equal opportunity to gain individual recognition by expressing their attitudes, feelings, intentions, and motives."

The Principle of a Full Complement of Norms and Expectations

"All participants have the equal right to give commands to others . . . and are required to justify their discourse and actions in terms of mutually recognized norms and rules of interaction"

Foss, Foss, and Trapp, 1985, p. 235.

the task itself. The achievement of these overlapping quality factors should be considered the overriding goals of your group. Thus our interpersonal or socioemotional ideal consists of dialogue that is supportive and confirming. The dialogue occurs within an ideal speech situation in which members participate under the assumption of equality. Our task ideal consists of a search for and subsequent use of a wide variety of high quality and detailed data from reputable sources that members subject to a reasoned process. Accomplishing these expected high levels of quality depends on equally effective levels of speaking, listening, and responding. The following case study illustrates the fact that a failure to communicate can have disastrous consequences.

SPEAKING

Verbal Messages

An indication of the importance of the spoken word to effective teamwork may be seen in the sheer volume of communication skills training paid for by American business and industry. Table 2.2 indicates the size of those training budgets.

CASE STUDY | **A COMMUNICATION FAILURE AT NASA**

On February 1, 2003, the space shuttle *Columbia* broke apart on re-entry into the earth's atmosphere, and the craft and all seven crew members were lost. After a seven-month investigation, the *Columbia* Accident Investigation Board (CAIB) published a report of findings about the causes of the disaster. Besides the primary physical cause, "a breach in the Thermal Protection System on the leading edge of the left wing, caused by a piece of insulating foam," the report described a number of organizational causes. Among these causes may be found "organizational barriers that prevented effective communication of critical safety information and stifled professional differences of opinion." Although engineers on the ground had tried without success to convey their fears to project managers, these messages were not "heard." Phone calls were not returned; e-mail messages were not answered. The report concludes that "[m]anagers' claims that they didn't hear the engineers' concerns were due in part to their not asking or listening" (CAIB 2003, pp. 9, 170).

Discussion Questions for Case Study

1. In a class discussion, apply the concepts of one-way and two-way communication found in Figures 2.1 and 2.2 to this case study.

2. For a deeper analysis of the case, apply the principles of the "General Symmetry Requirement."

TABLE 2.2 | **HOW IMPORTANT IS TRAINING?**

Company	Number of Employees	Percent of Payroll	Annual Training Hours Per Employee
Motorola	107,000	3.6 percent	36 hours
Anderson Consulting	26,700	6.8 percent	109 hours

Henkoff, 1993.

If you wonder why so much time and money are spent on such training, think about the limitless potential for things to go wrong between individuals based on "what you said," "what you didn't say," and "what you should have said." Now multiply those instances by five or more and add in the complication of **message sequences,** or the groupings of types of messages by various team members. Sykes (1990) illustrates the difficulty we face in trying to understand each other by comparing message sequences with music, as shown in "The Ephemeral Nature of Messages."

The Ephemeral Nature of Messages

Our domain is complex, not only because individual messages are tremendously varied, but also because messages occur simultaneously and in sequence. Like notes sounded on a piano, they are heard and then gone, to be succeeded by many others. It is their interrelation, their patterns, that ultimately we seek to describe and understand in the same sense a musician seeks to understand both chords and progressions. — Sykes, 1990, p. 206.

More significant than training dollars spent, perhaps, is the fact that even during the hiring process, employers say they are looking for prospective employees who already possess "good communication skills" (Panepinto, 1994). What do they mean by this phrase? In terms of selection, Toyota, for example, looks for individuals with interpersonal skills. Once hired, employees are supported in the practice of "open communication," "mutual trust," and "respect" (Toyota, "Hiring process . . .", 1994; Toyota, "Human Resource Management . . .", 1994; Stinson, 1995).

Certainly our word choices, or our **message variables,** influence whether we are understood or not (see Knutson, Wheeless, and Divers, 1977). Being understood, however, is no simple matter, because word meanings vary so widely from person to person and culture to culture. No dictionary can adequately capture the meanings people assign, consciously and unconsciously, to words. Bruce Gronbeck (1983) gives us a wonderful example, appearing in "A Cow?", of the complexity of such meanings.

A Cow?

Everyone knows what a cow is! Wrong. To a child on an Iowa farm, a cow is a friend to be cared for when it is weaned, a means of economic livelihood, and a source of sex education. Some of these cows have distinct personalities, especially those raised for a 4-H show; others are mere objects to be bought and sold, to be regulated by the government and turned into cash. In contrast, to a child reared in inner-city New York, a child raised on pavement, a cow is a wild animal kept in zoos along with lions, tigers, and tapirs. Milk, after all, comes in cartons, and meat comes in monofilament plastic from a grocery store. A cow is a mere animal, to be examined quizzically and to be ridden by cowboys . . . on TV. And to a Hindu child of India,

*a cow has a religious meaning. Linked with the divinity Krishna,
who was a cowherd, the cow is a sacred animal to be venerated
and to be worshipped in some religious ceremonies.*

   A cow? Everyone knows what a cow is? Not really. — Gronbeck,
1983, p. 85.

Our word choices also determine how we are perceived, in terms of our attitudes toward our teammates, our prejudices and biases, our knowledge and intelligence, our interests and personalities, and our level of interest in and concern for the group and the task. To others we are not only our physical presence and appearance, we are the constructions of our words and deeds. In the past perhaps the majority of individuals had little opportunity to "speak" in the workplace. However, in today's team environment, speaking is the norm. With that opportunity has also come the obligation to speak and the consequent need to do it well.

Not only do employees speak across the organization to their teammates, they also speak up and down the organization to those at different levels in the hierarchy. Some companies stress the importance of recognizing internal and external customer and vendor relationships and provide communication training to help build those sorts of ties. In typical teamwork environments, teams meet and talk by phone, fax, and e-mail with their counterparts at the companies that purchase their products. Companies cannot afford to jeopardize such precious contacts by poor interaction any more than by poor quality merchandise, so companies take great care with communication training before such connections are made.

In decision-making and/or problem-solving groups verbal messages generally serve procedural or substantive task **purposes.** In other words they structure and organize the group's procedures or processes so that a typical work session has a beginning, a middle, and an end. Verbal messages also create the substance or content that the group utilizes to make its decisions or solve its problems. Verbal messages can also serve relational purposes by enhancing the socio-emotional qualities of the group and building the ideal speech situation described earlier. Unfortunately, messages can have negative as well as positive effects in procedural, substantive, and relational realms.

Nonverbal Messages

Whole books and long courses of study have been devoted to **nonverbal communication systems,** or what we might think of as everything other than the words, as described in Leathers's classic text (1976) on nonverbal communication. We know as a result that no matter how artfully your words are crafted, if your facial expression or tone of voice fail to match your words, your listener will not believe your message. Likewise, the level of trust others place in you may be affected by your willingness to "look them in the eye," though the appropriateness of **eye contact** differs from one culture to another.

Your self-concept or confidence level may be likewise perceived as lacking if you exhibit downcast eyes or if your posture is closed rather than open. Closing the arms across the chest, for example, might mean any number of things: you could be angry, disappointed, deep in thought, or merely cold. To others, however, this gesture might seem defensive. Although the popular press has turned some of our knowledge of nonverbal messages into clichés, perceptions still matter.

Your sense of self-importance may be judged by your appropriation of space. People who enter a room only to take up more than their share of table space by spreading out their books and notes will be perceived far differently than those who claim little or no territory at all. Both perceptions can work to your disadvantage, though neither may reflect what you "mean" by your behavior. Remember that though you may not agree with or even be aware of others' perceptions based on your nonverbal behavior, those perceptions may guide others' treatment of you and relationships with you.

Think of the differences you have observed through interpersonal contacts, or even through the media, in another of the nonverbal elements, speaking rates, or the speed at which people speak, from one part of the United States to another. Then think about your judgments of persons who speak faster or slower than you speak. Simple awareness of how differences have been turned into stereotypes will help you guard against jumping to erroneous conclusions about others. Remember that your judgments may have been based on insignificant differences in nonverbal communication patterns.

If we believe, as communication scholars assert, that people communicate constantly, even when they don't mean to, and even in **silence,** then what does our silence mean? If one doesn't speak up in a meeting, that silence may be taken as agreement with a decision being made. But silence can also conceal disagreement if unspoken pressure to conform exists among the members. It can also serve as a sign of fear of speaking. As Linda Lederman (1982, p. 280) has explained, for some individuals, "silence is not a choice; it is a necessity." To them "talking carries with it an internal experience of anxiety." We'll look more closely at this condition, known as communication apprehension (McCroskey and Richmond, 1976), in Chapter 9, "Obstacles and Challenges to Teamwork."

LISTENING

The counterpart of speaking, of course, is listening. Although effective listening brings many benefits to the listener, such as clarity of information, understanding of others' points of view, and full knowledge of the situation one is in, listening may often serve as a gift you give to others. Although many pride themselves on being good listeners, others seem oblivious, not only to the words, but also to the nonverbal gestures, postures, or facial expressions that could and should be speaking volumes to them.

We listen for all sorts of reasons and thus a full range of **listening styles** and listening skills is needed to support those reasons. Listening for comprehension, or understanding, requires full attention, perhaps taking notes, asking questions, and clarifying what you think you have heard. Listening for evaluation requires all of these processes, plus comparisons of what you are hearing to your internal values or other criteria for judgment of the information. Listening in support of other speakers requires eye contact, as well as other nonverbal signs of attention and even empathy with their feelings or experiences. We are not speaking here of sympathy, or feeling sorry for the other person, but of **empathy,** the effort to "see as they see." Thus empathic listening and informational listening require different behaviors and attitudes. Because it is almost as hard to hear praise as it is to hear blame, listening for feedback on our own performance requires enormous patience and openness to the messages being sent.

As we noted earlier in our exploration of supportive and defensive communication climates, listening to others for evaluative purposes and then discussing what we have heard requires the most delicate concern. In a direct application to classroom groups, Anne Sullivan (1994, pp. 61–63) has these suggestions for us: Practice a "language of response," she urges, that looks first for strengths, not weaknesses; that describes rather than judges; that "speculates" on the quality of contributions without demanding change; and that makes one's listening obvious nonverbally, not just for listening's sake but as a sign of "respect for the work under consideration."

In the busy world we all share today, we often fall victim to **partial messages.** It takes a great deal of time to wait for the **whole message.** Some members of your group may be so impatient, or so uncomfortable with silence, that they will fill in the gaps in discussions or conversations with everything from "um's" and "uh's" to nervous laughter. This behavior may become increasingly common when the group is under the stress, perhaps, of the impending due date of an important assignment or of an evaluation process for the group itself or its members individually. One researcher found, however, that the most productive groups practice a listening rather than a speaking norm (Barge, 1989). In a perfect world with a perfect team, all members would be equally and highly skilled in listening. If you are highly skilled, you can serve as a valuable resource in an imperfect world.

RESPONSIVE COMMUNICATION

At the beginning of this chapter, we learned that early communication models concentrated generally on a one-way process. Certainly today we appreciate not only the two-way nature of the process but the crucial significance of response. From a **systems perspective,** which accepts the interconnectedness of all parts of a team or an organization, **feedback** derives from the output of a system and may be put back in to improve the system. Early studies in psychology referred to feedback as knowledge of results, which, if accurate and timely, improved later performance of tasks. The outcomes of some simple tasks, like hitting a target, are easy to measure and report. The outcomes of complex work tasks prove much more difficult to determine.

This difficulty, along with the top-down nature of most organizations, has resulted in the failure of those organizations to provide adequate feedback to employees, and more importantly, failure to receive adequate feedback from both employees and customers. Messages have traditionally flowed from the top to the bottom of the organization and have become increasingly more distorted along the way. Relatively little information ever came back up the chain of command.

Organizations that have moved to a teamwork environment, especially to self-managed teams, are changing these old assumptions. Traditionally, they communicated through print media: "newsletters, bulletins, magazines, brochures, posters, and annual reports . . . transmitting information . . . geared to a large audience . . . on a fixed schedule" (Dulye, 1993, p. 25). Now one Fortune 100 firm has established a "two-way communication flow" in order to "fill the pipeline—continuously and with accurate information" about business goals and progress toward them. This system required "alterations in the management fabric—from rigid and tight-lipped to open, candid, and receptive to interaction" (Dulye, 1993, pp. 25–26).

CONCLUSION

How does this information relate to you as a student of small group communication? It alerts you, of course, to the problems to be faced in the organizational world. But beyond that, it provides concrete evidence that in your future leadership roles you will need to understand and practice responsive and inclusive communication. Practicing now with your team will give you insights about the power of messages to influence outcomes.

Perhaps if we practice the ideals spelled out earlier in this chapter, we can learn to give and receive messages and feedback and thus improve our individual as well as our team performance. We will remember that communication is at the very least a two-way process. We will engage in dialogue that is both confirming and supportive. We will expect and encourage equality among our members. We will accept the fact that messages, both verbal and nonverbal, are complex and fleeting, and we will practice patience in listening so that we fully understand what our colleagues are trying to convey. And now we have come back around to the point made at the beginning of this chapter: Communication is the central axis around which the world revolves. Communication is so important that the group's very identity is formed by communication among its members.

COLLABORATIVE LEARNING ACTIVITIES

1. Before you divide into randomly selected groups or into your now permanent groups, note on a slip of paper three words that result in an emotional reaction in you (you like the word, you dislike the word or the connotation of the word, it makes you happy or sad or angry, it is loaded with meaning, it is biased or highly persuasive). Then, without signing your name to your list, place the lists in a stack and redistribute them among your group members. Choose one from the list you receive and describe to your group why it is an emotion-laden, or loaded, word. If you can't see why it was chosen, ask the group for help in understanding. As a group, discuss the effects of the use of these words in a team environment. In a round-robin discussion, present one word from your group's list to the class. This process involves teams taking turns giving one word each and summarizing their reasons for choosing that word.

2. Note individually at least one instance in which confirming or disconfirming responses affected your work or school performance either positively or negatively. Be sure to label your example according to the categories found in "Confirmation/Disconfirmation." Divide into randomly selected groups to compile a list of such instances. Decide as a group which three examples are most compelling and present these to the class. Hold a brief class discussion in which you analyze the examples for their commonalities.

Chapter 3

Teamwork and the Need for Diversity

Image provided by PhotoDisc © 2002

Personal, Cultural, and Organizational Differences

KEY WORDS AND CONCEPTS

collectivist cultures

communication styles

community

complementary relationships

cooperation v. competition

culture

diversity and differences

equality of opportunity

ethnicity

geographic origin

heterogeneous v. homogeneous groups

Hofstede's cultural categories

individualism

individualist cultures

instrumental v. expressive orientation

intercultural communication

locus of control

managing v. valuing v. celebrating diversity

masculinity v. femininity

minority

power distance

rapport

social construction of difference

status differences

uncertainty avoidance

values

voluntary associations

 To find out more about the Key Words and Concepts discussed in this chapter, use InfoTrac College Edition. Type in the keywords and subject terms. You can access InfoTrac College Edition from Wadsworth/Communication homepage: http://communication.wadsworth.com.

CAREER APPLICATION

"HE COULDN'T WORK WITH THE WOMEN AND MINORITIES ON OUR TEAM."

This justification for a personnel decision comes from a teamwork environment in which the team itself has the power to hire and fire its own members. Because the member described above could not see those different from himself as his equals, and because he refused to treat them as equals, he was fired.

"Each person brings her own expertise into the group; we are all equal." This quotation came from a hospital patient-education team composed of both nursing and administrative staff members. Working closely together, they began to appreciate the differences each one could contribute to the team's overall success.

Now that we have described the team concept, clarified the place of the individual in a team, and looked at the importance of effective communication practices, we can begin to understand the need for different skills, personality types, interests, and backgrounds among team members. Nowhere does the adage "Variety is the spice of life" apply more clearly than among team members. However, the word *diversity* has sometimes been misunderstood or even purposefully misused in our culture, such as to stir up fears among those who distrust change. So what do we mean by diversity, and why do we need it?

MEANING OF THE TERM *DIVERSITY*

In general usage, **diversity** today means **difference** in terms of race, class, gender, and **ethnicity.** Some would add "age, education, sexual orientation, **geographic origin,** or employment tenure" (Thomas, 1996, p. 6), others include religious preferences or beliefs (McEnrue, 1993, p. 27), and still others add language (White, 1994; Bantz, 1993) and physical ability (Hart and Williams, 1995). A more inclusive definition refers to "any combination of items characterized by differences and similarities" (Thomas, 1996, p. 6).

Whether we think simply of differences or of differences and similarities, each of these groupings has been used by people to explain divergences in appearance, economic or physical condition, language, culture, or behavior. We must remember, however, that the categories of similarity and difference have also been created by people. Once we saw race, social class, gender, and other human variations as simply existing realities that could not be questioned or challenged. However, because of the work of thinkers ranging from philosophers and scientists to language and communication theorists, we have come to see these groupings quite differently—indeed, to see them as symbolic products of human effort (Rorty, 1979; MacIntyre, 1984; McGee and Nelson, 1985; Simons, 1989). As our creations or **social constructions,** they have been used, often, to enable one group to gain and hold power at the expense of others.

DIVERSITIES

Where once only a part of the population was allowed to take part in many of the more advantageous sectors of the American economy, today we are making progress toward living up to the "American Dream" of **equality of opportunity.** As members of a multicultural society, we will have the chance more and more often to work closely with a wide variety of people. As one communication scholar asserts, if we accept multiculturality as the "key to difference and diversity," we can see both "the enormity of the differences" and the "problems of communicating across cultures" while bringing "pluralism into focus" (Johnson, 1988, pp. 39–40). Johnson urges us to seek differences rather than ignore them, to find pathways across cultural gaps, and to try to see variety in human life and experience as normal. Rather than fearing difference, through communication we can come to appreciate and respect, perhaps even to know and understand, others who will enrich our lives with their humor, their subtleties, their words, and their ways.

Personal Diversities

The American workforce consists of men and women, Asians and African Americans, those above and below any arbitrary standards of annual income, and those who came or whose ancestors or parents came from all parts of the globe. We are different in many other ways as well. In regard to individual personal characteristics, we may be "baby boomers" or "Gen-Xers." We may have eight, twelve, sixteen, or any number of years of schooling.

How likely are your class teams or groups to consist of diverse members? If you were a student at Queens College in New York City, you could hear sixty-six languages spoken. You might watch an Indian cable channel or eat at a neighborhood IndoPakBangla restaurant. You might walk by an Ecuadorian travel agency on your way to class; you could have responded to a sign advertising music lessons in the window of a local music store written in both Spanish and Chinese (Siegel and Adams, 1999). Even if we move away from the big cities of the East Coast, perhaps far inland to Western Kentucky University, you could still share the classroom with students from China or Turkey; with native-born students of Hispanic, European, African, or Asian descent; with traditional and nontraditional age students; and with those who live in dormitories and those who commute from both rural and urban locations. In short, diversity is normal.

Regardless of ethnicity, we differ in our preferred learning or working styles. Some study or work steadily day by day while others are driven only by deadlines. Our perceptions of the proper timing of work guide our work habits but may also lead to misperceptions of our commitment to work as compared with others. North Americans today are sometimes looked upon by those from other cultures as "multitaskers" who try to accomplish three jobs at the same time. The perfect example here would be the person who commutes to work while sending fax messages or e-mail from a laptop computer or talking on a cell phone. Some think nothing of working through lunchtime, while others carefully separate work or school from meals and from other facets of their lives (Bantz, 1993; Partlow and Wynes, 2002).

We have different **values,** or those elements of life that we "hold dear." Some will put work first while others place the highest value on family, school, religion, money, or pleasure. In terms of group work, recent studies have shown that women and men may differ in the value they place on **cooperation** versus

competition, which in turn may determine how they communicate in meetings. Indeed, much of the early research on group dynamics started from the values perspectives of middle-class white males who were both the researchers and the research subjects (Meyers and Brashers, 1994; Wyatt, 1993; Gearhart, 1979; Borisoff and Merrill, 1985; Allen, 1995). The resulting high value placed on persuasion has led to the belief that those group members who do not engage in persuasive or "competitive tactics" are not effective participants (Meyers and Brashers, 1994, p. 72; Gayle, Preiss, and Allen, 1994). If we can appreciate difference, however, we can recognize that cooperative strategies may have even more productive results. Kohn (1992; 1993, p. 88) has compared the effectiveness of competition and cooperation and found that those who work in cooperative environments learn more, produce more, and benefit personally from seeing themselves "as part of a **community.**"

We have differing **communication styles.** We all know people who just say what they think; they seem either uninhibited by convention or oblivious to the effects of their words or nonverbal signals. These free-spirited communicators are, of course, markedly different from closed, noncommunicative, perhaps fearful individuals who seem reluctant even to look you in the eye. (Actually, the ability or willingness to make direct eye contact, considered a sort of test of confidence in male, middle-class, white American society, does not at all mean confidence among other cultural groups in America and elsewhere.) Although most of us probably fit somewhere between these two extremes of seemingly open and closed communicators, during your working life you will, no doubt, need to learn to work productively with such team members (Partlow and Wynes, 2002). We'll talk more in Chapter 9 about a potentially serious difference in communicative style brought on by communication apprehension (McCroskey, 1977), defined as "the experience of anxiety associated with real or anticipated oral interaction with others" (Lederman, 1982, p. 280; McCroskey, 1977).

Differing communication styles may also reflect personality differences. Although we've probably all had the experience of feeling comfortable immediately with a new acquaintance, that instant **rapport,** rare though it is, may not hold as much potential satisfaction as the long-term relationships we can form when at first we struggle to "see as others see" and finally manage to do so. Some group members strongly guard their own independence and exhibit "little desire for involvement"; they may become impatient with the "frustrations of group decision making" (Webb, 1988, p. 51). Others enjoy close cooperation with teammates. Psychologists speak of **complementary relationships** that form among people who are different but who may each possess traits that the other lacks. A fully functioning team consists of members who complement each other in all the ways they are different and fill in the gaps as they learn about each other. As you learned in Chapter 2, complex relationships exist among communication styles, personality types, and effective teamwork.

Team members may also come from differing, perhaps contrasting, backgrounds. Few, if any, cultures actually exist as monoliths, or structures in which all members are alike, but studies have been done that seek broad differences and similarities within regional, national, and other defined groups. The Hispanic culture, for example, has been described as "close-knit," as compared with a stereotypical U.S. "American culture," where the "emphasis is on the individual rather than the team or the group" (Figueroa, 1992, p. 26). Those who have grown up in this or other such **collectivist cultures** may experience discomfort in highly competitive, winner-take-all **individualist cultures** that often characterize the corporate world in the United States. The connections between personal traits and cultural background require greater exploration.

Cultural Diversities

Researchers in **intercultural communication** often turn to the work of Geert Hofstede (1980, 1991) for his four-dimensional category system that locates **cultures** in terms of **power distance, uncertainty avoidance, individualism,** and **masculinity.** Although the U.S. culture is generally characterized as highly individualist, certainly not all of us fit the category; we vary by gender, race, age, and ethnicity, at the very least.

A short description of Hofstede's system illustrates its relevance to small groups or teams. As Bantz (1993, p. 2) suggests, "the concern is not solely the characteristic of the members' cultures . . . but also the mixture of those characteristics within the group." Hofstede relates power distance to inequality, or how we interact in the face of differing distributions of power in society or in organizations. In some cultures, powerful leadership and wide gaps in power levels between groups are considered normal and even desirable; in others, higher value is placed on the distribution or even the equalization of power. In your class groups, some may value equality of members while some may prefer strong leader and follower roles that distribute power unequally.

In terms of uncertainty avoidance, cultures place varying degrees of emphasis on maintaining stability, even at the expense of potentially beneficial change. Some members of your team or group may feel comfortable working with few rules while others may need to establish clear and concrete patterns of behavior. Once these rules and roles have been established, those who fear ambiguity or uncertainty will likely attempt to enforce them. Another aspect of uncertainty avoidance relates to differing levels of need for information about others. In their efforts to get to know each other, some of your group members may ask questions that seem inappropriately probing to others. Only through communicating about these differences can team members come fully to appreciate and trust one another.

Cultural differences may be most clearly seen through the individualism versus collectivism construct, or the relative importance placed on the person as compared with the group. A significant difference in your class groups may emerge in relation to whether individuals can and will put the group's needs above their own yet not end up resenting their teammates. Closely related to this contrasting set of values lies the concept of internal or external **locus of control,** or one's view of whether life's events are controlled by oneself or by others (Borden, 1991). Those in your group who see themselves at the mercy of "fate" will certainly interact differently than those who see themselves as affecting fate.

TABLE 3.1	CULTURAL SOCIALIZATION'S EFFECTS ON YOUR TEAMS

Students in your groups may have been brought up to think in the following ways:

Collectivist	Individualist
Look after your extended family, and they will look after you.	Look after yourself and your immediate family.
Your identity depends on your social network.	Your identity depends on you.
You should think in terms of *we*.	You should think in terms of *I*.
You must maintain harmony.	You should speak your mind.
Relationships are more important than tasks.	Tasks are more important than relationships.

Adapted from Hofstede, 1991.

Table 3.1 presents Hofstede's individualism versus collectivism categories from a classroom perspective.

Hofstede's (1984) fourth factor, masculinity (as opposed to **femininity**), is discussed by Bantz (1993, p. 5) as an **instrumental** versus **expressive orientation.** According to Bantz, the instrumental (or masculine) person has been socialized to be "assertive, seek advancement, and strive for earnings" while the expressive (or feminine) person has been brought up to be "nurturing, to be oriented toward providing service, to emphasize interpersonal needs, and to be concerned about the physical environment." Think of the differences these personal characteristics based on cultural norms will make in your group processes and outcomes. "Hofstede's Cultural Dimensions and Their Relationship to National Cultures" lists selected nations or regions according to Hofstede's cultural category system.

If collectivist cultures place a high value on the group, and individualist cultures place a high value on the individual, then a seemingly obvious question can arise. Do collectivists have an advantage over individualists in their ability to work together in teams? Or, to complicate matters further, do individualists have the advantage because of the higher value they would place on the task over the relationships? Of course this highly complex issue has been the object of much academic disagreement, with some theorists even proposing that teamwork may be unsuited to individualist cultures such as those listed by Hofstede (Earley, 1989). A recent study that compared student teams in the United States with similar teams in Korea came to different conclusions, however. Sosik and Jung (2002) found that individualists "reported higher levels of functional heterogeneity and group potency and attained higher levels of group performance than did the collectivists." Functional heterogeneity refers to the level of diversity of experiences and skills found within the group. Group potency may be thought of as "team spirit." Group performance was measured by evaluating the teams' solutions to business problems presented to all groups.

HOFSTEDE'S CULTURAL DIMENSIONS AND THEIR RELATIONSHIP TO NATIONAL CULTURES

Power Distance

Countries rating high exhibit large differences in wealth, power, and status between members of their cultures. Some regions with high ratings include Mexico and most of Central and Latin America. The United States and most countries of Western Europe have low ratings on power distance.

Uncertainty Avoidance

Cultures rating high exhibit a low tolerance for ambiguity and prevent uncertainty through many rules and regulations. Greece, Portugal, Guatemala, Uruguay, Belgium, El Salvador, and Japan rate very high while Singapore, Jamaica, Denmark, Sweden, Hong Kong, Ireland, and Great Britain rate very low. The United States rates fairly low.

Individualism

Cultures rating high, for example, the United States, Australia, Great Britain, Canada, the Netherlands, and New Zealand, place autonomy in the hands of the individual. Those rating low, such as South Korea, Taiwan, and Central and Latin American nations, value the group, the family for instance, over the individual.

Masculinity

Referred to in more recent writings as instrumentalism or achievement/ambition, this dimension reflects the value placed by the culture on individual success versus nurturance of others. It also reflects strongly differentiated gender roles versus more flexible roles. Areas rating high in this dimension include Japan, Austria, Venezuela, Italy, Switzerland, Mexico, and Ireland. Countries rating low in this dimension include Sweden, Norway, the Netherlands, Denmark, Yugoslavia, Finland, Chile, and Portugal. The United States rates fairly high.

Adapted from Hofstede, 1991.

NEW ZEALAND'S CULTURAL DIVERSITY

*D*uring the spring semester of 2002, I had the opportunity to teach my course in small group communication while on sabbatical at Waikato University in Hamilton, New Zealand. My students were interesting, my colleagues were welcoming, the weather was perfect, and I could not have asked for more from the experience. I received more personal learning than I could ever have had just from teaching the course "as usual." This benefit came from a perspective gained through seeing cultural diversity in a different light.

Students at this university are accustomed to taking classes with many international classmates. New Zealand contains within its own borders two major ethnic groups, Maori (or people who migrated from other parts of the Pacific islands and arrived earlier than the Europeans) and Pakeha (or European New Zealanders), as well as multiple ethnicities stemming from previous historic migrations. Thus, language differences, food preferences, religions, lifestyles, and other diversities abound.

The class met for four-hour sessions, two days each week, for six weeks plus an exam week. Each student functioned as a member of one four-to-six-person team throughout the course. In response to the question, "What region do you consider 'home?'" I received the following answers: 76 percent (twenty people), New Zealand; one person, Africa; one person, South Africa; one person, Texas; one person, Eastern Europe; one person, Asia; and one person, Central America.

In response to the question, "What is your nationality?" I received the following answers: thirteen people, New Zealanders; one person, Kiwi; six people, Pakeha/European New Zealanders; three people, Maori/New Zealanders (two listed themselves as partially Maori); one person, South African/European; one person, Namibian; and four people, Chinese. (The totals do not add up because "home" and "nationality" are not necessarily the same.)

As the above information shows, even the majority experienced some uncertainty about their identities, though perhaps multiplicity would be a better word than uncertainty. Although twenty of twenty-six considered New Zealand to be "home," only those who had been born elsewhere clearly identified their nationality. The New Zealanders named themselves Kiwis, Europeans, and Maoris as well. The South African found it important to identify as a European South African, whereas the Namibian was simply a Namibian. Although the Chinese were from three areas, Taiwan, mainland China, and Hong Kong, they all merely said they were Chinese. I later learned that the one person claiming to be a Kiwi was a native of India whose parents had brought him to New Zealand as a small child.

(Continued)

CASE STUDY	**NEW ZEALAND'S CULTURAL DIVERSITY (CONTINUED)**

Discussion Questions for Case Study

1. New Zealand culture generally features a very low level of power distance. The Pakeha culture derives from an individualist British colonial heritage, whereas the Maori culture is collectivist. For additional insights, find New Zealand and the other countries mentioned in this case study among Hofstede's country identifications (in "Hofstede's Cultural Dimensions and Their Relationship to National Cultures") and compare the "home" areas of these students in as many ways as possible.

2. Should their classroom teams be heterogeneous or homogeneous in terms of cultural backgrounds? On what basis do you make these judgments?

3. Suggest some strategies these teams could adopt to help enhance their chances for successful intercultural team communication.

Sosik and Jung (2002) sought to determine whether teamwork was viable in both environments, not to find whether one type of culture is "better" or "worse" than another. Looking at their "practical implications," we find useful suggestions, considering the increasing prevalence of global teamwork. First, they conclude that "managers should view work groups as appropriate means to perform organizational tasks in individualistic countries." Managers of "virtual teams and other long-distance collaborative work structures," however, should "pay attention to how group characteristics differ across cultures" and "how such variables may improve group performance." They suggest, for instance, that "patience makes perfect" might be watchwords for teams in individualist cultures where the task might threaten to overwhelm the relationship aspects needed for longer-term working groups. The case study on page 45 reveals the complex nature of cultural diversity in a country that has a remarkably similar history, yet interesting differences, when compared with the United States.

Organizational Diversities

Regardless of their orientation to teamwork, all organizations consist of power relationships and consequently of **status differences.** The most obvious manifestation of this difference relates to compensation, as determined by one's place on the organizational chart. Some analysts measure the values or the level of democracy of organizations by looking at the wage or salary differences between the highest- and the lowest-paid employees. Organizational clothing expectations can range from a required uniform to an appropriate three-piece suit. Some companies create teams consisting of employees from both of these groups without regard for the potential discomfort they might experience. Others, such as Saturn, provide casual attire featuring the company logo to everyone from the top down in order to reduce the impact of status differences.

With wage and salary diversities often come vast differences in employees' abilities to control their time and thus their lives. Some must clock in, are allowed scheduled fifteen-minute breaks, and have just thirty minutes for lunch. Others work according to a schedule they create, and thus they are free to arrange and attend meetings at times that suit their own needs. Certainly those at various organizational levels must be available to answer telephones, for example, to serve walk-in customers, to staff emergency rooms, or to install windshields as vehicles go by on the line. Working environments may range from a private, air-conditioned corner office with windows to a spot on an assembly line on the factory floor or a cubicle surrounded by other cubicles in a huge, open, noisy room. Employees also vary in terms of their formal memberships; for example, some teammates may also be union members while others are members of management. Cross-functional or cross-departmental teams are often formed to solve specific problems. As they come together, they may find that their members possess few similarities in their experiences even within the same organization (Alderfer, 1987).

Team meeting space, a significant organizational resource, may be similarly varied. At an aluminum mill, for instance, where huge metal ingots are transformed into can stock or aluminum foil, planned team meetings occur in comfortable conference rooms while impromptu, "we have a problem; let's fix it" meetings happen wherever the work of the plant is under way. Such meetings occur in glass-walled areas where computers and their operators control mill processes, out on the plant floor where an unusual noise or vibration may have been detected, or in the offices of accountants and MIS (management information systems) specialists going about the business of cost containment.

In any teamwork environment, opportunities must be available to relieve employees of their normal duties to make time for their team meetings and, indeed, for their team training. A trend toward hiring part-time employees to fill in the gaps and even toward job sharing has resulted in teams that consist of members who work only on Tuesday afternoons, Monday nights, or Sunday mornings along with the full-time "nine-to-fivers." You may find yourself among either of those groups; you may be a full-time student and part-time employee, or vice versa. Members of your class, and consequently members of your team, may be traditional or nontraditional students. You may work nights, come to school in the morning, and sleep in the afternoon. You may be a commuter who only comes to campus three days a week. You may have child-care concerns, and you may find yourself bringing your first-grader to class on "snow days." The mere fact that some of you can relate to the geographic and personal significance of snow days while others cannot indicates the level of diversity likely to occur within your groups.

WHY TEAMS NEED DIVERSE MEMBERS

Member Needs

In companies or institutions that operate twenty-four hours a day, every day of the year, scheduling of work is often a source of conflict. In the past, managers simply assigned some people to work days and others to work nights, some to work overtime and others to work holidays, some to work weekends and others to work weekdays. Increasingly, however, teams are scheduling their own hours and attempting to meet individual needs of employees, not to mention customer-service needs, at all organizational levels. As we can see from the discussion, real teams make decisions that impact the everyday lives of individuals, and they must take individual differences into consideration.

To make fair and equitable decisions, teams (and managers of all sorts) need multiple perspectives from as wide an experience base as possible. "Multiprofessional" teams are needed in health care, for instance, so that patients may be seen as something other than the site of a specific illness or condition (Harrison, 2002, p. 46). Teams need "the ability to accept more than one view, more than one language, more than one culture, and more than one way of solving a problem" (Figueroa, 1992, pp. 26–27). Only then can they make humane and effective decisions that actually solve human and organizational problems. They must not rely on old assumptions. Indeed, according to one writer on diversity, "the greatest barrier to understanding cultural differences is the delusion that we already do" (Strenski, 1994, p. 35).

Organizational Needs

The idea that organizations are made up of interconnected parts that affect each other has gained wide acceptance today. This systems approach to organizational theory tells us that organizational needs must be coordinated with individual needs and now with team needs. So what are the diversity needs of organizations? Business literature refers to them as needs for "**managing diversity,**" defined as "creating a working environment that allows every person to work to his or her potential" (McNerny, 1994, p. 22). A more enlightened view would insist that mere management is insufficient to the task, and that appreciating, **valuing,** or, indeed, **celebrating diversity** is required.

If we look at the statistics, we find that the concepts of majority and **minority** populations have been turned upside down. One hospital director in New York describes both his workforce and his patients. Those in clinical or administrative leadership positions are 80 percent minority, those classified as professional are 65 to 70 percent minority, and clerical and housekeeping positions are 100 percent minority. He defines *minority* as "Latino, Asian, Pacific Islander, Black." The ethnic profile of their 50,000 patients per year is 50 percent Latino, 30 percent Asian, 10 percent African American, and 10 percent other (Ferran, 1994, p. 2).

What are the organizational benefits of valuing diversity? As we have noted above, utilization of the brain power of diverse individuals simply adds to the store of knowledge and creativity available. There are other benefits, however.

In a global economy, organizations have expanding needs for understanding how to appeal to varying sorts of markets. In order to sell products, services, or ideas, companies must practice a "multicultural management philosophy" by which they are able to "translate" their values yet "still respect the various cultures" they seek to enter (Sunoo, 1996, pp. 38–44).

Companies and institutions that serve only domestic markets must also value diversity, of course, because of the diversity of the domestic population. Not only is the creation of a "responsive" working environment for all our people "a good thing in itself, particularly in a country as heterogeneous as the United States," but such an environment also fosters the "democratic and egalitarian ideals" that the nation "strongly espouses" (Gummer, 1994, p. 124).

Still, idealism aside, there are significant bottom-line or financial reasons as well. Paul Fireman, board chair of Reebok, has referred to valuing diversity as "an idea whose time has come." He says that effective decision making is best done by "a working team . . . that has the vision to give birth to an idea and the grasp and understanding to make the idea work." However, he says, "that kind of working team cannot be a team of clones." What we need instead are "people of different strengths and talents—and that means, among other things, people of different backgrounds" (Makower, 1995, pp. 48–54).

This sort of thinking is not new. These conclusions, reported fairly recently in the popular press, have been a part of the group communication research literature for many years. As long ago as 1961, psychological studies were conducted that showed the superiority of **heterogeneous** over **homogeneous groups** in terms of creativity and quality in both problem solving and decision making. These early studies have been consistently confirmed since then (Hoffman and Maier, 1961; Janis, 1982; Guzzo, 1986; Lichtenstein et al., 1997). What do the findings imply for your team? The more heterogeneous your group, or the more differences among you, the greater will be the possibility for you to produce creative and high-quality team results.

Much of the emphasis in this chapter thus far has been on business or other organizational groups. However, group activities and memberships, as we noted in Chapter 1, are much more pervasive than that. Not all groups perform tasks for which they are compensated. As Meyers and Brashers (1994, p. 76) point out, "women traditionally congregate or gather" in "**voluntary associations,** women's health clinics, rape crisis centers, battered women's shelters, cultural organizations, parent-teacher associations, . . . church groups, junior women's leagues, play groups, single-parent groups, exercise groups, friendship groups, or the family." Because such groups are typically loosely structured, members themselves must learn to recognize, value, and thus reap the benefits of diversity in achieving the group's goals. Group survival will likely depend on the cooperation and participation of diverse members.

In the same way we looked at the benefits of teamwork to clients as an ethical consideration in Chapter 1, we can look at the benefits of diversity to clients as an ethical consideration here. If all members of a health-care team, for instance, are "Caucasians and the patient is a member of a minority group," how comfortable might the encounter be (Coppola, 2002, p. 25)? If such considerations seem unnecessary because we believe that "race is no longer much of an issue in our society," we simply deny Gallup poll data, for instance, that shows continuing disparities in income levels for whites and blacks with similar educational backgrounds and other lingering discriminatory practices (Bailey, 2000, p. 2).

HOW DO WE VALUE DIVERSITY?

In the corporate world, as is always the case, the resources needed for training employees lie in executive organizational levels and must be communicated through a company's or institution's vision. However, the people who occupy positions within the organization will determine the success or failure of that vision through their day-to-day interactions. The ways they choose to communicate with one another, and thus to work with one another, will make all the difference. So what can we learn to do in response to the challenge that diversity brings?

A number of writers in the field of human relations have offered suggestions for both organizational and personal action plans. The choice of organizing into self-directed work teams, some claim, can do more to promote understanding of difference than any other single corporate strategy (Hayes, 1995, p. 230). Table 3.2 provides Roosevelt Thomas's nine options (1996) for managing diversity.

TABLE 3.2   THE DIVERSITY PARADIGM'S ACTION OPTIONS

Option	Description
Include/Exclude	Include by expanding the number and variability of mixture components, or exclude by minimizing the number and variability of mixture components.
Deny	Minimize mixture diversity by explaining it away.
Assimilate	Minimize mixture diversity by insisting that minority components conform to the norms of the dominant factor.
Suppress	Minimize mixture diversity by removing it from your consciousness and by assigning it to the subconscious.
Isolate	Address diversity by including and setting different mixture components.
Tolerate	Address diversity by fostering a room-for-all attitude, albeit with limited superficial interactions among the mixture components.
Build Relationships	Address diversity by fostering quality relationships characterized by acceptance and understanding among the components.
Foster Mutual Adaptation	Address diversity by fostering mutual adaptation in which all components change somewhat for the sake of achieving common objectives.

Thomas, 1996, pp. 6–8.

Although exclusion, denial, suppression, and isolation are neither desirable nor legal in most cases, an old assumption about assimilation, commonly found in the "melting pot" metaphor of American life, has also gone by the wayside. Indeed, diversity means "recognizing the uniqueness of another person; . . . it means acknowledging their right to be who they are" (Kluge, 1997, pp. 171–75). Certainly mere tolerance will not work any more. No one wishes to be "tolerated. . . . They want to be valued" (Strenski, 1994, p. 35). Valuing others' uniqueness helps to build relationships, and in the process each learns to adapt and, perhaps, to grow.

M. P. McEnrue (1993), who has studied the interracial climate in Los Angeles, describes the "Personal Qualities Associated with Effective Cross-Cultural Communication" that we might think of as starting points for ourselves. As you look at these eight qualities, found in the corresponding list, think about how you might convey each as you communicate with your friends and classmates.

It is clear that effective teamwork in a culturally diverse society depends heavily upon the communicative behaviors of individual members, which mutually build the culture of the team. Charles Bantz (1993) has developed strategies and tactics for improving intercultural communication based on his experiences as part of a research team made up of members living in Britain, Israel, Germany, the United States, and South Africa. Table 3.3 shows these methods of dealing with problems arising from the cultural characteristics outlined by Hofstede, mentioned earlier.

In Chapter 1 we found the word *flexibility* among the attributes employers are seeking in their pools of potential employees. We find the same word in the suggestions above. Clinging to old ways, old assumptions, and old attitudes and behaviors toward those we may have perceived as different from ourselves

PERSONAL QUALITIES ASSOCIATED WITH EFFECTIVE CROSS-CULTURAL COMMUNICATION

- The capacity to accept the relativity of one's own knowledge and perceptions
- The capacity to be nonjudgmental
- Tolerance for ambiguity
- The capacity to appreciate and communicate respect for other people's ways, backgrounds, values, and beliefs
- The capacity to demonstrate empathy
- The capacity to be flexible
- A willingness to acquire new patterns of behavior and belief
- The humility to acknowledge what one does not know

Reprinted from *Organizational Dynamics*, Vol. 21, Iss. 3, M. P. McEnroe, "Communication from managing diversity," pp. 18–29, p. 26. Copyright © 1993 with permission of Elsevier.

only makes us inflexible. Success in our new world requires that we "truly value variety of opinion and insight" (Thomas and Ely, 1996, p. 86).

CONCLUSION

In this chapter we have explored diversity as a positive and needed attribute of successful teams, organizations, and societies. The term *diversity* contains multiple meanings rather than being narrowly constrained by race or gender. Cultural classifications, such as individualism and collectivism, while useful as explanations for some differences, should not be thought of as "boxes" in which to put people. As the world grows smaller, perhaps such large difference categories will evolve and blur.

Organizational diversities in status and power, however, remain as potent ways to maintain cultural hierarchies. Teamwork initiatives that blend and value individuals at all levels challenge assumptions based on old conceptions of social class distinctions. We conclude the chapter with strategies for making the best use of and providing the most value to our diverse human resources for the good of ourselves, our organizations, and those served by our teams.

TABLE 3.3	STRATEGIES FOR IMPROVING INTERCULTURAL COMMUNICATION
Cultural Dimension	**Method**
Power Distance	Distinguish between tasks and practice different leadership styles with each.
Uncertainty Avoidance	Establish a common long-term goal or deadline, but leave short-term goals flexible.
Individualism	Retain individuality of members, but work closely together to establish a common group goal.
Instrumentalism	Alternate task and social behaviors; solve disputes in supportive ways.

Adapted from Bantz, 1993.

COLLABORATIVE LEARNING ACTIVITY

1. Use the "Inventory of Team Member Characteristics" in Appendix A to determine the level of diversity among the members of your class. For classes larger than thirty members, divide into groups of approximately twenty-five to thirty for this activity. Once results are determined, divide

into randomly chosen small groups and discuss the benefits of these diversities to your potential performance. Present your ideas to the whole class.

2. One way to begin the process needed for valuing diversity is to challenge stereotypes and assumptions about others. Develop a list of such stereotypes and assumptions about traditional and nontraditional college students. Once the two lists have been completed, examine them for their flaws and fallacies. What sort of evidence exists for their truth value? How much truth or falsehood did each contain? Hold a class discussion about your findings from this exercise.

Chapter 4

Establishing a Team Identity

Jon Feingersh/Corbis

Who We Are and What We Do

KEY WORDS AND CONCEPTS

action plans

bona fide groups

equality

ethical perspectives

ethic of caring and openness

group or team goals

group or team identity

group or team objectives

group or team phases

individual identity

managerial bias

metaphor

mission statements

mutual respect

narrative theory

rhetorical visions

sense of belonging

shared responsibility

social identity theory

team building

values

vision statements

voluntary associations

work ethic

To find out more about the Key Words and Concepts discussed in this chapter, use InfoTrac College Edition. Type in the keywords and subject terms. You can access InfoTrac College Edition from Wadsworth/Communication homepage: http://communication.wadsworth.com.

CAREER APPLICATION

Individual and group identities change when teamwork becomes a part of the culture. Hospital employees answered as follows when asked, "What if you had to give up teamwork?":

- "I was opposed to teamwork when the idea was first introduced, but now I'd never go back to the old way."

- "I would hate to go back to having a supervisor who told us what to do and we had nothing to say about it."

- "As a nurse, I would never want to go back to having no say-so in my day-to-day work."

- "Although I was a supervisor myself, I would never want to go back to that life."

- "Before, we were not asked; we were told. It didn't work."

Quotations obtained from various research sites whose locations will remain unidentified here because of the proprietary nature of the information.

In Chapter 3 we learned that the cultures we live in have been constructed socially by the attitudes and behaviors of their past and present inhabitants. In the same way, our **individual identities** and our small **group** or **team identities** are constantly "under construction," along with the larger organizations within which individuals and teams function (Koch and Deetz, 1981). If we go beyond work teams to consider formal and informal voluntary groups, such as study groups, singles groups, religious groups, hobby or sports groups, and support groups, four out of ten Americans regularly participate in these identity-building projects (Wuthnow, 1994).

HOW ARE TEAM IDENTITIES CREATED?

Studies of group identity often begin with an explanation of Henri Tajfel's (1978, p. 63) **social identity theory.** Tajfel defines social identity as "that part of an individual's self-concept which derives from his knowledge of his membership of a social group (or groups) together with the value and emotional significance attached to that membership." Tajfel claims that group identity is based on comparing the social status of one's own group to that of other relevant groups. In subsequent studies Tafjel and his colleague J. C. Turner have refined the theory by differentiating social and individual identity, for instance (Tajfel and Turner, 1979; Tajfel, 1982; Turner, 1982; Tajfel and Turner, 1986; Turner, 1987). Turner (1982, pp. 17–18) also showed the importance of the **sense of belonging** that can come with group membership as a result of internalizing or "locating oneself . . . within a system of social categorization."

Social identity theory has been challenged by a number of communication scholars as being too deterministic, that is, of giving too much credit for group identity to the place of the group in an organizational hierarchy. Scholars have done much theorizing about the power of organizational or group narratives, or stories, to create organizational realities and help members make sense of their lives.

An application of **narrative theory** to decision-making small group identities may be found in Ernest Bormann's (1972) study of student groups at the University of Minnesota. Bormann combined his analysis of group meeting transcripts with Robert Bales's previously published descriptions (1970) of the ways groups "created their social realities, their 'culture, motivation, emotional style, and cohesion' through 'discourse'"(Bormann, 1972, p. 396). Bormann concluded that groups create **"rhetorical visions"** of themselves from narrative themes that develop in their conversations about "a recollection of something that happened to the group in the *past* or a dream of what the group might do in the *future*" (p. 397). The rhetorical or persuasive aspect of the group's vision means that the ways the members choose to talk about themselves can affect the group's self-concept. Groups or teams can thus create their identities out of their own experiences and expectations. Seyla Benhabib (1999, p. 345), writing about "ethnic and nationalist" groups, shows that though our languages and our cultural narratives may limit our possibilities for identity construction, they do not "determine" our life stories. Perhaps you will see yourselves among more current storytellers in the case study on page 58.

Lembke and Wilson (1998) have sought to apply identity theory to human resource management of work teams. Building on a study by Sundstrom and others (1990, p. 120), who define work teams as "small groups of interdependent individuals who share responsibilities for outcomes," Lembke and Wilson (1998, pp. 928–929) conclude that interdependent identity must be created by members' attitudes toward each other or toward the group's work itself, described as "emotional attachment." This bonding, they find, often results in high performance, especially if the unifying connection among members is based not on personalities but on identification with and attraction to the group's common purpose.

In actual organizational contexts, teams of employees are identified first by the normal work they have been hired to do. At a hospital consortium, for example, some teams consist entirely of cardiac care nurses while others include accountants, secretaries, or administrators. At a large Midwestern firm specializing in mail-order sales of merchandise to outdoor enthusiasts, teams consist of telemarketers, customer service representatives, and technical-support persons. In the manufacturing environment, members may have been hired as technicians, engineers, or mainframe computer operators. However, as the technological needs of the business have changed, these persons have been retrained or new members have been added to the team in technical areas that were unknown a few years earlier.

At the same time these team members go about their "normal" work, they also, particularly in self-managed teams, assume management functions formerly held by a supervisor, manager, lead person, or department head. These functions might include hiring, assigning and scheduling work, choosing how resources should be used, or making a variety of other decisions. Some teams share these functions; others choose to rotate them among the members according to a specific time schedule, such as every six months or once each year.

At the General Motors Saturn Plant in Spring Hill, Tennessee, employees are organized into "self-directed work teams consisting of from six to fifteen members who are given responsibility and authority to meet their goals." On the list of "Thirty Work Unit Functions" of each team appear such items as "make their own job assignments, . . . plan their own work, . . . design their own jobs." They also control their own material, keep their own records, select new members, control quality, contain cost, improve the work environment, integrate their work with that of other teams, seek out resources, arrange for their training, and take responsibility for corrective action (Saturn, 1990; see Stokes, 1994, for service-sector examples).

Besides these managerial activities, work groups often take on projects or solve problems related to their work, their team's functions, or their organization. Corporations are always looking for ways to improve processes for getting the job done, and it is reasonable to assume that employees performing those processes every day would understand them best. In order to improve

A BRAND NEW TEAM HITS THE ROAD

*O*nce upon a time the administration at a university decided to create a new program in forensics and to invite students to participate in inter-collegiate competition in debate and individual events such as informative, persuasive, and after-dinner speaking and poetry and prose interpretation. They assigned a faculty member with no coaching experience to serve as advisor to this team. In due course, a total of twelve students signed up for the forensics team: five in debate, three in public speaking, and four in interpretation. During the third week of the semester, with little training or coaching, they set out in a university van for their first tournament, a nine-hour road trip away. Of course, they won no events and were quite a dispirited group as they boarded the van for the long trip home.

At first there was much grumbling, some napping, a little studying, and a good deal of staring blankly out the windows. No one talked about the future of the forensics team; indeed, a future seemed unlikely. About halfway back, the weather took a turn for the worse; rain fell in torrents. Then a student came down with a urinary infection, which required stops at each exit for many miles. The group decided that the best course of action was to return to the nearest city for which a hospital sign had been noted along the interstate. Some waited in the van while others accompanied their teammate to the emergency room. Then they all waited. And waited.

At last they departed once more for home in the dark and the rain for at least five more hours of driving. For no apparent reason, someone began to sing. Others joined in, and they sang their way home, took turns at the wheel, and laughed at the ridiculous variety of songs they all knew the words to. Strange as it may sound, they became a team through adversity and merely smiled that week when the school newspaper featured an article titled, "Forensics team off to slow start!" To every new member who joined after that, the tale of "our first tournament" was told and retold. And they lived happily ever after.

Discussion Questions for Case Study

1. Divide the class into groups of five members and share your "bonding experience" stories. Come back together as a whole class and share the most compelling stories.

2. Find the common themes in the stories you share and then apply social identity theory and narrative theory. Did you find rhetorical visions either of the past or of the future? Did you find evidence that narratives can be significant features of team identities?

coordination among departments, employees may find themselves on cross-functional teams or task forces designed to eliminate bottlenecks and thus save time and money. Project teams are often formed to find ways of promoting the safety or well-being of employees. For example, an ergonomics project team might seek ways to prevent repetitive motion injuries by redesign of tools or other equipment (Stys, 1994).

The Saturn Corporation gives us a "real-world" prototype project team in its Facilities Core Team. Because the Saturn plant was designed with a team-work philosophy from its beginning, the facility itself resulted from this team's research and planning project (see "Saturn Facilities Core Team Project").

Saturn Facilities Core Team Project

In designing the roadway to the complex, [the vast property containing the plant where the automobiles are assembled, administrative buildings, parking facilities, and so on] many people's needs had to be considered. From a transportation end, we needed a design that would permit a heavy flow of traffic daily onto the pad [ground level] without interfering with pedestrian traffic. Security needed a method of enforcement. . . . And team members and others wanted to preserve the environment. Given all these and financial considerations, the Core team was able to blend the concerns together.

They were able to design and implement a roadway system which was compatible with everyone's needs in a cost-effective manner. With it, trucks and construction workers are able to have direct access to the plant on the pad [ground] level. Team members and others travel on a completely separate road, gaining access to the complex via overhead walkways. And security is able to monitor both roads through designated checkpoints. — from Saturn News Release, Sept. 18, 1990, p. 29. Used with permission.

If we put aside the work group model for a moment, we can begin to see ourselves involved in other types of group activities such as those found in the community-based **voluntary associations** that were listed in Chapter 3. For these groups, "continuity and interdependence" and, indeed, "group survival" are the most significant concerns; communication patterns turn on ways to meet others' needs and to fulfill the "obligations of relationships." Identities both in terms of the groups themselves and their individual members are constructed out of "connections . . . with others" (Meyers and Brashers, 1994, p. 77; Shepherd, 1992; Ferguson, 1984).

Some theorists refer to these as bona fide groups (Putnam and Stohl, 1990) whose tasks comprise "information dissemination, coordination, organization, motivation, and affiliation" (Meyers and Brashers, 1994; Scheerhorn, Geist, and Teboul, 1994). Bona fide groups are characterized first by "stable but permeable boundaries," that is, by a clear identity within a larger organizational or cultural setting that is able to change without dissolving. Second, bona fide groups share an "interdependence with their immediate context." In other words, they depend on the larger group or organization of which they are a part, but at the same time the larger organization likewise depends upon them (Putnam and Stohl, 1990, pp. 256–259).

A typical example of a bona fide community group might be a local youth soccer league, founded and organized by parents whose children want to play the game. Over the course of time, as these children grow and change and as the needs increase for raising funds, buying uniforms, providing playing fields, coaching, and even selling refreshments, volunteers will come and go. The organization itself and the voluntary groups within it must learn ways to adapt and survive changes in membership. Creating and strengthening the groups' identities through effective communication will enhance their chances of survival.

The same is true, of course, of student groups in the classroom. Whether group membership is assigned or self-selected, identity formation begins with the first meeting. Groups may not consciously consider the question, "Who are we?" The process of "becoming," like communication itself, has no discernable beginning or ending point. The suggestions for effective group communication that include valuing members equally and thus building a sense of community will get you started. The identities you create for your groups will be influenced, as we have seen, by your perceptions of yourselves as compared with others and by the events in the group's experiences together that you choose to highlight or to dramatize. In the next section of the chapter you will find an example of how status and narration can come together in unexpected ways.

HOW DO TEAMS THINK OF THEMSELVES?

Thus far in this text, we have learned effective practices from good examples. In progressive organizations, managers recognize the importance of treating employees with the respect that enhances self-respect. However, sometimes bad examples make good lessons. Let's look at one such bad example.

In a training class attended by two newly formed teams from one company, one a group of hourly workers and the other consisting of their managers, all were instructed in brainstorming techniques and urged to try in this way to develop lists of business problems to solve. A member of the management team said aloud, in a joking manner, that the hourly team members were not capable of brainstorming, that they "couldn't stir up a slight breeze." During their next team meeting, the hourly team members decided to try out this brainstorming technique to generate a list of suggestions for their team name. As it turned out, they took the idea that had been used to dismiss their abilities and cleverly turned it around. After compiling a considerable list of possibilities using weather metaphors as a play on the word *brainstorm,* someone noted that powerful storms are designated according to a numbering system, and that Category 5 is the most powerful. Their team name, thus, became Category 5, or C5 for short.

In good times and bad, groups often describe themselves metaphorically. A **metaphor** is nothing more than a figure of speech through which we make a very strong comparison of one thing with another by equating the two and often identify and clarify a vague concept (in the above case, the new team's identity) in terms of a highly concrete concept (here, a hurricane). Not only could their team achieve results, the hourly team members were saying, it could blow the company away if it wanted to.

The most common metaphors for teams, even work teams, revolve around the concepts of families or communities and recognize, perhaps, the bonding that can occur as a result of spending as much time with our co-workers as with our families. Indeed, teams that terminate members, or teams that are taken apart and put back together with new members, often go through a grieving process and speak in terms of "divorce" or even "death." In teams formed across cultural differences, the metaphors used to characterize the teams during teamwork training can influence expectations among new team members either for good or for ill. For instance, if an organization headquartered in the United States speaks of its teams in terms of sports or military metaphors, its employees from regions that value cooperation may find such images threatening or alienating (Gibson and Zellmer-Bruhn, 2002). Giving early attention to the ways you speak of your teams may have long-term benefits for all of your members.

MISSIONS → VISIONS → GOALS → OBJECTIVES → ACTION PLANS

Any number of strategic planning theories and other management theories, such as Total Quality Management (TQM), as well as organizational theorists, such as Peter Drucker or Steven Covey, urge organizations (and individuals) to

---

CRITERIA FOR JUDGING MISSION STATEMENTS

1. Inspiring: Must be positive so that members can see their participation as worthwhile

2. Readable: Must be understandable to all members; often measured by an instrument such as the "Fog Index," which "takes into account sentence length, the total number of words, and the number of words with three or more syllables"

Gunning and Mueller, 1981.

CRITERIA FOR EVALUATING VISION STATEMENTS

1. Clarity: The degree to which the vision is readily understandable

2. Visionary Nature: The extent to which the vision describes a valued outcome for individuals in the group and thus engenders their commitment to group goals

3. Attainability: The practical likelihood that the team can achieve its goals

4. Sharedness: The extent to which the vision gains acceptance by individuals within the team

Adapted from Burningham and West, 1995, p. 107.

---

develop both **mission** and **vision statements** to clarify their identities. While the vision describes what the future can be like for the company in terms of a "valued outcome" that serves as a "motivating force" (Burningham and West, 1995, p. 107), the mission indicates its current reason for existence. Cochran and David (1986, pp. 108–109) describe mission statements as "planning documents" and suggest that effective statements define the "fundamental, unique purpose" of an organization.

Laurer's example (2002, pp. 1–2) illustrates that understanding the mission is not a simple matter. He cites a nearly bankrupt airline whose board brought in a new CEO to "save the day." At a meeting of executives, the new leader asked what sort of business they were in and got a standard answer: "the airline business." Not satisfied, the CEO suggested that they find a way to reach consensus on their particular airline's mission. After several days and much discussion, they decided their mission was "to take passengers from one location to another safely and on time." The company eventually regained its profitability by concentrating on customer service. "Criteria for Judging Mission Statements" provides two standards for evaluating mission statements.

The vision statement for General Electric's Appliance Park in Louisville, Kentucky, consists of only eleven words but contains lofty ideals: "One team, better and faster than anybody else in the world" (*GEA Today*, 1994, p. 1). The mission statement for a group of hospitals, also in Louisville, is both narrower and more focused on the present: "to provide high-quality, comprehensive health care in Kentucky and the surrounding area" (Alliant Health System, 1997). "Criteria for Evaluating Vision Statements" provides four standards for judging vision statements.

As we move from the corporate level through department levels and to team levels, missions and visions must be aligned. In other words, the team's mission supports the department or division's mission, which supports the organization's mission. To see how this works, note how a cardiac rehabilitation team's mission statement, "to provide a progressive, supervised, exercise program to

THEY MUST BE ALIGNED

Mission

The current reason for existence of an organization, department or division, team, or individual.

Vision

A desired future state of existence for an organization, department or division, team, or individual.

Goals

Future targets for organizational, departmental or divisional, team, or individual activity. Goals can be reached, but they cannot be performed.

Objectives

Activities performed as steps toward reaching goals.

Action plans

Layout of objectives to be performed in order to reach goals in key results areas. Action plans must specify who will do what, when.

individuals with coronary artery disease, stable angina, and/or increased risk factors for coronary artery disease," supports the Louisville hospitals' overall health-care mission above. "They Must Be Aligned" shows the relationships among mission, vision, goals, objectives, and action plans.

Once a team has arrived at a clear sense of its own purpose, not the purpose of its department or its company but the team's reason for existence, it can begin to lay out goals and objectives. **Goals** focus on the future, typically in reference to problems or obstacles that prevent the accomplishment of the vision, while **objectives,** sometimes in terms of key results areas (KRAs), outline the intermediate steps to be taken to achieve the goals. "Cardiac Rehabilitation Team Goals and Objectives" illustrates the types of goals a hospital team may develop.

With all of this preliminary planning finished, the team then puts together its **action plan,** which should include communication elements, such as how often and by what means the members should communicate with each other and with those to whom they report (Partlow and Wynes, 2002, p. 15). To be effective, the action plan describes who will do what, by which specific target

---

CARDIAC REHABILITATION TEAM GOALS AND OBJECTIVES

1. To provide a safe environment for cardiac patients to exercise in
2. To provide education to patients
3. To provide quality care as a team by maintaining certification
4. To provide adequate discharge planning
5. To function successfully as a shared-directed work team

"Cardiac Rehabilitation . . . ," 1994.

---

date, and to achieve which objective or KRA (see "Clinical Quality Improvement Plan/Report").

As you can see from these complex plans, team processes are not a simple matter. Some might wonder about the value of the high level of interaction and participation that goes into this extensive planning process. However, we have long known its importance. In a 1970 study done of 9,796 white-collar headquarters employees of a large industrial organization, researchers tested and confirmed the hypothesis that those who clearly perceive "the overall objectives or mission" of their work would also perceive a "high degree of cohesiveness, teamwork, and cooperation" (Maher and Piersol, 1970, pp. 127–128; Stayer, 1990). Not only do morale and commitment increase with "participation in goal setting," but improved work processes also result because team members achieve clarity of "focus and direction" (Burningham and West, 1995, pp. 107, 115).

A recent study by Hoegl and Parboteeah (2003) tested the relationships between goal setting and team performance. They found that for teams engaged in innovative projects, in this case software development, goal setting accomplished through collaboration of all members of the team was "an important success factor." Goals that are "clear and accepted" improve team performance by "directing attention, mobilizing effort, increasing persistence, and motivating strategy development" (Locke et al., 1981, p. 125). Cox (2003, p. 58) takes the concept of goal setting to its next logical step, that is, to "tracking results" and "sharing best practices."

How can we apply the concepts of vision, mission, goals, objectives, and action plans to student groups? Groups can clearly differentiate between what they would like to achieve by the end of the term or semester, their vision, from the reason they have been assigned or chosen their membership at the start, their mission. The mission, of course, is to learn and practice the principles of effective group communication so that they will become a cohesive, productive, and satisfied team. In my classes I urge students to think of their two overriding and interconnected short-term goals as to answer their research questions while maintaining good interpersonal relationships. Their objectives on a day-to-day basis appear on their task lists or their action plans as items to be checked off.

CLINICAL QUALITY IMPROVEMENT PLAN/REPORT

First Phase

Corporate Goal: Identify key processes.

Department Goal: Identify key clinical processes in Cardiac Rehabilitation.

Indicator: Key clinical processes are identified and communicated to all members by 4/1.

Action Plan: Members LH and MW will map all processes by 2/1; Members KP and SH will isolate key processes by 2/14.

Actions Taken: LH and KP reported results of mapping and narrowing processes to team on 2/21.

Monitoring Plan: Team meeting agendas will include standard item related to goal between 1/1 and 4/1.

Impact: All members will be able to prioritize clinical care processes and perform them accordingly.

Second Phase

Corporate Goal: Achieve quality improvement in at least one key process, resulting in significant improvements in service or clinical outcomes.

Department Goal: Achieve quality improvement in patient discharge process.

Indicator: An individualized discharge plan is developed for every patient by 7/1.

Criteria: Upon discharge the patient shall be able to (1) demonstrate the ability to monitor own pulse; (2) demonstrate knowledge of medications presently taking; (3) demonstrate knowledge of signs and symptoms of angina and appropriate actions.

Action Plan: Members KP and SH will coordinate efforts of this team to develop and implement a process for individualized discharge planning by 7/1.

Actions Taken: Process developed and implemented; three clinical indicators of quality all measured 100 percent by 3/1.

Monitoring Plan: Team meeting agendas will include standard item on individualized discharge planning process through second quarter of the year; team will review all discharged charts monthly.

Impact: All measures of quality for patient discharge process will rise to 100 percent.

"Health System . . . ", 1993.

They might include such things as: choose and seek approval for our topic for the assignment, brainstorm for a list of possible sources of information on our topic, set criteria or standards for acceptable types of information, and set a date and time for our weekly meetings. We will learn more about brainstorming and criteria setting in Chapter 5.

HOW DO TEAM FUNCTIONS AFFECT TEAM IDENTITIES?

Day-to-Day Interactions

In business and industry some teams meet on a daily basis, perhaps for five minutes to talk about safety or for half an hour to discuss productivity or problem solving. Others may meet weekly for two hours. However, official meetings are not the only settings in which team members work together. Certainly nurses providing cardiac rehabilitation work together and with their patients constantly. At the aluminum plant mentioned earlier, those who operate the cold mill's computerized, high-speed system congregate in a protected area, called "the pulpit," raised above floor level, while the enormous piece of equipment does its work. This room features every imaginable communication device, from a bank of computer screens showing stages of the mill's operation and providing access to both e-mail and production numbers to an intercom and several telephones for talking to other teams. In this room they listen for unusual noises or vibrations in the mill, talk about "how it's running today," or discuss how close they are to making their monthly production goal.

Team Building

Teams also participate in **team building** sessions, where they work together to improve their communication or their cohesiveness, or they learn how to avoid such obstacles as groupthink, a potentially serious problem faced by groups that become too cohesive (Janis, 1972; see Chapter 9 for a detailed discussion). They ponder the likelihood of meeting their goals, they set new goals, and they may even develop new ways of looking at goals as the company or the economy changes. At some team-building sessions, they extend and find ways to align their individual mission statements with each other and with the organization. These activities are often held off-site in order to help members break free of old thinking habits.

GROUP PHASES

One theoretical perspective on team identity focuses on how teams change over time, the so-called phasic model. Fisher (1980) traces the development of phasic models from Bennis and Shepard's 1956 model, through Tuckman's 1965 model, to his own 1970 model of decision emergence. According to Fisher, his four-phase model developed as a result of his observation of decision-making groups. Fisher's first phase, orientation, or "forming" in Tuckman's terminology, represents the experience of newly formed groups who struggle with who they are and what their task consists of. They "search tentatively for ideas and directions," and they are "unaware of the direction the group will eventually take" (p. 145). The major characteristic of this phase is ambiguity.

In the second phase, conflict, members compete and argue over ideas, coalitions form, and emotions run high. Tuckman referred to this as the "storming" phase (Fisher, 1908, p. 140). If the group is to remain together, however, dissent must be replaced with consensus, and groups typically move in the direction of Fisher's third stage, "decision emergence" or "norming," according to Tuckman (p. 147). Here ambiguity returns, which allows a modified form of dissent to turn gradually toward agreement. In the final phase, which Fisher calls "reinforcement" and Tuckman calls "performing," the group reaches consensus on its decision and reinforces the decision's "rightness" by continuing to provide supporting evidence. The distinguishing characteristic of this phase is a sense of unity among the members (pp. 148–149).

This model may be useful in thinking about classroom team identity formation. In the course of a semester or other such time period, groups will come together tentatively at first, will struggle to work together, will come to see that working cooperatively is essential to their success, and will eventually reach decisions based on evidence and reasoning. Thus they will complete the four phases and adapt their behaviors and their team identities accordingly.

The phasic model in its simplified form may not be useful in understanding identity formation among longer-term groups. Work teams, for example, might constantly repeat the phases or might return to the orientation phase only when new members are hired. Conceivably all four phases could occur within a single meeting if the group were asked to tackle a novel situation or faced a crisis.

For virtual teams phases, particularly those that establish norms of behavior, or values, for the team, must occur without benefit of facial expressions or tone of voice clues so useful in deciphering the "shoulds and oughts" in face-to-face teams. Graham (2003) provides a useful study of norm development among student groups working in virtual teams. He found that "norms tended to evolve from a general state with fuzzy boundaries to a more operationalized state with clearly defined boundaries" (p. 329). For instance, an early norm of "we should communicate frequently" developed into one clarifying that "we should check and respond to e-mail daily" and finally became "we should check e-mail twice daily, a.m. and p.m." (pp. 330–332). The changes among the team norms generally came as a result of one or more of the following factors: "a past experience, an individual need, a team conflict, a traumatic event, or a norming activity for a new team" (p. 340). Because the "norming" phase, according to the models described above, comes after and as a result of the "storming" or conflict phase, Graham concludes that interventions built into teaching or training programs could help alleviate potentially harmful conflict. He further suggests that we should think of norm development as occurring throughout the life of the group, even during the "performing" phase, and that awareness of the significance of norms could improve group performance (pp. 346–347).

VALUES AND ETHICS

Overarching considerations in regard to team identity must certainly involve the **values** the members hold in common, meaning the things, ideas, or ideals they "hold dear," as well as the **ethical perspectives** they bring to the group, that is, the behaviors they think of as "right" (Johannesen, 1996). As we learned in Chapter 3, individuals of different cultures, genders, regions, ages, and so forth, may bring contradictory values and ethical perspectives to work with them. Team-building sessions are sometimes devoted to resolving or at least acknowledging those differences. Certainly team members are not required to change their deeply held values at the whim of their teammates, but members must find ways to agree on work values featuring **mutual respect** and **equality** and on the team's **work ethic.**

How do typical college-student group members differ in their values orientations? I often ask my classroom groups to think about and share their individual priorities in terms of the course. Such discussions often hinge on time and grades, especially at the start of the term. Once the members realize that time can be saved and grades can be improved if they work together, their priorities seem to change. Although I don't encourage it, competition usually develops between the groups as each resolves to be the best team in the class, and this goal turns into an unstated vision.

Organizations also talk about values and philosophies as they write their vision and mission statements. Management theorists claim that the "opportunity to participate in problem-solving and decision-making activities has become a core value in most enterprises, although the extent of that participation varies from organization to organization and manager to manager" (Stokes, 1994, p. 40). Alliant Health System's published list of values (1997, p. 1) highlights a customer focus on "respect for every individual, delivery of quality service, constant pursuit of excellence, and commitment to integrity." Some organizations have incorporated their teamwork initiative as a feature of their value system which, once publicized, would seem to mark a commitment; however, sometimes the differences are vast between the "talking" and the "doing."

Planners for the Saturn plant representing both General Motors and the United Auto Workers expressed their values in a philosophy statement, made before the plant even opened, that seems to have held true over the years. "Saturn's Corporate Philosophy Statement" presents it in full.

A number of organizational perspectives on ethics (which, in turn, provide a basis for small group ethics) have been criticized as having a **managerial bias,** meaning that the theories privilege corporate interests over those of organizational members or employees. Charles Redding's typology (1996, pp. 17–40) of unethical messages, which he labels "destructive, deceptive/manipulative, coercive, secretive, and intrusive," are described as unethical only because they lead to organizational ineffectiveness, according to Mattson and Buzzanell (1999, p. 55). These authors propose, instead, an approach that seeks a "value transformation" based on "equitable power sharing and decision making." They define unethical behavior as "communicative actions and processes that attempt to marginalize, silence, and disempower individuals or groups and that prohibit development of voice, or the ability to speak in organizational settings" (p. 62). The ideal speech situation described in Chapter 2 would seem to qualify as ethical communication by their standards.

Yet another way of thinking about ethical behavior can be seen in the work done by Littlejohn and Jabusch (1987, 1982). They propose an **ethic of caring and openness.** Figure 4.1 adapts their concepts to a model of ethical small group communication. As you can see, a high level of both attributes results in the most ethical position, that of ethical **shared responsibility** for the outcomes produced by group communication.

A study from Sweden provides an interesting variation on the theme of "care." Styhre, Roth, and Ingelgard (2002, p. 503) assert that care positively affects "team-based, knowledge-intensive work" in the pharmaceutical industry. While acknowledging that people create meanings and thus make sense of their workplaces by understanding the organization's "values, norms, and cultures," these authors suggest that meaning and sense-making are not enough for successful teamwork. Team members also need to share in the "experiences and know-how" of the organization that can only come through caring relationships and the "ability to establish interpersonal, sensemaking mechanisms."

CONCLUSION

How do teams establish identities that work for, rather than against, them? They start with the work they do or the purpose for their existence. How the members think and behave in regard to that purpose will affect the ways they

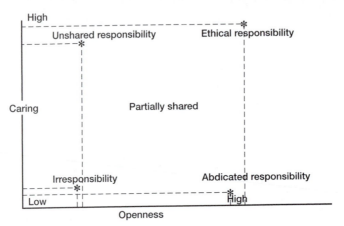

Adapted from Littlejohn and Jabusch, 1982, pp. 12–22.

think and behave in reference to their team. In the case of teams of employees, the organization they work for will treat them in ways that either enhance or detract from their self-concepts, which will further affect their team identity. Groups who go about their work confidently and successfully will have been given sufficient information about where they fit into the organization, they will know their value to the company, and they will work through their action plans and thereby accomplish their goals. They will solve problems, make decisions, serve customers, sell products, manufacture goods, and provide services together.

If, on the other hand, we speak of voluntary groups, their members may advocate a cause, raise funds, distribute flyers, provide assistance, or celebrate successes. Your class groups will, perhaps, choose discussion topics; gather, sort, and evaluate data; set criteria; and make decisions. Regardless of the contexts in which groups exist, the best chance for success comes to those who establish clear identities that foster agreed-upon values and ethical stances based on equality, participation, care, and excellence in communication.

COLLABORATIVE LEARNING ACTIVITIES

1. Randomly divide the class into groups of approximately five persons. Each group should create a model of the interrelationships between an effective team's mission, vision, values, goals, objectives, and action plans. Present the models to the class making sure all members take part in the presentation.

2. Re-divide the class into groups and create models of an ineffective team's mission, vision, values, goals, objectives, and action plans. Present the models to the class and then hold a discussion about the relative importance of fully understanding the mission.

Chapter 5

Team Cognitive Processes

Creativity, Criteria Development, and Critical Thinking

KEY WORDS AND CONCEPTS

argumentation

antithesis

backing

brainstorming

claim

creative thinking

creative problem solving

criteria

critical thinking

data

decision matrix

dialectical thinking

dialogical thinking

evidence

facts

inductive v. deductive reasoning

morphological analysis

nominal group technique

opinion

premise

qualifier

reservation

reverse brainstorming

source bias

synthesis

thesis

warrant

To find out more about the Key Words and Concepts discussed in this chapter, use InfoTrac College Edition. Type in the keywords and subject terms. You can access InfoTrac College Edition from Wadsworth/Communication homepage: http://communication.wadsworth.com.

CAREER APPLICATION

In a hospital teamwork environment, these are the training courses required for employees ranging from nurses to accountants:

CRITICAL TRAINING AREAS

1. Group problem solving
2. Conducting effective meetings
3. Communication skills
4. Handling conflict
5. Roles and responsibilities
6. Quality tools and concepts
7. Evaluating team performance
8. Work flow and process analysis
9. Selecting team members
10. Presentation skills
11. Leading and influencing others
12. Budgeting

Health System, 1994.

Now that we have looked at the purposes for which groups of people come together, it is time to explore the cognitive elements, or thinking processes, that can set a truly effective team apart. In years past, we thought of creativity, the first of these elements, as innate, that is, as something only some people possessed. It has been shown, however, that individuals, though perhaps creative in different ways, can be shown how to develop their creative potential. The same would be true, of course, for groups made up of variously creative members. Johnson and Hackman (1995, pp. 12–13) explain **creative thinking** as "original thinking" that is both "relevant" and "divergent." Others define creativity as "linking two seemingly unrelated things" (Barker, 2002, p. 168), or "building a relationship between two disparate entities by finding the unseen connection that joins them" (Nucifora, 2002, p. 18). In other words, creative thinking results in new ideas that are useful in problem solving in that they take the group in a direction not previously considered.

In this chapter we begin with the concept of creative thinking, then we see how it can be used in a team setting to generate ideas and to develop **criteria,** or standards for making judgments about ideas. The process of developing these criteria provides a bridge linking creative thinking with **critical thinking,** or careful analysis and judgment based on a reasoned process. Through critical thinking we can not only judge ideas but also compare and contrast ideas and evaluate information in preparation for completing the common team tasks of decision making and problem solving.

CREATIVE THINKING

As Johnson and Hackman (1995, p. 4) assert, creativity is the "driving force in human history." In their book *Creative Communication,* these authors provide a number of idea-generation techniques that groups or teams could find quite useful. The most commonly used form is the **brainstorming** process developed by Alex Osborn (1957), which you read about in Chapter 4. Other methods, such as **reverse brainstorming,** the **nominal group technique, morphological analysis,** and **creative problem solving** may prove equally useful in any given group. Regardless of the methods used to stimulate new ideas, Thompson (2003, pp. 98–99) suggests that groups have more difficulty engaging in "divergent thinking," in which we must "put aside typical assumptions," than do individuals. She blames this problem on both organizational and team dynamics that encourage conformity and "convergent thinking," in which we work toward a "single answer." If this is the case, teams must have sufficient strategies available to overcome the tendency toward conformity.

Brainstorming to Generate Ideas

The purpose of brainstorming is to get out as many ideas as possible. In order to do that, the rules require that no one make any judgments about an idea; groups simply list the ideas in rapid-fire order. This rule may be the most difficult one to follow because our first inclination is to evaluate ideas as good or bad and espe-cially to agree or disagree almost immediately with those giving their ideas or opinions. However, to say "I like that solution" cuts off further discussion. Such evaluation not only stops the process but also prevents members, knowing oth-ers are making such judgments, whether good or bad, from contributing for fear of embarrassment (Barker, 2002, p. 168). Some researchers even go so far as to suggest that the stress of being evaluated affects brain functioning and shuts down the "cerebral cortex, inhibiting creative thought" (Nucifora, 2002, p. 18).

Other proponents of brainstorming suggest that members try to think of odd ideas, "the crazier, the better," and that they build one idea on another. In preparation for brainstorming, companies sometimes send people out to seem-ingly unrelated industries to gather some "crazy ideas." For instance, General Mills's chief technical officer observed the processes of a SWAT team, a NASCAR pit crew, and stealth-bomber mechanics to help his company create the "best supply chain in the world" (Gogoi, 2003, p. 74). Organizations also put together people who do not normally work together and ask them to "do some-thing unexpected" (Barker, 2002, p. 169). Other suggestions include presenting "impossibilities" to the group and asking them to find ways around them (Thompson 2003, p. 98). After all, it was once impossible to have the knowledge contained in the world's great libraries available on your own desk, but the con-tinuing development of the Internet brings us more accessibility every year.

Finally, brainstorming requires that you "wait out the pauses." Although people generally find these periods of silence uncomfortable, often the best ideas emerge after a long pause when you have a chance to "see" patterns or themes that have developed. You could also engage in a process of "brainwrit-ing" during the pauses, that is, asking participants to write their own thoughts in silence. Subsequent "round-robin exchange," either by the writers them-selves or after an exchange of papers, can serve as a stimulus for divergent thinking. Even taking short breaks can provide the pauses needed for new ideas to emerge (Thompson, 2003, p. 104).

Reverse Brainstorming to Isolate Weaknesses

Reverse brainstorming, on the other hand, is designed to find as many weak-nesses as possible in a plan, proposal, or policy option so that unworkable solu-tions can be discovered early enough for other solutions to be considered (Whiting, 1958). If a campus group composed of faculty and students were asked to develop a parking policy agreeable to all, for example, they could use reverse brainstorming before narrowing their choices to a final decision. During the process they could take their potential choices one at a time and generate a rapid list of the potential pitfalls of each before moving on to the next. They would follow the same rules of brainstorming, that is, they would neither agree nor disagree with ideas listed; they would try to think of unusual ideas, in this case flaws in the proposals; they would seek a large number of ideas; and they would build ideas one upon the other. By comparing their lists, they might dis-cover whether their plans were ultimately too costly, unfair to one group or an-other, or not practical or feasible.

Nominal Group Technique

Another method of promoting creative thinking avoids one of the problems that has been associated with brainstorming, that is, the blocked thinking that results from pressure to initiate uncommon ideas in an open group setting. The nominal group technique creates a setting that is a group process in name only, thus its title "nominal." This process represents an effort to concentrate simply on the idea-generation task and consists of the following steps:

1. Individuals work silently to develop lists of alternatives.
2. The group creates a comprehensive list through a round-robin session.
3. They hold a brief clarification session so that all members understand all items on the list.

These three steps could be quite useful as a method of brainstorming for groups whose members have generated few ideas because they feared disapproval (Guzzo, 1986, p. 59).

Morphological Analysis

A morphological analysis requires that groups take ideas apart and put them back together in different ways so that previously unrecognized relationships may be discovered. The term morphology relates to the "form and structure" of a concept or problem (Miller, 1987). If a group were engaged in solving a problem, such as the campus parking issue noted above, they would break the situation down into its logical parts then list subdivisions of those major parts. Table 5.1 illustrates this creative-thinking method.

By taking the problem apart and listing its components, the group might be able to see it in a new light. Perhaps the long-term standard solutions, covering more green spaces on the campus with asphalt or building a parking garage, would not be necessary in the long run if it could be shown that the student population were changing demographically or that the university planned to move more swiftly into electronic instruction.

Creative Problem Solving

This method, developed by Sidney Parnes at the State University of New York at Buffalo, consists of six steps related to the concept of "finding" (Parnes, Noller, and Biondi, 1977). First the problem solvers engage in objective finding, or determining the positive or negative situation in question. They develop questions such as "Wouldn't it be nice if (WIBNI)?" or "Wouldn't it be awful if (WIBAI)?" to represent outcomes. They then move to data finding to figure out what they already know and what they need to know to answer their research question or solve their problem. Next comes problem finding, similar to the morphological problem analysis mentioned above. Idea finding, perhaps through brainstorming, comes next, to be followed by solution finding through criteria generation and convergence, or listing

TABLE 5.1	**MORPHOLOGICAL ANALYSIS**

Question: How can we solve the campus parking problem?

Groups Affected	Space Available	Needs	Hours
students on campus	large lots	safety	morning
faculty	small lots	convenience	lunchtime
staff	parking structure	sufficiency	afternoon
commuters	curb/free	accessibility	evening
people with disabilities	distant space	short- or long-term	varied
		overnight	ability to come and go

Severity	Considerations	Instructional Delivery
minor inconvenience	fairness	daytime
moderate concern	equality	evening
major significance	cost	weekend
	population rising or declining	electronic

criteria for judging solutions and then refining the list. In the final stage, acceptance finding, the group attempts to ensure that the solution chosen will be acceptable to all members and is actually possible (Johnson and Hackman, 1995, pp. 134–137).

CRITERIA DEVELOPMENT

Groups that create lengthy brainstorming lists of problem characteristics, problem solutions, or policy options must find ways to narrow them by eliminating those that, indeed, are "too crazy" and by categorizing and measuring the ideas against criteria or standards. The development of these criteria requires cognitive processes that are both creative and critical. An example of how this procedure works will clarify these cognitive processes.

Project Criteria

At a plant in Tennessee that makes steel racks that display merchandise in large warehouse stores like Wal-Mart, the Roll Mill Team developed a seventy-three-item "problems" list in a one-hour meeting. Over the course of the next few weeks, they gathered information, thought through what was possible under current conditions, and categorized the items as follows: thirty-nine items that the "team can solve," twenty-one items that "will need outside help," seven items that are "beyond the scope of the team," and six items that are "high priority safety concerns" (Steel, 1994).

By narrowing the seventy-three items to the thirty-nine they could actually solve and then by highlighting the six related to safety, they could see more clearly what to do. The team then spent one more meeting prioritizing the problems remaining on the list by holding each item up for view against a series of questions:

- Does this problem stop our production?
- Does this problem reduce the quality of our product?
- Would solving this problem also remove other problems from our list?
- What is the worst thing that could happen if we do not solve it?
- What is the best thing that could happen if we succeed in solving it?

As this team worked through process improvements that could result from their meeting discussions, they held each potential problem-solving project up to their criteria, that is, to standards related to safety, workability, authority (or whether the team had the power to change a particular process), significance, and impact.

The loss of the space shuttle *Columbia,* unfortunately, provides process criteria that make chillingly clear the need for standards to be met before U.S. spaceflight resumes. The *Columbia* Accident Investigation Board Report (2003) lists a total of twenty-nine recommendations that resulted from its lengthy study of the causes of the shuttle disaster but separates out fifteen recommendations that must be carried out "before return to flight." These are related to safety due to the "physical cause of the accident, and include preventing the loss of foam, improved imaging of the Space Shuttle stack from liftoff through separation of the External Tank, and on-orbit inspection and repair of the Thermal Protection System" (p. 9).

Problem Solution Criteria

Once problems have been isolated and chosen for solution, projects have been assigned, or new product needs have been outlined through brainstorming or other creative methods, teams must engage in the process of data gathering and narrowing. "Brain Data Lets Daviess Rethink Curriculum" describes an example from a public-school setting that broadens our understanding of teamwork in action.

As we see with the Daviess County administrators, once they have evaluated information and created lists of possible solutions, teams must establish additional criteria to judge potential solutions, projects, or products. One standard for alternative problem solutions could be cost effectiveness: when benefits exceed the costs of the solution. They must also decide whether these criteria or standards are essential or merely desirable.

If one possible solution meets three out of five essential criteria and three out of six desirable criteria while a second solution meets all five in the essential category but none labeled desirable, how will they choose? If the team agreed fully on their essential criteria ahead of time, this decision should be

BRAIN DATA LETS DAVIESS RETHINK CURRICULUM

By Charles Wolfe, Associated Press

OWENSBORO, Ky.—All children in Daviess County's elementary schools got piano lessons this year. The idea was to build up brains, not strictly to make music.

For the same reason, students began learning to play chess. They were regularly exposed to the visual and performing arts. Kindergartners were taught their ABCs, as one would expect—but in Spanish as well as English.

Everything was calculated to increase neuron connections—literal pathways in the brain—for learning, remembering and solving.

There is research to show that each activity enhances brain development in childhood, the only stage of life at which some kinds of learning can occur. Daviess County arranged its elementary curriculum around that research. It apparently is among a handful of districts in the nation doing so.

The project was named Graduation 2010. It was born, fittingly, in a brainstorming session two years ago, when [Superintendent Stuart M.] Silberman and other administrators floated ideas about how to increase student achievement.

Some in the group delved into brain research and came up with concepts. The county school board signed on. Later, 200 people came to a town meeting, at which committees were formed to turn the concepts into action plans. Corporate sponsors and a local charity, the Hager Foundation, agreed to help underwrite it.

The project so far covers only the elementary grades, which have 4,200 of the district's 10,000 students. This past year's kindergartners—the high school class of 2010—are the center of attention.

A Western Kentucky University research team plans to study them for the next 12 years. It will look for ways in which achievement is affected by the project.

fairly simple. What are some examples of essential criteria? For most businesses, answers such as "cost-effective," "environmentally sound," "does not privilege one employee group at the expense of another," "is actually doable," or "fits within a specific time frame" generally make the essential list. Desirable criteria might include such items as "would solve more than one problem," "would significantly cut costs," or "would provide an innovation no other company has thought of using." Table 5.2 presents a **decision matrix,** which illustrates one way to compare alternatives with criteria for judging them.

TABLE 5.2	A DECISION MATRIX

Question: What should be our school's policy in regard to the allocation of scarce parking spaces?

Alternative	Meets Criterion			
	A (cost)	B (choice)	C (solve)	D (fair)
1. Low/no fees, first come/first served	no	yes	no	?
2. Sticker price based on proximity	?	yes	?	?
3. Reserved spaces at high prices	yes	yes	?	no
4. Freshmen cars prohibited	?	no	?	no

Alternative 1: Low fees or no fees; first come, first served

Alternative 2: All sticker prices based on proximity to campus

Alternative 3: Reserved spaces available at high prices

Alternative 4: Freshmen prohibited from having cars on campus

Criterion A: Cost effectiveness*

Criterion B: Freedom of choice

Criterion C: Will solve the problem

Criterion D: Fairness

*Cost effectiveness determined by comparing the cost of the project itself with the gains to be made from it. Remember that monetary costs are only one type. How else would these solutions "cost" the university?

Fortunately, the characteristics Johnson and Hackman (1995, pp. 137–147) list for the most creative groups, namely, a cooperative orientation, a concern for excellence, a supportive rather than defensive communication climate, a cohesive and noncoercive relationship among the members, a significant role for minority influence, and an encouragement of productive conflict, also characterize the most effective groups in organizational studies, as you shall see throughout this book. The delicate balance between creative thinking and critical thinking that teams or groups must maintain requires vigilance on the part of all members but is well worth the effort. Criteria setting may be understood as both a creative process and a critical process that bridges the gap between the free-flowing energy needed for idea generation and the sound and careful judgment needed for high-quality decisions.

CRITICAL THINKING

Data Evaluation Criteria

Regardless of the setting—manufacturing, education, health care, or retail sales—forward motion by the team toward its goal requires information gathering. However, with today's information explosion through electronic dissemination and other technologies, the ability to sift through massive amounts of data and choose not only the "right" information but also the "best" grows ever more valuable. Thus, teams must establish criteria or standards by which to judge information.

For example, one standard for information could be based on recency: Information used should be no older than, say, two years or six months or three days, depending on the situation. Another criterion for data, credibility, requires that the information be derived from sources that are knowledgeable and reputable because of expertise in the subject area. If your group were looking for information of a medical nature, for instance, you would choose professional or scholarly medical journals instead of popular magazines as your sources.

This criterion is closely related to yet another, source bias, which deals with the degree to which the source can be objective about the topic or is relatively free of a vested interest in the topic. If your team were gathering information on the subject of school violence, you could find a wealth of information from the Web sites of lobbying groups, but you should consider the built-in bias of the information. How would you proceed? You could, perhaps, think of equally biased groups with equally vested interests in the topic but with different positions on the issues and seek information from those sources as well.

In many cases all sources are biased, so your best choice is to try to balance the biases. You might look at government documents, such as the *Congressional Record* because Congress holds complex and lengthy hearings on national problems while they write bills to create national policies. Still, as they hear testimony from many sides of controversial issues, they too must attempt to sift through biased information.

Warnick and Inch (1989), in their book, *Critical Thinking and Communication,* show that information, or **evidence,** is "not simply concrete facts or observable behavior." Evidence, rather, derives from three sources. The first is "objectively observable conditions in the world," such as "what we can see and hear, feel, touch, and smell" (p. 66). A second source of evidence would be "beliefs or premises generally accepted as true," though this would be a difficult use of evidence if there were fundamental and deep-seated differences among decision makers. A third source of evidence consists of "conclusions that have been previously established," in this case established by the group or team (p. 67).

Warnick and Inch (1989, p. 69) further divide evidence into two categories, that is, "fact and opinion as to fact." They define **facts** as "things people believe to be true either because they have experienced them or because they regard them as the truthfully reported experiences of others." Such facts can be obtained from a number of sources including reports and descriptions, or "nonnumerical or narrative accounts of some object or occurrence" that provide examples and illustrations.

TABLE 5.3	CRITERIA FOR ANALYZING EVIDENCE

Criteria	Questions
Reliability	Has this source of information been correct in the past?
Expertise	Does this source of information possess sufficient competence in the specific content area under consideration?
Consistency	Does this information seem to be generally in agreement with other sources on this topic? If not, why not? Does this source or piece of information remain the same throughout or does it contradict itself?
Recency	Is the information the latest available on the topic? If not, does it fit the time period for which it is being considered?
Relevance	Does the information actually apply to the topic under discussion or does it merely "seem like" good information?
Access	Has the source of the information actually had access to the relevant experience forming the basis for the data?
Accuracy of Citation	Is all of the information presented and is it presented in the context for which it was designed?
Source Itself	Is the information from a primary, or original, source or from a secondary source that combines or reports information from primary sources?

Adapted from Warnick and Inch, 1989, pp. 71–77.

Facts may also be represented by statistics, or "a quantitative summary of the characteristics of a population or a sample" (p. 70). Facts may also appear in the form of artifacts, or "physical evidence that helps to prove an argument." An **opinion** represents an "interpretation of the meaning of factual evidence" or a "judgment about how an event or state of affairs is to be understood, evaluated, or dealt with."

Warnick and Inch (1989, pp. 71–77) provide evidential criteria that groups would be wise to use in determining answers to their research questions. These criteria include reliability, objectivity, relevance, consistency, expertise, and recency, among others. Table 5.3 illustrates the kinds of questions, based on these criteria, that groups should ask themselves about the evidence they intend to use.

Reasoning with Data

Once a group has chosen a question to answer and gathered data from many sources, they must continue to practice critical thinking as they work with the information. Even though we are interested here in a cooperative discussion model of member behavior rather than an adversarial debate model, the concept of **argumentation** can help explain how critical thinking works in this phase. When we speak of argument, we do not mean the sort that children have on the playground; we do mean the use of structured proofs through which we can reach conclusions. Let us begin with some terminology.

Data, besides being the pieces of information gathered through research, are, according to Ziegelmueller, Kay, and Dause (1990, p. 56), "the starting points of argument, the substance from which we reason." These authors divide data into two kinds: **premises,** "the fundamental assumptions or beliefs that we bring to a situation and that we accept without external support," and **evidence,** "source materials that are external to us and that are used to lend support or proof to a conclusion" (p. 57). An argument, or a "complete unit of proof," contains three elements: "data, the reasoning process, and the conclusion" (p. 55).

Other authors use terminology from the classic Toulmin (1958) model of argumentation and replace the term reasoning with **warrants** and the term conclusion with the **claim;** add in **backing,** or support for the warrants; add **qualifiers,** or words that modify the claims, such as "probably" or "possibly"; and add **reservations** that give exceptions, expressed often as "unless" (Warnick and Inch, 1989, p. 167; Ericson, Murphy, and Zeuschner, 1987). Figure 5.1 illustrates the basic model.

Although data, claims, qualifiers, and reservations may be fairly easy to understand, the reasoning process—whatever we call it—needs more explanation. Reasoning is the key to moving from the evidence to the claim, or in the case of making a policy decision, the key to deciding on the basis of information gathered which of the alternate policy proposals would be best. Reasoning has traditionally been divided into inductive and deductive processes for establishing "relationships among data" (Ziegelmueller, Kay, and Dause, 1990, p. 59).

Inductive reasoning is often described as a process that moves from the specific to the general; **deductive reasoning** is moving from the general to the specific.

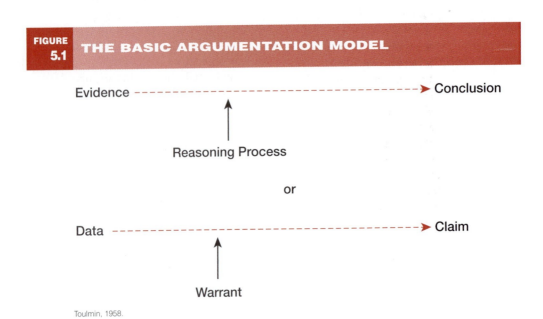

FIGURE 5.1 **THE BASIC ARGUMENTATION MODEL**

Evidence - ➤ Conclusion

↑

Reasoning Process

or

Data - ➤ Claim

↑

Warrant

Toulmin, 1958.

However, these descriptions are incomplete in that they do not explain how the reasoning process allows our thinking to move from the data to the claim. Ziegelmueller, Kay, and Dause (1990, pp. 60–61) define inductive reasoning as "the synthetic process used in moving from particulars to probable conclusions" and deductive reasoning as "the analytic process used in moving from generalities to structurally certain conclusions."

A synthetic process "involves the bringing together of elements into a whole," and induction does seek to bring many specifics together and establish the relationships between them. In order to make such connections, we draw inferences, educated guesses, from the specifics, which themselves may have been expressed as statistics. The use of statistics to summarize data means that we have not presented information about each specific instance, and so our conclusions or claims based on statistics go beyond the concrete data we have available from the sample we have studied. Our claims or conclusions reached by this type of reasoning process can only be expressed as probabilities, not as certainties (Ziegelmueller, Kay, and Dause, 1990, p. 60). Figure 5.2 presents an inductive argument in the form of a complete Toulmin model.

FIGURE 5.2 **AN INDUCTIVE TOULMIN MODEL**

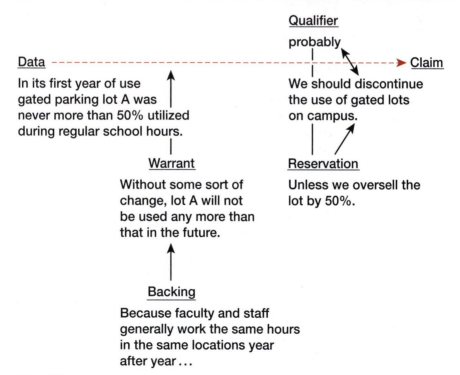

Qualifier
probably

Data -- ▶ Claim

In its first year of use
gated parking lot A was
never more than 50% utilized
during regular school hours.

We should discontinue
the use of gated lots
on campus.

Warrant

Without some sort of
change, lot A will not
be used any more than
that in the future.

Reservation

Unless we oversell the
lot by 50%.

Backing

Because faculty and staff
generally work the same hours
in the same locations year
after year . . .

Toulmin, 1958.

A DEDUCTIVE SYLLOGISM

Major Premise

All of the gated lots on campus were underutilized by at least 30 percent in their first year of use.

Minor Premise

Lot A is a gated lot.

Conclusion

Gated lot A was underutilized by at least 30 percent in its first year of use.

An analytic process, conversely, "is concerned with the breaking down of a whole into its parts," or it "relates parts to the whole through inclusion in, or exclusion from, a class." Deduction does move from the "more general to the less general," but its conclusions are "not necessarily specific," though they might be (Ziegelmueller, Kay, and Dause, 1990, pp. 61–62). If our beginning general statement is true, and if our parts actually are contained in the general statement, then a conclusion reached through this type of reasoning process may be expressed as a certainty.

Deductive arguments are often expressed in the form of three-part syllogisms, which contain a major premise for the "whole," a minor premise for the "part," and a conclusion based on their combination. "A Deductive Syllogism" illustrates this process. As you can see, the conclusion may be expressed as a certainty.

I often advise my students as they try to differentiate between these two types of reasoning to think of Sherlock Holmes. The great detective always discovers the certain identity of the murderer through deductive reasoning. He investigates all of the suspects (the whole) for motive and opportunity. Then he eliminates them one by one (the parts) until he has only one left. At the end of the book or the film versions, Holmes's colleague, Dr. Watson, always says, "Brilliant deduction, Mr. Holmes," to which he replies, "Elementary, my dear Watson."

Critical Thinking in the College Class: Skills and Attitudes

Short of taking an entire course on formal logic or argumentation, what do members of effective teams need to do to be able to think through their problem-solving or decision-making processes? Robert Ennis (1962, p. 84) provides a list (see Figure 5.3) of "aspects of critical thinking" you might find useful in evaluating your individual or group skill levels in this vital activity.

FIGURE
5.3 **ASPECTS OF CRITICAL THINKING**

1. Grasping the meaning of a statement
2. Detecting ambiguity in a statement
3. Judging whether given statements contradict each other
4. Judging whether a conclusion follows necessarily
5. Judging whether a statement is specific enough
6. Judging whether a statement is actually the application of a given principle
7. Judging the reliability of an observation
8. Judging whether an inductive conclusion is warranted
9. Judging whether the problem has been identified
10. Judging whether something is an assumption
11. Judging whether a definition is adequate
12. Judging whether a statement made by an alleged authority is acceptable

Ennis, 1962.

Skills in critical-thinking processes, though essential, must be accompanied by a critical attitude or a healthy skepticism about the nature of information. That does not mean group members vie with each other to see who can destroy the most evidence, but it does mean that they work together to weed out information that does not stand up to scrutiny. This cooperative critical process may be best accomplished by what Richard Paul (1987, p. 127) calls **dialogical thinking,** which, for its completion, must be subjected to a **dialectical thinking** process (p. 128).

As you saw in Chapter 2, dialogue, as opposed to monologue, requires that we open our thought processes to more than one alternative. In dialogic communication, we seriously consider the position or attitude of our communication partners and work through both our and their perspectives until we reach a view acceptable to both or to all, in the case of a team. In dialogic thinking, we seriously consider two or more different, perhaps opposite, possibilities and work through them until we reach a conclusion.

In dialectical thinking, we "reflect critically" on our own way of thinking and "reason sympathetically within frames of reference distinct from, and even opposed" to, our own (Smith, p. 51). According to Paul (1987), we must set these frames of reference "dialectically against each other so that the logical strength of one can be tested against the logical strength of the contending others by appealing to standards not peculiar to either" (p. 128). In a group or team setting, to practice dialogical or dialectical thinking would require members to question their own pathways to conclusions and to try to understand the pathways of others.

Although the term *dialectic* is sometimes simply equated with logical argument, explained above through use of the Toulmin model, here dialectic takes on an additional meaning that ties it more closely to the concept of dialogue. Start with one point of view and call that view the **thesis.** Think of the opposite of that view and label it the **antithesis.** If two persons with these two opposing views work together to resolve the differences in the views, seeking common ground, for instance, they might be able to find a **synthesis,** or a composite view. Dialectic is the process by which the thesis and antithesis find resolution in a synthesis. At the group level, the existence of more than two points of view will require genuine dialogue in order to achieve consensus.

CASE STUDY   **ARGUMENTATION IN THE *COLUMBIA* ACCIDENT REPORT**

This case study consists of excerpts from the *Columbia* Accident Investigation Board (CAIB) Report.

"The Columbia Accident Investigation Board's independent investigation into the February 1, 2003, loss of the Space Shuttle Columbia and its seven-member crew lasted nearly seven months. A staff of more than 120, along with some 400 NASA engineers, supported the Board's 13 members. Investigators examined more than 30,000 documents, conducted more than 200 formal interviews, heard testimony from dozens of expert witnesses, and reviewed more than 3,000 inputs from the general public. In addition, more than 25,000 searchers combed vast stretches of the Western United States to retrieve the spacecraft's debris.

"Because the events that initiated the accident were not apparent for some time, the investigation's depth and breadth were unprecedented in NASA history. Further, the Board determined early in the investigation that it intended to put this accident into context. We considered it unlikely that the accident was a random event; rather, it was likely related in some degree to NASA's budgets, history, and program culture, as well as to the politics, compromises, and changing priorities of the democratic process. We are convinced that the management practices overseeing the Space Shuttle Program were as much a cause of the accident as the foam that struck the left wing."

CAIB, 2003, pp. 9–11.

Discussion Questions/Activities for Case Study

1. Using the components of the inductive Toulmin argumentation model explained in this chapter, find and diagram the board's argument.

2. Using the criteria for analyzing evidence found in Table 5.3, evaluate the board's argument, recognizing that you have only two paragraphs from a 248-page report.

CONCLUSION

In this chapter you have been challenged to learn to think both creatively and critically, which appear to be quite contradictory skills. Try to see them, though, as processes that follow along a continuum with criteria development leading from one to the other. All three processes are vital to the success of the activities characterizing the next level of teamwork, that is, making good decisions that can help solve real problems.

You have been introduced to several methods for generating creative ideas, and you should give them each a try to see which works best for you and your team. Once you've achieved a sufficient list of items, perhaps a list of potential topics for a research project to be undertaken by your team, you will then need to narrow the list by applying some criteria, say, likelihood that our teacher would approve this topic or originality, or uniqueness, of the topic. Finding a unique topic might keep the team's interest high, but if a search yields very little information, then a criterion of "accessibility" could prove more useful.

The last step, that of critically evaluating the data you have gathered, requires your understanding of both inductive and deductive reasoning processes. Furthermore, you must be able to judge the validity of others' reasoning efforts because much of your research will reflect that sort of evidence. In Chapter 6 we apply these skills, attitudes, and processes to decision-making and problem-solving tasks. The following case study illustrates the uses of argument and evidence in the investigation of a recent national tragedy.

COLLABORATIVE LEARNING ACTIVITIES

1. In a brief class discussion, choose a controversial campus issue specific to your school. Then proceed with the following steps:

    A. Using Figure 5.2, each person develops a model argument to justify one claim.

    B. Through class discussion, determine whether the arguments tend to cluster into patterns of pro or con or something in between.

2. Form groups based on those clusters and combine your arguments.

    A. Make brief presentations of each group's set of arguments.

    B. Discuss how you could reconcile the sides and resolve the issue.

Chapter 6

Team Decision Making and Problem Solving

Corbis

Types and Procedures

KEY WORDS AND CONCEPTS

basic problem-solving procedure

choice phase

constraint-free consensus

critical evaluation of data

decision by consensus

decision making

design phase

devil's advocate

driving v. restraining forces

force-field analysis

goal orientation

intelligence phase

interaction process analysis (IPA)

maintenance orientation

outcome criteria

performance strategies

problem solving

process mapping

question of conjecture

question of fact

question of policy

question of value

review phase

socio-emotional behaviors

task orientation

valence

 To find out more about the Key Words and Concepts discussed in this chapter, use InfoTrac College Edition. Type in the keywords and subject terms. You can access InfoTrac College Edition from Wadsworth/Communication homepage: http://communication.wadsworth.com.

CAREER APPLICATION

Advisory groups that are often asked to function as decision makers are sometimes given too little information upon which to base reasonable judgments. Take this example from higher education:

Both the faculty and staff advisory councils were given data comparing the benefits offered by two proposed health insurance plans for the coming year. They were asked to decide which plan would best meet the needs of the university's employees. Considering only benefits, both groups agreed that Plan A was much better than Plan B. The university went forward with Plan A, but when the cost details were included in the form of a rate schedule, it could quickly be seen that the lowest paid hourly employees could not afford the huge costs associated with the "best" plan and would thus be able to have no insurance at all.

Thus far in this volume, you have read many examples of the kinds of tasks teams accomplish. Some theorists divide member roles into those most concerned with the job at hand and have a **task orientation** and those who focus on interpersonal relationships and have a **maintenance orientation.** In the traditional small group literature, tasks generally fall into two categories: **decision making** and **problem solving.** Regardless of whether groups function as part of an organizational structure or independently in the community, they will all have problems to overcome and choices to make. As you saw in Chapter 5, cognitive elements of creative thinking and critical thinking are necessary in accomplishing those tasks. In this chapter we explore the methods used to complete decision-making and problem-solving tasks most effectively.

THE RELATIONSHIP BETWEEN DECISION MAKING AND PROBLEM SOLVING

Decision making may be defined as "the act of choosing among a set of alternatives under conditions that necessitate choice" (Gouran, 1990, p. 3). Problem solving is much more complex. Brilhart and Galanes (1995, p. 207) define it as "a multi-step procedure through which a group develops a plan to move from an unsatisfactory state to a desired goal." Although the two processes are defined differently, in practice they are highly interwoven. Many decisions may need to be made before a single problem can be solved. On the other hand, one organizational decision may solve numerous problems while, no doubt, creating new ones. An endless array of tasks—problems to solve, decisions to make, actions to take, evaluations to conduct, people to hire, schedules to change, prices to adjust, products to develop—present themselves to organizations worldwide every day.

Some decision makers or problem solvers concentrate sincerely on the task at hand and can be said to be task oriented. Burningham and West (1995, p. 107) define this term as "a shared concern with excellence and quality of task performance." Strongly task-oriented groups would emphasize accountability of their members; they would also find ways of measuring their progress. They would give and receive feedback on their performance. They would develop "clear **outcome criteria**"; that is, they would set standards for completion of their work that would help them decide when the task was actually completed, so they could move on to their next task. They would expect and value differences of opinion (Tjosvold, 1982).

DECISION-MAKING PROCESSES

Simon's Decision-Making Activities

Herbert A. Simon's Nobel-prize-winning work on decision processes (1977) presents us with four kinds of activity needed to make decisions: **intelligence, design, choice,** and **review.** These may be considered steps in a sequence.

Intelligence refers to the data-gathering stage, in which groups investigate not only the details surrounding problems that need solving, such as those involving airline safety, for instance, but also the circumstances that require decisions be made even when no problems seem to exist.

Design refers to the generation of possible alternative courses of action. Choice refers to the period when the alternatives are considered for selection. Once the choice has been made, the review process monitors the implementation of that choice for effectiveness. Indeed, the process of gathering intelligence may be said to have started once again during the review phase (Guzzo, 1986, pp. 35–37).

Gouran's Criteria

Dennis Gouran and his colleagues (1978, 1990) developed a process for evaluating the communicative behaviors of group members as they attempt to make effective decisions. His evaluation criteria, heavily weighted toward reasoning with high-quality information, asked questions about the performance of individuals such as the following:

- Were the member's contributions goal oriented?
- Did the member initiate topics relevant to the discussion?
- Did the member amplify topics through development of relevant data?
- Did the member contribute consistently throughout the discussion?
- Did the member present and cite data from qualified sources when appropriate?
- Did the member **critically evaluate data** by picking and choosing the best for use in decision making?

As you will see, these sorts of questions may be used to evaluate your performance as a decision maker. Because you may wonder just what you would say in order to accomplish those goals, the box "How Would I Communicate These Criteria?" provides examples.

Basic Types of Decision Questions

For decision-making processes to work well, group members must be skilled in conducting research to answer basic **questions of fact** (what has actually happened, as in the case of a plane crash) or **questions of conjecture** (what might have happened). This research process requires gathering data that itself must be measured against criteria, as we learned in Chapter 5, such as accuracy, recency, adequacy, credibility, trustworthiness, and reliability. These judgments about information were difficult enough in earlier times; with the massive data, both real and "unreal," available on the Internet, we must be even more vigilant about the quality of the data we choose for decision making.

Questions of value (what is the worth of something) involve exploration of the human or organizational needs or priorities that are at stake when decisions

HOW WOULD I COMMUNICATE THESE CRITERIA?

Goal Orientation

Begins, summarizes, or concludes the discussion; assists reticent members to enter the discussion; assists in management of conflict; orients the group to the agenda; notes and mentions the passage of time; moves the group along when necessary; monitors participation levels

Topic Initiation

Introduces content areas relevant to the research question under discussion; does not bring up extraneous elements that would take the group off the topic

Topic Amplification

Introduces details from his or her own research in the form of examples, illustrations, narratives, statistics, and so forth, that add to the group's understanding of the topic

Consistent Contribution

Participates in equal proportion throughout the discussion; is neither dominant nor partially absent

Source Citation

Provides name and credentials of sources of information; includes publication or other distribution data

Critical Evaluation of Data

Exemplifies critical thinking by means of reasoning—comparing, contrasting, concluding, predicting, asserting, and so forth—based on evidence presented by self or others during the course of the discussion

Adapted from Gouran, 1990.

are made or problems are solved in one way as opposed to another. Such questions of value, such as those provided in "Types of Decision Questions to Ask Yourselves," must be carefully thought through; their answers may serve as some of the criteria you need for judging your alternative solutions.

TYPES OF DECISION QUESTIONS TO ASK YOURSELVES*

Question of Fact

What is the nature of the relationship between perceived "natural" sleep cycles (work in the daytime; sleep at night) and worker productivity?

Related Question of Fact   What is the nature of the relationship between employee shift rotation and job satisfaction?

Question of Value

What is the worth or desirability (benefits and detriments) of employee shift rotation in twenty-four-hour, seven-day-a-week facilities?

Related Question of Value   What values are at stake when employers mandate three twelve-hour shifts to replace five eight-hour shifts?

Question of Policy

What should be Organization X's work scheduling policy?

* Notice that all questions are open (no yes-or-no answers possible) to generate as many answers as possible.

Questions of policy (what shall we do) require that you compile enough viable alternatives to facilitate a good final choice. Too often groups think only in yes-or-no categories and limit themselves to "this solution" as opposed to "that solution." One way to broaden your choices is to start with "everything" and "nothing." At one end of that spectrum lies an extreme solution; at the other lies the option of doing nothing at all. Think of the world of possibilities that lie between those two points. "Types of Decision Questions. . ." presents an organizational example of ways fact, value, and policy question types can interrelate.

Making a decision from among the choices available requires much time and effort in order to arrive at an answer to a question of policy. Often it is an organizational policy change that a group seeks in order to solve a problem. The different types of decision questions require different kinds of information gathered in a wide variety of ways. This information then must be synthesized into usable forms for workable and fair policies. Once a policy decision has been made, an action plan should be devised specifying who will do what, within what time frame, and with what expected results. Then after a reasonable period of time has passed, results of the new policy should be measured. The following case study illustrates a "real-world" project completed by a communication consulting company.

**HOW CAN WE BEST PRODUCE
PATIENT NEWSLETTERS?**

Those with careers in the communication consulting field often work in teams in order to find creative ways to serve their clients' needs. This case study gives you a "real-world" example of the kinds of decision-making and problem-solving tasks consultants must tackle.

*T*he manager of a communication consulting company was asked by her client to consider combining three quarterly patient newsletters into one consolidated newsletter that addressed diabetes, heart disease, and chronic obstructive pulmonary disease (COPD). The problems perceived by the client had to do with costs of producing three different newsletters, one for each disease, and the logistical complications of producing three different newsletters. The manager and her team considered the following three alternative solutions: combine all newsletters into one with separate sections for diabetes, heart disease, and COPD; combine newsletter schedules but keep the actual newsletters separate; include more general health topics and customize where possible; reduce the number of articles per issue; and continue to produce one newsletter for each disease to be sent to both patients and physicians with no changes.

The team developed a set of criteria against which to judge their alternatives, such as "continue to provide same high quality content to patients," "satisfy multiple reviewers from managed care organizations," "reduce costs to client," and "simplify project management requirements." Once they had gathered facts about each alternative, they applied their criteria to their data and began to see that the disadvantages for the "combining newsletters" option grew much faster than the advantages. By placing their question into a decision matrix, with alternatives on the vertical axis and advantages and disadvantages based on their criteria on the horizontal axis, they could clearly analyze their options. The team noted that the matrix also opened up "roadblocks that were not readily apparent when we just informally talked it through."

To conclude the decision about how to produce the newsletters, the team "provided the client with the grid and briefly explained our process for arriving at our decision." They then "walked the client through several scaled-back options." In the end, the client was "satisfied with our thought process and had no objections to following our recommendation, which was to leave the newsletters alone."

Personal Communication, Lori Poag, 2002.

Discussion Questions for Case Study

1. Of the question types explained in this chapter, which ones were the members of this team faced with in this project?
2. Is this case study best thought of as a decision-making or a problem-solving exercise? Why do you think so?

PROBLEM-SOLVING PROCESSES

Organizational problems range from the simple to the enormously complicated. One overriding problem that plagues almost every organization relates to the scheduling of work. The problem becomes especially acute in twenty-four-hour, seven-day-a-week operations such as medical facilities. Health care, of course, is not the only provider of round-the-clock service. With every increase in the globalization of the economy, more organizations find themselves staying up all night because it is daytime where their customers live.

Problem-Solving Examples

Some problems and problem solvers rise to the level of public awareness through the news media. The National Transportation Safety Board (NTSB), for example, a federal agency created to "promote transportation safety in the areas of civil aviation, highway, railroad, marine, pipeline, and hazardous materials," investigates airline crashes to determine their probable causes. In their "investigative phase," the board sends a "crash team" to the accident site to gather data from witnesses, survivors, voice and flight data recorders, and physical evidence, among other factors. They analyze potential causes such as weather and air-traffic conditions; aircraft operations, structure, systems, and maintenance; human error; and process error (Ray, 1999, pp. 305–306).

The NTSB may then hold public hearings to gather more information from witnesses whose "employees, functions, activities, or products were involved in the accident and whose specialized skills and knowledge can contribute to the development of evidence" (Ray, 1999, pp. 318–321). Once the NTSB completes the investigation and analysis and establishes probable cause, the board then makes recommendations, each of which "designates the person, or the party, expected to take action, describes the action the Board expects, and clearly states the safety need to be satisfied" (p. 321).

A final example from a corporate team illustrates the connectedness of problem solving and decision making. When the team lost a member through promotion, they developed a very complex and stringent set of criteria, analyzed the credentials of nineteen internal applicants, and found none who could measure up to their own 99.7 percent attendance record. They revised that standard, however, when they realized that their schedules allowed the luxury of flexibility that had never been available to other employees. They could, for instance, more easily schedule a dental appointment by knowing they could make up the time later. This team managed to solve their problem by deciding to rethink their attendance criterion. "Highly Successful Team's Criteria for New Member" illustrates this team's revised hiring standards.

HIGHLY SUCCESSFUL TEAM'S CRITERIA FOR NEW MEMBER

1. Matches their work style
2. Not shopping around for easier position in the company
3. Matches their 99.7 percent attendance record

Revised to say: Matches the company's average attendance record

4. Highly responsible
5. Cooperative
6. Good work ethic
7. A history of good work habits
8. Commitment to the team
9. Calm under pressure
10. Willing to help teammates

Hill's RMC Team, 1994.

John Dewey's Model

Many theorists have developed models of decision making or problem solving based on sequential steps. A commonly used process, John Dewey's problem-solving method (1910) contains the following steps:

1. Define the problem.
2. Analyze the problem.
3. Develop a set of criteria or standards by which to judge potential solutions.
4. List possible alternatives.
5. Evaluate all solutions.
6. Choose the best alternative solution.

"Basic Problem-Solving Procedure" provides suggestions for using Dewey's model.

The first two steps in Dewey's model may seem quite cut-and-dried, but we can see their relevance if we look again at the 2003 space shuttle *Columbia* accident. As we have noted before, the *Columbia* Accident Investigation Board's report placed blame on NASA's "culture," a nebulous term in this context. Chapter 6 of the report (CAIB, 2003, p. 12) clarifies the term as it "documents management performance related to *Columbia*" in regard to four specific issues: "the history of foam strikes . . . to determine how . . . managers rationalized the danger from repeated strikes on the Orbiter's Thermal Protection System"; the "intense pressure the program was under to stay on schedule, driven largely by the self-imposed

BASIC PROBLEM-SOLVING PROCEDURE

Define the Problem

This may be the most important step because, contrary to popular assumptions, all members will not understand the problem the same way.

Analyze the Problem

This step requires research into potential causes, symptoms, depth, and breadth of the problem.

Develop a Set of Criteria or Standards by Which to Judge Potential Solutions

Some examples might include cost effectiveness, basic fairness, feasibility, and workability; the list must then be divided into essential and desirable criteria.

List Possible Alternative Solutions

Strive for creativity through brainstorming, perhaps; find as many solutions as possible.

Evaluate All Solutions

Measure them against all final criteria; eliminate as you go along.

Choose Best Alternative Solution

The best solution may actually be a combination of possible solutions that meet the final criteria.

Adapted from Dewey, 1910.

requirement to complete the International Space Station"; the "effort by some NASA engineers to obtain additional imagery of *Columbia* to determine if the foam strike had damaged the Orbiter"; and "how management dealt with that effort."

The summary in Chapter 6 of the report (CAIB, 2003, p. 170) concludes as follows: "Perhaps most striking is the fact that management . . . displayed no interest in understanding a problem and its implications. . . . In fact, their management techniques unknowingly imposed barriers that kept at bay both engineering concerns and dissenting views and ultimately helped create 'blind

TABLE 6.1	A PROCESS MODEL OF TASK PERFORMANCE	

Processes	Simon's Activities	Dewey's Procedures
Research	Intelligence	Define problem Analyze problem
Creative thinking	Design	Develop criteria List alternatives
Consensus	Choice	Evaluate solutions Choose best solution
Implementation	Action Planning	
Measurement	Review	

Adapted from Simon, 1977, and Dewey, 1910.

spots' that prevented them from seeing the danger the foam strike posed." Certainly we cannot solve a problem if we will not recognize its existence, and here the failure first to define the problem and second to analyze the problem led to a human and technological disaster.

Dewey's and Simon's sets of steps are only two out of a multitude of similar models. However, while Simon leaves implicit the implementation stage and moves from choice to planning to review, Dewey's model never goes beyond choice. Table 6.1 folds them into a newer model that treats these activities not as a series of predictable steps but as different processes groups must learn to use. The processes include research, creative thinking, consensus, implementation, and measurement. For the implementation process, action plans like those we saw in Chapter 4 would be quite useful.

Interaction Process Analysis

Robert Bales (1950), an early group communication theorist, developed a method for studying the communicative interactions of members, especially as they relate to problem solving. His set of categories divided task-oriented behaviors into asking and answering and likewise divided maintenance or **socioemotional behaviors** into positive, negative, and mixed comments. Regarding the task, according to Bales, members ask for and provide information, opinions, and suggestions. In the social or emotional realm, individuals agree and disagree with each other and with information and positions taken, they help and reward each other or attack others and defend themselves, and they either create or try to reduce tension. Although Bales's clear separation of social and task categories has been criticized by scholars as too exclusive, his system has proven quite useful in helping students understand two general goals of most groups: to accomplish a task yet maintain harmonious, and thus productive, social relationships at the same time. Table 6.2 shows the types of communication acts Bales placed in each category.

TABLE 6.2	BALES'S INTERACTION PROCESS ANALYSIS CATEGORIES

Socio-emotional Area

Positive Reactions	Negative Reactions
1. Shows solidarity	Shows antagonism
2. Shows tension release	Shows tension
3. Agrees	Disagrees

Task Area

Attempted Answers	Questions
4. Gives suggestion	Asks for suggestion
5. Gives opinion	Asks for opinion
6. Gives orientation	Asks for orientation

Groups Work Through the Above Pairs in Solving Problems of:

1. Integration
2. Tension management
3. Decision making
4. Control
5. Evaluation
6. Orientation/information

Adapted from Bales, 1950.

Bales's system was designed for describing and recording what group members do, not for prescribing what they should or should not do. However, among the negative individual communication behaviors in the social realm, we find several that would be potentially quite harmful to your group outcomes. These range from withdrawing from participation with and withholding help from your teammates to actually attacking their status or credibility.

PERFORMANCE STRATEGIES FOR DECISION MAKING AND PROBLEM SOLVING

Guzzo (1986, pp. 55–57) provides five "essential considerations" that must be met by organizations and teams for effective problem solving and decision making. These include the nature of the task itself; the rewards provided for performing the task; the resources available to the task group; the team's level of autonomy, or control over their own work; and their use of appropriate **"performance strategies."** "Five Essential Considerations for Effectiveness" clarifies these factors.

The concept of performance strategies bears careful scrutiny. Indeed, your team's understanding of performance strategies may hold the key to your success at accomplishing your tasks in this course. This understanding will help you answer the ever-present question, "What should we be doing *now*?" When you work in class, your instructor is there to guide you through activities that prepare you to work alone. But during team meetings outside of class, a full set of strategies for action and an accurate sense of when each is appropriate will make all the difference. So what are your options?

Decision Phases

1. Intelligence Phase   Guzzo (1986, pp. 57–58) divides his set of strategies along the lines provided in Simon's four activities phases. In the **intelligence phase** the group must "adhere to a basic principle of detecting a discrepancy between *what is* and *what should be*" that is "predicated on agreement about goals and goal clarity." If goals are clear, the group may use **force-field analysis** to "define as precisely as possible the discrepancy between present and desired conditions." Here the group seeks out the driving forces, or "those things that help bring about the desired end," or even those that support a current bad situation. The group also seeks the **restraining forces,** or those that prevent either the desired end or the bad situation. Then the group

---

FIVE ESSENTIAL CONSIDERATIONS FOR EFFECTIVENESS

1. The Task: Is it different from that of other groups? Is it motivating and meaningful? Is it a whole task? Is it overly stressful?

2. Rewards: Pay, recognition, and time off must be distributed equally if a high degree of coordinated effort is needed.

3. Resources: Resources (membership resources such as skill, expertise, and strength; organizational resources such as training and development, advice, and planned interventions such as team-building experiences; and decision support systems) affect the group's sense of potency, or the "collective belief by a group that it can be effective" (Guzzo, 1986, p. 55).

4. Autonomy: This critical factor "can determine their membership, rules for meetings, division of labor, rules for selecting one alternative over another, and methods of reviewing past choices" (p. 56).

5. Appropriate performance strategies: Choice of strategy depends on which part of the decision-making process the group is conducting.

Guzzo, 1986.

compares the relative strengths of these opposing forces. Groups may also use brainstorming, the creative thinking technique we learned in Chapter 5, as a performance strategy during this phase (Guzzo, pp. 57–58). Table 6.3 illustrates a force field analysis created by five student groups in their efforts to answer a question of fact comparing causes of school violence. Their final goal if they were engaged in a policy discussion would be to devise a school policy to help alleviate the problem of violence.

TABLE 6.3	CLASSROOM EXAMPLE OF A FORCE-FIELD ANALYSIS

The Question

What forces are holding student-to-student violence in place in high schools, and what forces are inhibiting it in colleges?

The Process

1. Class is divided into five small groups of five members each.
2. Groups use brainstorming to generate lists of factors.
3. Lists are then compiled to find common threads.

The Analysis

Accelerators in High Schools (driving forces)	*Inhibitors* in Colleges (restraining forces)
Group 1	
TV violence	more freedom
lack of supervision	more challenges
Group 2	
media influence	less TV watching
cliques	old cliques broken up
Group 3	
adolescence	older students
intolerance of difference	more differences
Group 4	
in-group/out-groups	more opportunities
hate groups	more people
Group 5	
depression	optimistic environment
drugs	culture

One other performance strategy potentially useful in the early stages of problem solving, **process mapping,** consists of literally drawing on paper all the steps needed to complete a process. By mapping, simplifying, and then simplifying again, tangled processes can be improved. Let's take a hypothetically tangled registration process for college classes. While some schools get it right, others enforce antiquated control mechanisms that require tracing and retracing many unnecessary bureaucratic approval steps. If your team took on the question, "What should be our school's registration process?" your best first step would be to map the existing process (Stewart, 1991).

2. Design Phase   In the design phase groups can use brainstorming or the nominal group technique as performance strategies, or they could proceed with criteria development, Dewey's third step of the problem-solving procedure.

3. Choice Phase   In the choice phase Guzzo suggests that, on the one hand, groups could simply use a voting procedure such as unanimity or majority rule. On the other hand, they could choose among the alternatives they have listed in the design phase by looking for **valence,** or the accumulation of positive and negative comments made about each alternative during discussion. Choices could be made through the use of a decision matrix (see Chapter 5) in which the alternatives are listed along with their positive and negative attributes. A multi-attribute decision analysis, which adds a weighted value for each of the various attributes, could provide an even more complex means of choosing among the alternative problem solutions or decisions.

If teamwork is the goal, an equally complex yet essential performance strategy would be **decision making by consensus,** a word often misused and misunderstood. Glassman (1992, p. 6) explains that consensus is not "a unanimous vote. It is a decision that the majority favors, and that the minority, after being heard and having had ample time to persuade and influence the majority, agrees to support and implement." According to Caws (1991, pp. 378–379), consensus is

---

MOMENTS DISCERNABLE IN A CONSENSUS-SEEKING PROCESS

1. The Initial Situation: The group must agree, at the least, on procedures they will use to make their decision. They must agree, at the least, that something in the situation needs to be addressed.

2. Changes in Positions: Observer could see points at which individuals change from opposition to support and vice versa.

3. Emergent Collective Judgment: The group makes a judgment that a course of action is *right*, though not necessarily a collective judgment about *why* it is right.

Moreno, 1988.

"something more than acquiescence or compromise" because "the expectation is that the members . . . will all agree that the outcome is, if not the very best in the opinion of each, at least thoroughly acceptable to each."

Achieving consensus requires time and discussion. In fact, Habermas (1975), whose speech acts theory we studied in Chapter 2, insists that consensus can only be found through discourse, to him a special kind of communication found in an ideal speech situation. Only when team members speak as equals, without concern for power differences, and only when they communicate about the relative merits of the proposals under consideration, can they arrive at a **constraint-free consensus.** This consensus "expresses," Habermas says, a "rational will" that "permits only what *all* can want" (pp. 107–108).

Why would we wish to spend the time and effort needed for consensus? For one thing, decision making, once the province of those in authority, now is handled more and more often by groups whose members possess differing backgrounds and experiences. Caws (1991, p. 376) gives us the example of a medical team composed of "a physician, a nurse, a social worker, a representative of a patients' advocacy group, a lawyer, an administrator, and a philosopher." This group meets regularly to decide such matters as "admission and retention of patients with new and rare diseases and conditions and the provision or withholding of scarce drugs, therapeutic technologies, or basic life support." How could such significant decisions be derived from anything less than consensus?

Consensus also has the advantage of giving decision makers "confidence in the rightness of the result" (Caws, 1991, p. 385). It frequently produces the "most supported, most implementable, most liked plan" among the alternatives proposed (Glassman, 1992, p. 7). Most important, perhaps, it "ensures that the truth that lies in the minority is surfaced, heard, understood, and not lost" (p. 6).

HALL'S RULES FOR CONSENSUS DECISION MAKING

1. Avoid arguing for your individual judgments. Approach the decision on the basis of logic.

2. Avoid changing your mind only in order to reach agreement and avoid conflict. Support only solutions with which you are able to agree somewhat at least.

3. Avoid "conflict-reducing" techniques such as majority vote, averaging, or trading in reaching decisions.

4. View differences of opinions as helpful rather than as a hindrance in decision-making. Differences of opinion are natural and expected. Seek them out and try to involve everyone in the decision process.

5. Disagreements can help the group's decision because, with a wide range of information and opinions, there is a greater chance that the group will hit upon more adequate solutions.

Hall and Watson, 1970.

NEGATIVE ALTERNATIVES TO CONSENSUS

Near Consensus: Implied support created by pressure for agreement or acceptance of silence

Majority Vote: Coalition formation resulting in unwilling minority; winners and losers

Minority Wins: Action prevented, status quo preserved by powerful minority

Handshake: Two members agree and proceed to act, whether others support the action or not

Self-Authorization: One member makes a suggestion and acts on it when no one objects; perceives silence as support

Glassman, 1992.

Consensus achievement is a process rather than a product, though certainly a decision product results from the process. As a process, it too features stages or steps. See "Moments Discernable in a Consensus-Seeking Process" for three in the course of consensus gathering. As a performance strategy, consensus may be achieved more efficiently if the team avoids certain pitfalls. "Hall's Rules for Consensus Decision Making" presents five concrete guidelines.

Other writers provide additions to our list of performance strategies, some positive and some negative. Think about the unfortunate frequency with which the examples found in "Negative Alternatives to Consensus" are actually used.

4. Review Phase   In the review phase groups often rationalize, or try to find good reasons for, the choice they have made, which serves to build commitment for carrying through on the decision. However, such rationalizing may prevent the group from seeing that its choice was poor and thus cause them to cling to it too long. Guzzo (1986, pp. 61–63) suggests that a "skilled" member may need to play the role of **"devil's advocate,"** a process discussed in Chapter 8, so that early favored choices can be challenged.

WHEN MAINTENANCE *IS* THE TASK

The above-mentioned separation of task from maintenance functions and the emphasis on rational models of decision making may in some cases be artificial and counter-productive to our understanding of group processes and needs.

For members of community associations like those found in Chapter 3 (Meyers and Brashers, 1994, p. 76), group maintenance or group survival becomes the task.

If these groups fail to ensure the quality of their interpersonal relationships, they may languish and eventually disappear. They certainly make decisions and solve problems as do work teams, but they may go about those processes differently. Think of the positive changes possible in the business world, however, if we could incorporate the values prevalent in those volunteer settings, that is, harmony, community, group concerns, relationships, continuity, and interdependence (Kanter, 1972; Buzzanell, 1994). Much research remains to be done before we understand fully the procedures needed for task completion in voluntary associations.

CONCLUSION

This chapter has been designed to focus your attention on the assortment of tasks, "how-to's," processes, and strategies needed by members of successful teams. In addition to task needs, we must think about the maintenance, or socio-emotional, needs of effective teams. Indeed, we have found that for some community groups, survival depends on serving the emotional needs of their members.

For a problem to be solved, we must first recognize, acknowledge, and explore the problem itself. Only then can we ask the right kinds of questions and make the most appropriate kinds of decisions about how to solve it. However, even the best processes or strategies cannot guarantee that your team will succeed if your member interactions fail either to accomplish the task or achieve positive interpersonal relationships. Consensus decision making, the ideal we strive for, cannot be achieved without good socio-emotional relationships, but neither can it be achieved without careful deliberations over the task. In the next chapter we will explore the role of leadership in fostering both task and interpersonal achievement.

COLLABORATIVE LEARNING ACTIVITIES

1. Begin a problem-solving process using the first two steps of Dewey's procedure for the following question: "How shall we deal with the problem of lack of access to higher education on the part of nontraditional students?" Continue the problem-solving process using steps three and four of Dewey's procedure for the same question. Finish the process using steps five and six for the question.

2. Conduct a decision-making process for the following question of value: "What important features of our campus would be at stake if we chose to offer classes only from 8:00 a.m. to 3:00 p.m., Monday through Friday?

Chapter 7

Teamwork and Leadership

Corbis

Theories and Their Applications in a Team Environment

KEY WORDS AND CONCEPTS

autocratic style

born-leader or trait theory

leadership
  charismatic
  distributed
  maintenance
  servant
  shared emergent
  symbiotic
  traditional
  transactional
  transformational

power
  coercive
  expert
  legitimate
  referent
  reward

contingency theories

democratic style

egoless leader

ethic of equality

functional theories

great-man theory

laissez-faire style

leadership as coaching

leadership as empowerment

leadership as facilitation

leadership theories

maintenance leadership

rotated-role leadership model

self-management leader

servant leadership

shared emergent-leadership

single-leader theories

situational-leadership theory

To find out more about the Key Words and Concepts discussed in this chapter, use InfoTrac College Edition. Type in the keywords and subject terms. You can access InfoTrac College Edition from Wadsworth/Communication homepage: http://communication.wadsworth.com.

CAREER APPLICATION

School systems are beginning to adopt site-based management, in which councils of faculty, staff, parents, and students participate in decision making. At one school which has never had a principal, the following communication guidelines help ensure the shared-leadership model:

- We are all part of the same team; we collectively own the problems, and we collectively solve them.
- We will allow conflict and differing ideas to exist.
- We will help and support others.
- I will be honest and I will commit to practice these guidelines.

    As they point out, the "us-versus-them dynamic doesn't materialize, because there's no them—just us."

Barnett, McKowen, and Bloom, 1998, pp. 48–50.

The new emphasis on teams in the workplace has resulted in a questioning of our older views about the nature of **leadership** in a small group or team. In this chapter you will be introduced to the **shared-emergent-leadership** style, one quite applicable to both a teamwork and a learning environment. The term *style* has been chosen because in a team, as in life, we need a range of behaviors to select among as our groups or situations change. The dynamic nature of teamwork requires that all members of the team understand these possible choices and practice them to the group's advantage when needed.

Learning environments require opportunities to practice what we teach. Unfortunately, classroom group activities sometimes go one of two ways. In the first scenario, a student who is highly motivated by good grades will do most of the work, will resent and be resented by the remainder of the group, and all will come to dread the phrase *group project*. In the second instance, little motivation exists, little is accomplished, and all perceive the activity as something merely to get through. These problems can be predicted and avoided if, from the very first day, the culture of the class is built on the philosophy of reward for equal participation, avoidance of dominance, and high-quality leadership resulting in positive outcomes. If one of the goals of the course is to foster leadership skills in each student in the class, then through the use of shared emergent-leadership, all students may learn to lead by leading.

UNDERSTANDING THE TERMS

Understanding of Leadership Common to the Culture

Let's begin building our understanding of leadership by reference to an American cultural icon, the television and film series *Star Trek*. If, like many in the United States and around the world, you have absorbed the lore of the starship *Enterprise,* you can no doubt hear the voices of Captain Kirk, Scotty, Dr. McCoy, and Mr. Spock debating the finer points of leadership. To Spock, logic should always prevail; for the captain, however, emotion often takes precedence over logic. Even so, Kirk's judgments inevitably prove sound, and we know why he is the captain. In one television episode, Spock expresses his puzzlement that the three earthlings seem to admire the villain Khan. Captain Kirk explains that humans all have within them a "streak of barbarism," which allows them to abhor, yet respect, the successful, though ruthless, use of power (Coon and Wilbur, 1966). Captain Kirk serves nicely here as our model for a **traditional leader.**

A newer version of *Star Trek*, featuring Captain Jean-Luc Picard, provides a glimpse of the possibilities of teamwork. This captain exercises leadership, but he actively pursues a policy of group decision making. Sharing the power to act in the best interests of the ship and its crew, he trusts his colleagues' skills and training. He removes obstacles from their path. Picard serves us well as a model for **leadership as facilitation.**

Turning from TV and movies to the world of sports, think of the role of a coach. Here is a person who both leads and follows, and who, while standing apart, still functions as an integral part of a team. The coach assists others in learning how to do their best work, sets rules, and encourages high performance standards. A swim team coach never gets in the pool during the swim meet but still deserves thanks at the medal ceremony for helping the team to reach its goal.

These images clarify three key terms regarding the differences between traditional and team leadership. A traditional leader, typically hired or appointed for a particular level of technical or managerial expertise, ostensibly knows what should be done and issues directives to others. A facilitator, typically part of a personnel, human-resources, communication, or training department, but perhaps formerly a leader, acts as a resource to the team (Bach, 1967). The facilitator helps the team both determine and accomplish its goals by interceding, for example, with the larger organization when the team meets with impediments. And someone practicing **leadership as coaching** guides, encourages, and teaches.

A return to the *Star Trek* model with which we began our exploration of leadership provides a synthesis of leader, facilitator, and coach in the person of Kathryn Janeway, captain of the starship *Voyager*. In the pilot episode of this newer *Star Trek* series, Janeway "boldly goes where no man has gone before" as the first female starship captain, and she invokes the concept of leader as teacher. One of the episode's plotlines involves a "Caretaker" who nurtures and protects the inhabitants of an alien planet to the degree that they cannot exist without him. He has kept all knowledge and power so much to himself that when he dies, they will perish with him. Janeway's solution lies in his teaching them how to survive on their own. Although she thus exemplifies the **empowering leader,** later, at a point of crisis, she orders the crew to violate the "Prime Directive" against interference in the life course of other cultures. When the chief engineer questions her power to be "making these decisions for all of us," the first officer replies simply, "She's the captain" (Piller and Taylor, 1995). Table 7.1 compares **leadership theories** with these characters from popular culture.

Workplace Leadership Terminology

Does this new leadership concept exist only in the flickering images of televised science fiction or on the movie screen? Although Captain Kirk still personifies probably the most prevalent leadership style, Picard and Janeway types actually do exist in business and industry. At Saturn, for example, a "shifting leadership" pattern allows self-directed work unit members to perform their daily tasks without direction from above but with accountability. Team members, of course, must be committed to their unit's success in order to make effective operational decisions. With adequate training, each unit is considered capable of determining assignments, assuring safety, and distributing tasks equally to its own members. Saturn's philosophy that "people are our greatest strategic resource" and their "clean sheet approach" to each person's strengths combine to support each employee's efforts to learn and practice leadership (Saturn Corporation, 1990).

TABLE 7.1	THE EVOLUTION OF LEADERSHIP THEORY

Styles	Behaviors
Traditional Leader	"knows," directs, demands
Facilitator	serves as resource, helps remove obstacles
Coach	guides, encourages, teaches

Styles	Star Trek Captain
Traditional Leader	James T. Kirk, *Star Trek*
Facilitator	Jean-Luc Picard, *Star Trek: The Next Generation*
Synthesis of all three styles	Kathryn Janeway, *Star Trek: Voyager*

At Honeywell, as far back as the early 1980s, efforts were made to change from the "Patton style" of leadership, meaning, of course, a military style, to a "collaborative way of operating" (Boyle, 1992, p. 14).

Management communication scholar Ted Zorn (2003) suggests that social changes—including lifestyle patterns, media messages, and rapid technological shifts—require different types of leadership. Perhaps, he notes, even renowned past leaders such as Winston Churchill and Abraham Lincoln might not work so well in modern times. New terminologies have developed to describe both attitudes and processes needed to implement leadership transformations. The **egoless leader** is able to relinquish control to teams because she or he can take satisfaction from helping others develop their skills (Zawacki and Norman, 1991, p. 78). Those who favor **distributed leadership** view the attribute as "a collection of roles and behaviors that can be split apart, shared, rotated, and used sequentially or concomitantly" (Barry, 1991, p. 34). With all members equally authorized to lead, multiple and complementary leadership functions can be performed by those most adept. **Symbiotic leadership** promotes the interdependence of both labor and management in organizations that are gradually moving away from the hierarchical leadership paradigm (Edwards, 1992, p. 28).

COMPETING VIEWPOINTS

The leadership philosophy most useful in a team environment encompasses all of these terms. Leading, or knowing what to do and how and when to do it, underlies facilitating, coaching, and teaching. Differences between the single-leader and the teamwork models of leadership lie in two complementary features: a sharing of the power to direct the work of others and an absence of direction when none is needed. This concept of shared emergent-leadership has been a part of our theorizing about leadership since long before teamwork became a part of the workplace, but it has found its most profound application there. In this environment, leadership knowledge and power are freely held by all but exercised only when the necessity arises.

A Look at the Extremes

For a full understanding of this new leadership philosophy, we need a backward glance. Conventional wisdom has long endorsed the single-leader model and still predicts chaos in its absence. According to Pamela Roby (1998, p. 3) of the Society for the Study of Social Problems, "most of us have been deprived through authoritarian, competitive schooling, racism, sexism, classism, and so on, of the exercise and even knowledge of our real leadership abilities." A sense of helplessness may result from our cultural practices and institutions that seek to control our behaviors from an early age. Historically, schoolrooms have been places where children were seen and not heard while teachers were admonished to be good disciplinarians above all. The days of the silent classroom are passing by, however, as school systems move toward cooperative or collaborative learning. Here children discover how to function in groups, and even teams, by coaching each other, say, in the intricacies of long division.

At the opposite end of the spectrum lies the belief that we should have no leader. Those subscribing to this view claim that the presence of a leader destroys the equality that should be present among the members and promotes an unhealthy dependence on that leader. Such dependence reduces the competence levels of followers over time (Gemmill, 1986). A compromise between this and the single-leader extreme retains the egalitarian spirit and reduces dependency yet fills the power vacuum. That compromise may be seen in the concept of rotated-role leadership. The case study on page 112 illustrates the problems that can arise when a team has a very poor leader who has been appointed as a part of an organizational structure.

Rotated-Role Leadership Model

For this sort of leadership to work, employers must provide relevant information that allows employees to make rational decisions and education in teamwork, leadership, communication, problem solving, and decision making. Organizations instituting teamwork have explored the leadership question by breaking down management's roles into their component parts. Once they specify what managers do, they can begin training team members in those functions.

At the aluminum plant we've visited in previous chapters, a "star-point" system has been developed through which team members learn about and then take on the roles traditionally held by supervisors. In their first fully self-managed team, these roles are production, personnel, quality, team meeting director, administrative, maintenance, and site and safety star points (CM1C

THE CASE OF THE HIDDEN AGENDA

2:30 p.m.: A meeting of coordinators from eight different teams and their business-team leader began with some friendly banter. The leader provided pizza and soft drinks. The mood of the coordinators changed from friendly to wary when the leader abruptly took charge and asked that they go around the table and give one problem that they were concerned about. She indicated that once the items were listed on the board, they could then prioritize and discuss only the most important ones during the meeting. She started the process by calling upon the most vocal person. He had come prepared with a list of issues, and he gave all of them. Her assistant, a management trainer, listed items on the board. Although she and the scribe both agreed aloud that they should not discuss each item at the time but just list them, they all discussed as they went along and took an inordinate amount of time.

The team went around the room a second time and then concluded listing. Rather than prioritizing, which the coordinators resisted despite the team leader's insistence, the group started at the top of the list and began discussing the issues in order as listed. The leader gave input for each item, and the team members mainly listened. When they reached one item that seemed very controversial, and that the leader seemed unwilling at first to discuss, she took firm control of the meeting and spoke to the coordinators for at least half an hour on the topic. She repeated a number of times that she had taken the issue to her superiors and that they had been unreceptive and impatient. It seemed as if she was trying to elicit their sympathy or support because she had taken their issue forward and had been punished for it.

5:00 p.m.: Meeting adjourned without resolution of any issues.

This team meeting was "over-long," but was it "over-controlled" or "under-controlled"? The business leader had a hidden agenda that she attempted to fulfill, that is, to convey to "her team" that she was "on their side." She tried to show them that though she struggled on their behalf with upper management, those above her would not listen. She was frustrated by the coordinators' unwillingness to abide by the rules of procedure she laid down, so she simply talked at length about "their problem."

Discussion Questions for Case Study

1. What was the leadership structure like in this meeting? Who was responsible for its length and its outcome?

2. Would *no* leader have been better than *this* leader?

3. Once you have completed further discussion of this chapter, return to this case and explore whether you think this is the way a servant leader would behave.

FIGURE
7.1

ALUMINUM PLANT'S STAR-POINT SYSTEM

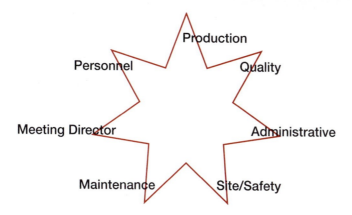

Each star point has a "back-up." The aluminum plant's CM1C team has sixteen members; eight are required to run the mill each day, and the plant operates twenty-four hours a day, seven days a week, 365 days a year. If nine are scheduled to work, the extra person floats (relieves others for breaks and lunch), trains, or attends meetings. The personnel star point coordinates days off, vacation days, and sick days among the sixteen team members. The team is arranged into "drop-out groups" who take the same days off. The star points rotate on an annual basis.

Watwood, 1994.

Team, 1993, p. 9). At the Louisville hospital consortium also discussed earlier, two configurations of teams have been developed: self-directed work groups consisting of whole small teams, such as the Cancer Registry Team, who work and meet together in a similar star-point system, and self-governed work groups consisting of larger teams that choose a council of ten people who rotate the star-point functions (Hospital Group Team Fair, 1994). Figure 7.1 illustrates the aluminum mill star-point system.

The method most frequently found to spread the expertise needed for team leadership to all team members is cross-training. The star-point positions described above rotate on a regular basis, with rotation schedules arranged to fit the needs of the specific team. For example, in a health-care team, job-related skills would take first priority; therefore, the teamwork- and management-related skills, such as budgeting, scheduling, or facilities coordination, could be rotated slowly, perhaps quarterly. In less crisis-prone environments, rotations may occur more frequently, and thus all could be cross-trained in these functions fairly rapidly. Once a full rotation of all functions has been completed in a team, shared leadership in decision making on a variety of issues could be achieved.

As the comparison above illustrates, a team's context plays a substantial role in determining its leadership style. In an emergency, certainly the directive leader who isolates the best possible path to take and urges others along it succeeds where the consensus builder fails. However, under most circumstances, the single powerful leader becomes incongruous in a team setting where all have been trained and informed.

Without training and information, crises can result in tragedy. On D-day, June 6, 1944, many of our troops who landed on Omaha Beach were scattered because of the tides and lost both their officers and their command structure. Time was wasted while they tried to regroup or simply to gather with other soldiers, whom they did not know, in order to decide what to do and which way to move inland (Clinton, 1994). Consider this chilling account: "Once aground only a hundred men of the 2nd Battalion reached the beach . . . , and they could advance no farther until a young officer walked to the barbed wire . . . and came back to say . . . , 'Are you going to stay there and be killed, or get up and try not to be?' Then he returned to the barbed-wire entanglement and cut a passage. All the men followed in single file, climbed the hill, and marched on to Colleville" (Boussel, 1966, pp. 123–124).

Of course, their adversaries were even less well-equipped to make decisions at lower levels of command, and the invasion force ultimately prevailed. However, as noted World War II historian Stephen Ambrose (1997, pp. 22–23) points out, German junior officers "were not only grounded in detail and doctrine, but were encouraged to think and act independently in a battle situation." Imagine what could have been the outcome had everyone at all ranks and on both sides, even those below officer level, been given both authority and training in leadership skills, decision making, and problem solving, so that each could lead when necessary.

APPLYING WHAT WE KNOW ABOUT LEADERSHIP THEORY

Single-Leader Theories

Our over-reliance on the **born-leader theory (traits theory),** or the norm of leaving leadership in the hands of an elite few, has perpetuated our struggle with the leadership concept more than fifty years after World War II. However, even traditional hierarchies have begun to change. For instance, retired U.S. Army General Hugh Shelton, who commanded troops in Vietnam and the first Gulf War, says today that he has found that people "respond to positive leadership" and to "people that don't abuse power." He says that even military commanders must learn to "back off," and that they can do that by developing others and then "not looking over their shoulder[s]" (Stamberg, "Interview with Retired . . . ", 2003). To foster that sort of development, the United States Marine Corps has instituted a training procedure, the Crucible, that distributes leadership among recruits during week eleven of their twelve weeks of basic training.

According to First Sergeant Frankie Holmes (1997), chief instructor at Parris Island's Drill Instructor (DI) School, the purpose of the Crucible is teamwork training, especially in problem solving. As he notes, the corps wants men and women recruits who have been urged to "use their brains." Each day an individual is chosen to be the leader for a particular activity, and if he or she fails, the instructors "sit them down and help them see how to do it better." Thus even a command-and-control culture can be seen moving to a shared-leadership model. A brief review of the theories that are being overturned will clarify their long hold over our thinking.

According to Warren Bennis and Burt Nanus's beautifully crafted visual image found in their classic book, *Leaders, The Strategies for Taking Charge* (1985), leadership theory may be seen as the "La Brea Tar Pits of organizational inquiry," that is, a sticky mess filled with the bones of dead ideas. Traces of the **great-man theory** intertwined with the trait theory linger in our culture as we assume that, historically, leaders were usually male, white, tall, intelligent, and attractive. Only when we factor in privilege do we begin to see that history in a different light. Moreover, when we look at history's notable exceptions, we feel justified in looking elsewhere for explanations of leadership.

LEADERSHIP AS A SET OF TRAITS OR STYLES

Great-Man Theory*

In difficult times, a great man will arise to lead the nation successfully toward its destiny.

Traits of the Great Man*

He will be dominant, bold, intelligent, handsome, brave, dynamic, tall, male (of course), and white.

Styles Possible for Designated Leaders**

Autocratic: Dominant, commanding, traditional

Democratic: Open to the wishes of a majority of followers

Laissez-Faire: Uninvolved, does not participate

* Consider the biases built into the trait theories.

** Consider behavioral limitations of the style theories. Hill (1976, p. 246), in his study of opinionated leadership, notes that "White and Lippitt (1960) concluded that democratic leadership was more efficient in contributing to the achievement of both work goals and social goals than either autocratic or laissez-faire leadership."

TABLE 7.2	TRAITS AND STYLES ONE CAN LEARN OR CULTIVATE

Traits	Styles
Appearance	Attentiveness to others
Confidence	Consideration for relationships
Knowledge	Concern for the task
Assertiveness	Participatory
Communication skills	Empowering
Motivation	
Maturity	

Style Theories

Theories based on styles generally feature three alternative models: **democratic, autocratic,** and **laissez-faire** (White and Lippitt, 1960). The democratic leader would practice inclusion and equality in regard to subordinates and would take their views and needs into account. However, this consideration may extend only as far as the leader's own ultimate decision-making authority. Autocratic leaders would simply order or direct subordinates' behavior with little or no consultation except upward through the chain of command. Laissez-faire leaders generally are leaders in name only. As their name implies, they leave their subordinates alone and give little guidance or support. "Leadership as a Set of Traits or Styles" summarizes these theories.

Table 7.2 presents features more recently added to the traits and styles literature. Think of them, however, as personal qualities that are not inborn but could be learned or cultivated.

Functional Theories

Early theories based on functions consider only task and maintenance, or socio-emotional, orientations. One either concentrates on "getting the job done" or on keeping harmony and balance within the group (Benne and Sheats, 1948). More current theories view the task and maintenance functions as being intertwined rather than mutually exclusive. Table 7.3 clarifies these two sets of functions that members may perform.

Contingency Theories

Contingency theories describe leadership behaviors considered appropriate or desirable depending upon the situation in which the group finds itself or the situation a leader can create or foster (Fiedler, 1967; Fiedler, Chemers, and Mahar, 1976; Hersey and Blanchard, 1982). As we noted earlier, the **situational-leadership theory** assumes that the designated leader can adapt to changing

TABLE 7.3	LEADERSHIP FROM A FUNCTIONAL PERSPECTIVE

Task Functions	Maintenance Functions
Initiating	Encouraging
Information giving	Harmonizing
Information seeking	Tension relieving
Opinion giving	Gatekeeping
Opinion seeking	
Elaborating	
Energizing	
Reviewing	
Recording	

contingencies related to members, tasks, relationships, and power. "Situational or Contingency Factors Affecting Leadership" offers some of the questions a situational leader could ask when deciding how to lead in various situations.

Let's look at an example of situational leadership. Leaders can offer tangible rewards for increases in productivity or quality of work, resulting in an exchange, or a transaction. As Bass (1985) shows, however, **transactional leadership** results only in "first order changes," or small, though significant, changes only in degree of performance.

Leaders would make a greater difference by becoming **transformational leaders,** a term first used by Burns (1978) and then adopted by Bass for his comparison with transactional leaders. Indeed, "second order changes—revolutionary changes in attitudes, values, and beliefs, and 'quantum leaps' in motivation and performance—result," according to Bass, "only from transformational leadership." Such leaders are, perhaps, **"charismatic,"** or "inspirational," they "'heighten expectations and engender excitement,'" and they "articulate [a] compelling rhetorical vision to focus followers' attention and energy, and to build commitment to organizational purposes" (Zorn, 1991, p. 179). Studies indicate that for organizations to foster creativity, they must have leaders who "stimulate others rather than order them around" and who give others "the freedom to explore and to fail" (Nucifora, 2002, p. 18).

Certainly we are familiar with this language and approach from our explanations of missions, visions, goals, and objectives in Chapter 4, but why would this leadership style be considered more "humane" or simply better than other single-leader theories? First, in order to succeed, the transformational leader must have "an intuitive understanding of the followers' needs," both "immediate self-interests, and . . . higher level needs," and he or she must practice what Bass (1985) calls "individualized consideration," or a "mentoring orientation

SITUATIONAL OR CONTINGENCY FACTORS AFFECTING LEADERSHIP

Relationships Among Members

- Are they coequal members?
- Are they from different levels of the organization?
- Do they have a past or current superior-to-subordinate relationship?
- Do they have assigned leadership responsibilities?
- Did other members have any authority over that assignment?

Member Attributes

- Are members skilled in group communication?
- Are they committed to the team's success?
- Are they competent in terms of task requirements?
- Have they had any leadership education or training?

Task Itself

- Is the task simple and repetitive?
- Is the task complex?
- Does it require coordinated efforts?
- Can it be accomplished by each member working alone?
- Is it a long-term or short-term project?

Power Distribution

- Are members in competition for power?
- Will successful completion of the task increase the team's power?
- Would sabotage of the task increase the power of any member?

toward followers." In addition, besides charisma and inspiration, the transformational leader must utilize "intellectual stimulation," defined by Bass as "the use of logic, convincing argument, and rational thinking to arouse and change followers' problem awareness, problem solving, thought and imagination, and beliefs and values." As you can see in "Characteristics of Transformational and Transactional Leaders," the concept of the transformational leader has moved our thinking a very long way from the early versions of the single leader.

CHARACTERISTICS OF TRANSFORMATIONAL AND TRANSACTIONAL LEADERS

Transformational Leader

Charisma   Provides vision and sense of mission, instills pride, gains respect and trust

Inspiration   Communicates high expectations, uses symbols to focus efforts, expresses important purposes in simple ways

Intellectual Stimulation   Promotes intelligence, rationality, and careful problem solving

Individualized Consideration   Gives personal attention, treats each employee as an individual, coaches, advises

Transactional Leader

Contingent Reward   Contracts exchange of rewards for effort, promises rewards for good performance, recognizes accomplishments

Management by Exception (Active)   Watches and searches for deviations from rules and standards, takes corrective action

Management by Exception (Passive)   Intervenes only if standards are not met

Laissez-Faire   Abdicates responsibilities, avoids making decisions

Shared-Leadership Theories

All of these approaches to the study of leadership assume that a single individual will either be designated as leader or will emerge out of an inevitable struggle for leadership among the originally coequal members. Leadership studies traditionally and overwhelmingly acknowledge that a great deal of energy must be devoted to this struggle. If the group's time and effort could be turned toward the creation of community rather than the competition for power, how much more could be accomplished? If members could be taught to evaluate and use their strengths, to understand and adapt their styles, and to recognize and attend to task and socio-emotional team needs under varying circumstances, how much better could they serve both themselves and their groups? Although not a panacea for the ills of the workplace, the development of group norms

HOW LONG DOES IT TAKE?

To Make a Decision

By a Single Leader of a Group

By a Group without Leadership

By a Group with Leadership

For the Group to Become Committed to That Decision

If Made by a Single Leader

If Made by the Group without Leadership

If Made by the Group with Leadership

For the Decision to Be Carried Out

If Made by a Single Leader

If Made by the Group without Leadership

If Made by the Group with Leadership

As you can see, it takes longest of all to implement or put into effect a decision made by a single leader. The group that tries to perform without leadership of any kind—shared, emergent, democratic, autocratic, or otherwise—does not fare well. However, the least time is needed to implement a decision that has been made by a group *with* leadership, though it takes the group longer to make the initial decision.

Adapted from Sashkin and Morris, 1984.

based on the shared-emergent-leadership concept could help redirect the energy of teams toward a democratic ideal heretofore unrealized.

"How Long Does it Take?" illustrates some differences in time needed to make decisions, to commit to those decisions, and to implement the decisions made under three different leadership situations (Sashkin and Morris, 1984). As you can see, it takes much less time for an individual to make a decision than it takes for a group to reach agreement, but once they have decided, their commitment will help make it work.

Leadership Power

In this chapter you have seen one of the key buzzwords of the era, empower, which implies that someone has power and chooses to pass it on to another. Our society maintains multiple sources of power, of course, ranging from financial to military, from economic to spiritual. In the classroom, the instructor leads, at the very least, through **legitimate,** or **position, power** and, in ideal cases, through **expert power.** Teachers who are well liked also have **referent power,** teachers who punish have **coercive power,** and teachers who use grades as motivators have **reward power.** These forms of influence, compared in "Types of Power," originated with French and Raven (1959).

A useful contrast can be made here between the historical, "dictatorial, even tyrannical" power thought to be needed by a symphony conductor in earlier days and the current view of the role by Marin Alsop, conductor of the Bournemouth Symphony Orchestra in England. She compares the relationship between conductor and orchestra as being similar to a corporate teamwork structure in that "without the musicians, the conductor has nothing." Instead of wielding power, the

TYPES OF POWER

Legitimate Power: Power comes from being hired or appointed to a position or comes with rights and privileges.

Expert Power: Power may come from special knowledge or from a special ability.

Referent Power: Followers identify with this person; others may follow this person simply because they like her or him.

Coercive Power: Power may come from the use of force or punishment or from making the work of others difficult.

Reward Power: Power may come from extending tangible rewards or from giving praise.

Adapted from French and Raven, 1959.

FIGURE 7.2

A SHARED-EMERGENT-LEADERSHIP MODEL

Although roles may be assigned and rotated among members for specific periods of time, in day-to-day activities such as team meetings, all members are empowered to engage in leadership functions related to the task and to the maintenance of harmonious working relationships. In a typical meeting, a team starts along a path marked by their agenda toward a goal, such as decision making or problem solving. Along the way a disagreement occurs, say, over information. A member (A) who is skilled in data analysis helps resolve the disagreement and thus helps the group get back on their path. Alternatively, this conflict or another may actually have been over job-related rivalries or competition between members. In this case, a member (B) skilled in interpersonal conflict resolution or human-resources issues helps the group return to the path. In another instance, conversation drifts away from the task itself and onto an unrelated problem. A member (C) skilled in orientation to the agenda helps the group return to the path.

Adapted from Gouran, 1990.

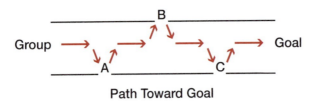

Path Toward Goal

conductor should possess "respect for the musicians, humility about oneself, and a sense of humor." Her role model for leadership is Leonard Bernstein, legendary leader of the New York Philharmonic, who exhibited the "greatest power one can have—to enable people to be better than they are" (Stamberg, "Interview with Bournemouth . . .", 2003).

These same sources of power apply in the workplace, with the manager or supervisor having access to their use. Linguist Deborah Tannen shows us that language itself both possesses power and reveals one's attitudes toward power. She compares a man's use of "clout," for example, with a woman's use of "relationships" as a source of power (Stamberg, "Interview with Linguist . . .", 2003). Building relationships with employees would certainly give a manager "clout," but where would the "power" lie? In an empowering organization, the sources of power mentioned above are distributed to hourly employees and to teams. If the old adage about the corrupting influence of absolute power is true, then this democratizing process may help alleviate the misuse of power. Much will depend on the communication ethic that develops in conjunction with a team's use of power. Figure 7.2 illustrates the model of leadership that guides this chapter, the shared-emergent-leadership or rotated-role model, based on an **ethic of equality** among members (Gouran, 1990).

Combination-Leadership Model

As previously noted, leaders have multiple power sources of various types that they can choose to keep or to distribute. The question of what role the leader of a self-managed work team should play has led to a number of research studies. The findings have resulted in a set of behaviors we might think of as providing a model for leadership focusing not on a single leader nor only on shared leadership but on a combination of the two perspectives. Manz and Sims (1987, p. 106) quote the ancient Chinese philosopher Lao Tzu (as quoted in Maccoby, 1981), who said, "The best of all leaders is the one who helps people so that, eventually, they don't need him."

So what does the **self-management leader** do? According to Manz and Sims (p. 118), this leader encourages team members to practice the following behaviors: self-reinforcement, self-criticism, self-goal setting, self-observation and evaluation, self-expectation, and rehearsal. This view of working oneself out of a job suggests not only the self-managed team leader role but also the coach-as-teacher role. Teaching team members to function independently may represent the most ethical use of teacher power possible, compared with those outlined earlier in this chapter. "How Do You Lead Others to Lead Themselves?" clarifies the meanings of these concepts.

A related combination theory, the concept of **servant leadership,** may be considered the most idealistic of the leadership theories currently practiced. This theory evolved from a number of philosophical sources and would seem to

---

HOW DO YOU LEAD OTHERS TO LEAD THEMSELVES?

- Encourage self-reinforcement so that team members find ways to identify and pursue meaningful, performance-contingent work outcomes for themselves.

- Encourage self-criticism, through which team members learn to diagnose inappropriate behaviors and engage in appropriate self-reprimands.

- Encourage self-set goals for the group by having team members identify and articulate key areas for progress.

- Encourage self-observation and evaluation, with team members controlling their own consequences only after assessing their own behaviors.

- Encourage high self-expectations, or self-efficacy, by developing a culture of risk taking and success.

- Provide opportunities for rehearsal prior to meeting final work demands so that team members can practice and further develop requisite team skills with less risk to success and self-esteem.

From Sims and Lorenzi, *The New Leadership Paradigm: Social Learning and Organizations,* p. 212. Copyright © 1992 Sage. Reprinted with permission of Sage Publication, Inc.

ACTIONS OF A SERVANT LEADER

The Servant Leader will

- put aside personal ego
- use position power "with, not over, followers"
- treat others equally
- balance task and social needs in the workplace
- make opportunities for participation
- recognize good work
- serve as peacemaker

Adapted from Holifield, 1993, p. 39.

---

be a reaction to the typical view of leadership as influence based on position power (Nair, 1994). One who accepts power but values justice and fairness will lead differently than one who values only power. Those differences will result in the leader's adoption of a servant's attitude, that is, in finding ways to assist followers in accomplishing their goals. "Actions of a Servant Leader" summarizes characteristics of this leadership style.

What a different organizational world we might all live in if our leaders practiced this attitude! According to Michael Holifield (1993, p. 40), their style would be based on "a human approach tempered with a task approach steeped in justice, defined as the fair application of fair rules in a fair game where fairly situating the least fortunate is a good."

An Important Postscript: Shared Leadership Still Requires Leadership

As we have seen earlier in this text, tragedies can result from lack of leadership or from a simple case of poor leadership. In the case of the space shuttle *Columbia* accident, the CAIB's *Report* stresses both problems. For instance, NASA created a Debris Assessment Team to investigate the foam strike that occurred on liftoff. However, the team operating at the highest level, the "Mission Management Team[,] . . . provided no direction for team activities, and Shuttle managers did not formally consult the Team's leaders about their progress or interim results." The managers of the mission itself "did not actively seek status, inputs, or even preliminary results from the individuals charged with analyzing the debris strike. They did not investigate the value of imagery, did not intervene to consult the more experienced Crater analysts . . ., did not probe the assumptions of the Debris Assessment Team's analysis, and did not consider actions to mitigate the effects of the damage on re-entry" (CAIB, 2003, pp. 170–171). Notice the number of "did not" assertions in the report. We need to remember that even high-powered teams will fail if their attitudes toward others, in this case others below them in the organizational hierarchy, will not allow them to do what needs to be done.

CONCLUSION

This chapter has explored historical theoretical approaches to the study of leadership in terms of styles, functions, and contingencies that have been commonly perceived as "best practices" over the years. However, the chapter has also proposed that in the teamwork environment under construction in organizations today, the shared-emergent-leadership style facilitates the most participation and the best learning. For everyday practical purposes, this style often manifests in the division and distribution of functional task roles, formerly held by managers or supervisors, and their rotation among team members over time. This style finds its most effective application in education in perceiving and practicing leadership itself as a skill in communication, data analysis, reasoning, problem solving, and decision making. Sharing leadership by distributing the so-called maintenance roles—encouraging, harmonizing, tension relieving, and gatekeeping, or regulating the flow of participation—has likely always been a part of our group existence in our homes, in our schools, with our friends, and at work.

In situations where single-leader models prevail, the transformational style would seem to be the most rewarding to followers, and to leaders, too, and could thus be considered the most ethical of all style choices. Models that combine the best aspects of single- and shared-leadership situations, the self-management and the servant-leader types, certainly require skill and patience by the leader but can foster the communication ideals we explored in Chapter 2 and the ethical inclusiveness needed for humane workplaces.

COLLABORATIVE LEARNING ACTIVITIES

1. Divide into randomly chosen groups of five members. Develop group leadership models based on current examples from film or television comparable to the *Star Trek* models in this chapter. Present the models to the class.

2. Divide into randomly chosen groups of five members. With the information available in "Characteristics of Transformational and Transactional Leaders," discuss the pros and cons of transformational and transactional leadership. Incorporate any experiences your members have had in being a part of or working with either of these types of leaders. Present your conclusions to the class.

Chapter 8

Effective Team Meetings

Image provided by PhotoDisc © 2002

Face-to-Face and Virtual Meeting Processes and Practices

KEY WORDS AND CONCEPTS

agenda	goal-path model
chat room	hidden agenda
computer-mediated meetings	information sharing
counteractive influence	meeting ecology
debriefing session	meeting effectiveness
decision conferencing	meeting leadership
Delphi technique	minutes
devil's advocate	parliamentary agenda
electronic brainstorming	production blocking
electronic bulletin board	standard agenda
equalization effect	threaded discussion board
evaluation apprehension	time shifting
face-to-face meetings	virtual meetings

 To find out more about the Key Words and Concepts discussed in this chapter, use InfoTrac College Edition. Type in the keywords and subject terms. You can access InfoTrac College Edition from Wadsworth/Communication homepage: http://communication.wadsworth.com.

CAREER APPLICATION

At the hospital group mentioned earlier in the text, meetings are normally structured around functional issues, but the Cancer Registry Team, for instance, keeps a small file box available to receive agenda items from all members in preparation for their two-hour weekly meetings. The Center for Bone and Joint Disorders Team holds weekly meetings in which members report on their star-point functions, such as budgeting. Because these teams also conduct their own hiring and peer evaluations, space must be provided on agendas for discussion of how to handle such procedures, criteria for screening applicants, group interviews, items to include in discussion of review results, suggestions for growth, and myriad details of the team's "real work," or "task," that is, patient education.

Many research studies have shown that a large percentage of a typical workweek will likely be spent in meetings. Although once this could be said only of upper-echelon managers, now employees at all levels and in all types of jobs, whether in manufacturing or finance, health care or computer programming, will find themselves around conference tables to wrangle with facts and figures and make decisions.

Likewise, those who choose to participate in voluntary associations or advocacy groups, or to serve as members of local school boards or in other elected positions, will gather periodically for meetings. Although many of these types of groups have adopted a **parliamentary agenda** format featuring a call to order, new and old business, motions, amendments, and votes, others have adapted meeting procedures to their own unique needs. Support groups, twelve-step groups, and special-interest groups, for instance, follow practices that resemble counseling sessions more than business meetings.

Some of you may have experienced a decision-making class assignment relating to a question of fact. If not, think about work, school, or community meetings you have attended, especially those that were problematic. No doubt you remember from typical meetings that some members participated more than others, perhaps more than necessary. You may have discovered at eight minutes into a ten-minute meeting that you were not even halfway through your agenda. Or you may have run out of things to say at the five-minute mark. These and other common experiences may serve as goal- and objective-setting devices for your team. Here we consider ways to improve **meeting effectiveness,** especially as related to meeting purposes, environments, procedures, and communication behaviors.

WHY DO WE HAVE MEETINGS?

In previous chapters we saw the benefits of teamwork to both organizations and individuals. However, these benefits will fail to materialize if team members cannot spend enough time together in structured and focused meetings. They must be able to share information and solve problems; only then is employee involvement worth the time and expense required for teamwork.

Teams that meet daily most likely spend their time in three activities: reporting, discussing, and coordinating. For instance, at the aluminum company, twice-daily staff meetings are held at the beginning and end of each of three shifts. At these overlapping shift meetings, representatives from various departments share numerical production data and describe specific problems that have arisen and measures taken to solve them. At the hospital consortium, one team meets daily at lunchtime to coordinate the next day's schedule and weekly for other purposes.

Special weekly or monthly meetings, such as those of an advisory group in any organizational setting, could be held for the purposes of reviewing progress, discussing whether goals are being met, and developing suggestions.

Business teams that meet weekly would satisfy a variety of situational purposes, such as identifying customer needs; calculating the budget impact of satisfying those needs; reviewing the team's past and current use of resources; deciding on changes in their practices, processes, or structure; or setting new goals or objectives. At other times they might meet to write up job postings, to screen applicants' credentials, or to write a budget proposal or plan an oral presentation to upper management.

Student groups may be assigned to develop explanations that compare and contrast specific communication theories, perhaps like those we saw in the previous chapter on leadership. One class meeting could be devoted to this project. A task list that would serve as an agenda for the day could be posted on the board. It could suggest that the groups begin by listing the defining characteristics of their assigned leadership theory. Then they could list ways in which their theory differs from theories assigned to other groups. They could create a scenario based on a business or organizational problem through which to portray their specific leadership theory in action. Finally, they could assign a role for each member in the presentation to the class. This class meeting example illustrates a collaborative learning model practiced in many classrooms today.

Voluntary association meetings may serve any number of purposes. One particularly common purpose would relate to the lifeblood of such groups, fundraising. Because new ideas in fundraising are always needed, a good brainstorming session may start off the project. Unfortunately such group discussions sometimes wander for hours while members suggest ideas, others claim that they won't work, and eventually the meeting adjourns in frustration. However, one effective meeting per year devoted solely to the planning process could result in a completed and satisfactory plan. Once the group compiles a list of possibilities, criteria based on what the group could actually do, considering its limitations, should be used to narrow the list. Once the group makes a decision on what they will actually do, then they can outline an action plan that designates who will do what by when, and the project is underway.

MEETING ECOLOGY

Face-to-Face Meetings

Michael Schrage (1995) has coined the term "meeting ecology" to describe "the interplay of ideas, personalities, and environment" that affects meeting outcomes. We'll talk more about ideas and personalities later in this chapter, but the environmental concept bears special consideration. Schrage, writing about face-to-face meetings, suggests that warm hospitality should characterize meetings and their locations. This hospitality is shown by the presence of "creature comforts" and is lacking when the meeting room is too cold, too cramped, or when all members cannot maintain visual contact with each other and with needed materials (Clark, 1998, p. 40). Others have shown that meeting spaces should not be "too stimulating" or contain "piles of work lying around" but should be "comfortable, quiet, and spacious" (Anderson, 1998, p. 117).

Creation of an atmosphere where all those in attendance can feel equally welcome, regardless of status differences, can be accomplished, in part, by room arrangements. Placing identical chairs in a circle or around a large table "sets the stage for the desired interaction among participants" (Coppola et al., 2002, p. 20) and eliminates the implications of a "head table" versus "observers." Planners should even consider the lighting adjustments needed for the occasion (p. 21), especially if the meeting will include computer graphics, slides, overhead projections, or video or film clips. But what happens to this environmental concern when meetings are held not in a meeting room but among people in different neighborhoods, cities, states, or nations in the form of virtual meetings?

Virtual Meetings

Virtual meetings, sometimes called "distributed meetings," are held by means of e-mail; Internet **chat rooms,** forums, **bulletin boards,** or Web pages; voice mail; conference calls; teleconferences; or other technologies and provide advantages to business and voluntary-association groups or teams. They allow **time shifting** so that employees of multinational corporations can participate in problem solving or decision making during their normal waking and working hours. They save both the time and cost of travel. Some of these technologies eliminate scheduling conflicts because members can respond at times convenient to themselves. The University of Georgia's Institute for Community and Area Development (ICAD) uses "interactive computer technology in its '**decision conferencing**' work" to help "community, regional, and state groups solve problems . . . through collaboration" or through "designing a process that gives the group a shared vision." For example, ICAD has developed a "collaboration center" that is "used by such groups as advocates for the homeless to resolve highly controversial issues" (Knack, 1994, pp. 19–20). In another instance, local government in Fairfax County, Virginia, has used electronic citizens' focus groups in conjunction with the county park board to "narrow down a list of capital projects to be funded with proceeds from a bond issue (pp. 20–21).

Computer-mediated or other virtual meetings and processes have their disadvantages, of course. The costs of establishing and maintaining such systems are enormous, and thus community groups must rely on publicly funded resources. Learning and using the technologies also present complex problems and sometimes require the services of communication and technology experts as facilitators. Interpersonal problems may surface as well. For example, in groups that meet only electronically and who have had no previous face-to-face interaction, the trust vital to teamwork may be completely lacking. So what does small group research have to say about the effectiveness of virtual meetings held by computer-mediated groups or teams?

Advantages and disadvantages seem tied to the nature of the task. For example, in experimental or laboratory settings, "computer-mediated groups appear superior at generating ideas, but face-to-face groups appear superior on problem-solving tasks and tasks requiring the resolution of conflicts"

(Hollingshead and McGrath, 1995). Virtual groups seem to have specific advantages in a number of areas, however, especially in adding structure to the decision-making process, which always seems to enhance group effectiveness (see Guzzo and Dickson, 1996, pp. 320–323, for a full discussion of structure).

Other advantages include improving creativity particularly in brainstorming groups or procedures. Why might this be true? Two problems characterize brainstorming procedures in face-to-face organizational settings: **production blocking,** or the inability to speak simply whenever someone else is already speaking, and **evaluation apprehension,** or the withholding of ideas by lower-status members for fear of higher-status members' disapproval. The sheer number of ideas generated by **electronic brainstorming** can be greatly increased because

---

CASE STUDY   **VIRTUAL PROJECTS FOR LARGE NATIONAL ORGANIZATIONS**

*L*arge national associations that are organized to bring attention to particular interest groups and their problems or needs have wide-ranging memberships. One such group, the American Diabetes Association (ADA), headquartered in Alexandria, Virginia, has a one-thousand-person staff as well as volunteer groups, one consisting of "parents of children with Type I diabetes and pediatric endocrinologists," for instance. This particular group of volunteers works with association staff members to create "kits, booklets, stickers, games, and other items to be used by newly diagnosed youth with diabetes." In the past they have met once face-to-face and then relied on sporadic conference calls to keep the group moving along. Recently, though, the association established a listserv that allows virtual meetings. According to Rick Johnston, ADA vice president for constituent relations, "There was almost daily communication, so the team was able to exchange ideas, bounce back feedback, [and] review materials." As a result, he concludes, "The project turned out exceptionally well, and the fifteen people who worked on it liked the process."

Johnston, 2002, p. 35.

Discussion Questions for Case Study

1. Do any members of your class belong to voluntary community associations like the one mentioned here? Explore the actual or potential uses of technology to enable these associations to serve their constituents best.

2. Do any members of your class belong to voluntary student associations or student government associations on campus? Do these groups use technology to reach the entire student body with information or with calls for participation?

one member's contributions do not interfere with those of any others and because anonymity can be ensured.

Experimental studies have also shown that more unique ideas and more high-quality ideas can also be generated through this process, perhaps because anonymity also makes it easier for any member to play the role of **devil's advocate,** or to scrutinize, probe, or question others' ideas (Gallupe et al., 1992; Dennis and Valacich, 1993; McLeod, 1992; Valacich et al., 1994). Several studies have shown that electronic decision processes result in the so-called **"equalization effect,"** or more equal levels of participation regardless of status (Dubrovsky et al., 1991). This latter idea related to equality of participation leads us to a consideration of the other disadvantages of virtual meetings and processes besides costs, mentioned earlier. Dubrovsky and colleagues (1991) also found that "differences in influence based on differences in expertise were less pronounced" in virtual groups. Does that mean that less-expert members were too influential, or more influential than their knowledge would justify? Perhaps so. Kiesler and Sproul (1992) found that groups communicating by electronic means alone experienced "more extreme or risky decisions, and more hostile or extreme communications . . . than in face-to-face groups." The most serious problem, however, may lie in the research that shows quantity of work over time, or productivity, was greater in face-to-face groups than in computer-mediated groups, especially when the tasks required "higher levels of coordination among group members" (Straus and McGrath, 1994). The case study on page 131 gives you an example of how important virtual meetings have become for large associations.

WHAT ARE EFFECTIVE MEETING PROCEDURES?

Agendas

Perhaps the most frequent problem that dooms meetings, whether face-to-face or virtual, is the failure to plan adequately; the most likely missing link is the fully and collaboratively developed agenda. In the staff meetings described earlier, a semi-standard agenda meets the needs for an organizing pattern, though the schedule should be flexible enough to allow for the unexpected. A true **standard agenda** consists of the same items for every meeting of the same type. We'll see examples of standard agendas later in the chapter.

What characterizes an effective agenda-setting process and, indeed, an effective agenda? Agendas must be flexible and thus able to adapt to unanticipated needs of the group. At the same time, though, they must be planned and distributed in advance so that all those attending the meeting can be prepared with information, materials, and at least a little prior thinking about the issues to be discussed. Certainly agendas must be prioritized with items arranged for maximum input.

At a typical team meeting, most members arrive generally on time. A few minutes are spent in small talk; this is normal and even beneficial. Depending on the time of day set aside for meetings compared with the other work—the real work of the team members—the most significant items should be placed first or last on the agenda. On the one hand, if the members are just arriving for the day, they may need some warm-up time before discussion of top-priority items. If, on the other hand, they have just completed eight hours, or in some settings, twelve hours of work, first things must come first before fatigue takes its toll. Some meeting specialists suggest that you "hold knotty or difficult issues for the middle of the meeting when the group's attentiveness and energy are at their height" (Ephross and Vassil, 1988, p. 142).

In the same ways that managers once controlled and arranged agendas to serve their purposes, self-directed team members today construct agendas to serve team purposes. If the members rotate management functions around a star-point system, as described in Chapter 7, daily meetings generally follow a semi-standard agenda with items arranged according to that team's priorities: safety first, production second, quality third, and personnel fourth, for example. At other meetings, items could be arranged in yet another standard form you have no doubt used, that is, into old and new business. In this form, the group could handle a recurring set of long-term issues under old business and then move on to short-term or unique items under new business. If problem solving were the sole purpose of the meeting, the agenda could be structured around John Dewey's model (1910), illustrated in "Basic Problem-Solving Procedure" in Chapter 6.

Dewey's system, based, he said, on "how we think," has proven so useful for many different types of groups that it has been considered by some to represent a true standard agenda. Let's see how it could be used for a meeting called for discussion of a campus issue, traffic congestion, for example. Perhaps individuals who live in a neighborhood near the campus have complained about dangers posed to pedestrians; perhaps students have been victims of accidents themselves. A simple call on authorities to solve the problem is insufficient because the problem itself has not yet been defined. A community forum could be held in order to gain insights on the problem from all those affected. To ensure participants came prepared, public notice could be made of not only the time and place but also of the problem-solving agenda itself. Therefore, anyone choosing to attend would see that he or she should be prepared to discuss the nature of the problem itself, its possible causes and significance, and potential solutions and standards by which to judge each of them. Although it would be difficult to manage the entire process in one large public meeting, smaller groups could, perhaps, be chosen to gather the information needed in order for the whole group to make a decision on the best alternative solution at a future meeting. This process of problem solving, following the standard agenda format, alerts groups to the need for careful definition and analysis of the problem before they attempt to solve it.

Under other circumstances or for purposes other than problem solving, you will need to construct agendas appropriate to the types of meetings you schedule. In the early stages, when you develop your mission, goals, and objectives, such planning meetings benefit from open-ended processes such as brainstorming.

"Agenda for a Thirty-Minute Planning Session" provides a suggested schedule for such a meeting.

Later, after you have gathered research data, information-sharing sessions would be more appropriately structured. As you move into problem solving or decision making, more formal arrangements of agenda items may be called for. "Agenda for a Thirty-Minute Information-Sharing Session" provides a suggested plan for a data-sharing meeting.

Regardless of the life history of the group, however, the existence of a plan for discussion that has been cooperatively constructed clearly separates successful from unsuccessful groups or teams. "Agenda for a Two-Hour Meeting

AGENDA FOR A THIRTY-MINUTE PLANNING SESSION

Because the following agenda is constructed for the purpose of structuring a planning session, an inherently open process, we first review the components of brainstorming:

- Generate as many ideas as possible in the form of a list.
- Do not evaluate any idea as either a good or a bad idea.
- Build one idea upon another.
- Seek odd, unusual, or untried ideas.
- Wait out the pauses while making the list. Give yourselves time to think.

Agenda

9:00–9:05: Explanation of meeting purpose: to develop list of possible goals for your class team; clarification of terms such as vision, mission, goals, objectives

9:05–9:20: Brainstorming session: follow guidelines above for brainstorming; a member writes down all ideas expressed on a white board, chalkboard, poster, large sheet of paper, or whatever is available; all should contribute ideas, including the member writing them down; all must be able to see list

9:20–9:25: Conclude list; short discussion to generate reasons for eliminating items, such as "not possible in class context or in one semester, quarter, or term"

9:25–9:30: Eliminate items based on reasons found above

9:30: Adjourn

AGENDA FOR A THIRTY-MINUTE INFORMATION-SHARING SESSION

Hypothetical situation: Your team decided to tackle the following research question (a question of fact): What is the relationship, if any, between parking problems and the cost of parking passes on your campus? Once you chose the topic and narrowed your question appropriately, each of you gathered data separately. The purpose of this meeting is to pool your recently acquired knowledge.

Agenda

9:00–9:05: Open with a short discussion to clarify the research question and clarify any necessary terminology, etc.

9:05–9:25: Discussion of the following topics in this order:

- Actual number of parking spaces available
- Number of restricted-use spaces
- Number of parking passes sold per term or year
- Categories of passes and numbers in each category
- Cost of passes in each category
- Limitations on driving and parking on campus
- Alternate off-campus parking availability
- Other transportation availability
- Survey data: Student, staff, and faculty answers to the question, "At what level would the price of a parking pass be prohibitive; that is, at what level would you seek other means of transportation?"

9:25–9:30: Summarize findings

9:30: Adjourn

of the Board of Directors, Metropolitan Youth Soccer League" illustrates a schedule for the voluntary association fundraising meeting described earlier.

Minutes

Once a group has met, they need a record of their actions. Minutes are kept in order to document decisions, plans, and perhaps a summary of the main points and dissenting views made in discussion. See "Minutes of a Morning Staff Meeting in the Manufacturing Sector" for an example of minutes resulting from a twenty-minute staff meeting.

AGENDA FOR A TWO-HOUR MEETING OF THE BOARD OF DIRECTORS, METROPOLITAN YOUTH SOCCER LEAGUE

Time: 7:00–9:00 p.m., Thursday, May 12

Place: Parks and Recreation Department Conference Room

Meeting goal: To develop the league's annual fundraising plan

Objectives:

1. To generate a list of possible fundraising strategies
2. To set standards or criteria for their eventual choice
3. To choose one strategy based on these criteria
4. To outline an action plan for the fundraising project
5. To set a timeline for completion of the project
6. To establish commitment for individual responsibilities

7:00–7:10: Clarify meeting goal and objectives; clarify rules for brainstorming

7:10–7:50: Generate list of fundraising project possibilities

7:50–8:00: Break

8:00–8:15: Discussion of criteria for choice of project; answer questions such as how many will participate, is it doable with our time and human resources, etc.

8:15–8:30: Measure possibilities against criteria; choose one project or a combination of activities

8:30–8:45: Construct action plan complete with timeline

8:45–9:00: Fill in names of those responsible for each action item, go over verbally, and seek commitment

Minutes to be written up and sent to all league members within one week.

Indeed, "precedents contained in minutes" often serve as "building blocks" for future decisions (Ephross and Vassil, 1988, p. 141). Minutes that facilitate "follow through" keep groups from having "the same meeting" every week for months on end. Still, the need for a note taker, who necessarily does more listening than speaking, prevents free discussion by all members.

In your groups, if you are evaluated largely on the quality of your verbal contributions to the meeting discussions, the issue of who will take the minutes can become crucial. You and your instructor may decide to abandon minutes during the graded activities in favor of equal opportunity to participate. A second alternative could be rotation of the role of note taker. A third alternative, and one that could serve multiple functions, would be to devote the last five

---

MINUTES OF A MORNING STAFF MEETING IN THE MANUFACTURING SECTOR

- Meeting began at approximately 7:35 a.m.

- Those present: Production star-point representatives from three first-shift and three third-shift teams met to coordinate activities by sharing production numbers and describing problem issues that arose overnight.

- Reports were made of pounds produced, roll changes, percent of efficiency, downtime, and amount of scrap produced. Comparisons were made of numbers for the previous twenty-four hours.

- Short discussion was held regarding a vibration in the mill, its location, when it occurs in the roll cycle, its duration, what it sounds like, and what is being done about it.

- No further business; meeting adjourned at 7:55.

- Those in attendance: George, Jim, Mary Ellen, Gary, Roger, and Alice.

---

minutes of your meetings to generating minutes as a team, perhaps as a **debriefing session.**

MEETING COMMUNICATION

In traditional meetings, the leader called the meeting to order and then directed individuals to speak. In team meetings, a meeting director or other designated meeting leader might still do the same. Alternatively, no designated leader might be present, but **meeting leadership** is still needed. As we noted in the previous chapter, leadership has always involved directing, or knowing what to do and how and when to do it. Today, leadership, whether designated or emergent, also includes facilitating or enabling the work of others and helping or coaching others in their learning of what to do and how and when to do it. Teams in business organizations most often rotate their functional roles so that over time all members receive cross-training in many leadership skills, including that of meeting leader.

Effective teams strive to balance their members' roles and levels of participation. In small, "real-world" teams, all members are perceived as "key members." In larger groups where duties have been more clearly differentiated, all those who have responsibility for agenda items are key members. Although meeting directors or leaders may prepare agendas, they share both the obligation and the opportunity for discussion, problem solving, and decision making with the whole team. If the group's goal or vision is genuine teamwork, all members must be considered key members and must be equally authorized and accountable for leadership.

Leadership in Virtual Team Settings

As we learned earlier in this chapter, excessive risk-taking, hostile communication, and lowered productivity that are related to lack of coordination sometimes characterize virtual team meetings. All of these outcomes would seem to require better-quality leadership, and, once again, we find a place for shared leadership. According to Katzenbach and Smith (2001), what matters most in online teamwork is not technology but "real-time collaboration, multiple leadership, and the disciplined behavior of a real team." Online teams cannot, these authors assert, rely on "individual tasks and goals that members [can] achieve under clear single-leader direction." Accountability can come through jointly developing "behavior standards, ground rules, or group agreements" and ultimately giving adequate attention to "visually tracking results and recognizing those who make significant improvements" (Cox, 2003, p. 58).

Leadership in a virtual setting, shared or not, requires "particular attention to the challenges posed by the physical separation between members." The first challenge is to foster a "team" identity through a "common purpose" and "shar[ed] responsibility for specific outcomes." As Roger Ballentine of the Center for the Study of Work Teams at the University of North Texas notes, "[A] virtual team without the 'team' built in regresses to telephone calls and faxes pretty quickly" (Joinson, 2002, under "Not a Cure-All"). Instead of letting the team gradually fall apart, members should establish their own operating rules, such as how often to check and respond to e-mail, as we noted in Chapter 4. One software company manager suggests that members can "rotate the hosting of conference calls," which distributes leadership responsibilities. Segments of company Web sites dedicated to virtual teams can feature maps of team-member locations that link to individuals' photographs and brief biographies. Task leadership can be accomplished by helping the team focus on work expectations and team task goals and objectives the same as in face-to-face environments, but socio-emotional leadership might mean having a birthday cake delivered to a team member in Hong Kong (Joinson, 2002). So how does the shared-emergent-leadership model we learned about in the previous chapter look from the inside out, and how does it relate to communication?

Typical Meeting Problems

Think of a meeting you may attend. Important concerns are on the agenda, but obstacles continue to disrupt the flow of the discussion like boulders falling onto a mountain highway. Divisive personal conflict erupting between two colleagues hinders any forward motion. A third person attempts to take the group on a long, winding mental journey that most fear will lead only to a dead end. Outdated, irrelevant, or false information threatens to lead the whole team "down the garden path." In each instance, leadership from someone is vital either to remove the boulders from the roadway or to find an alternate route. This **goal-path model** of teamwork is especially useful for its explanatory power in terms of situational leadership as **counteractive influence** (Gouran, 1990, pp. 149–151).

Forcing yourself to remain in this imaginary but painful meeting for a while longer, think about what the outcome would be in a traditional, top-down staff meeting if the designated leader were actually responsible for these problems. Imagine the leader as contender in a power struggle with the vice-chair, for example, or the leader as a long-winded sermonizer or dispenser of false or incorrect data. Depending on the level of fear prevalent in the organization, members would suffer in silence or leave in disgust and chalk up the experience as yet another example of precious time wasted on endless meetings. Because the boulders in the path often are hidden by a screen of power, staffs, departments, and whole organizations keep running into them time and again. Only by authorizing all members to see and attempt to remove the impediments to teamwork—to use counteractive influence—can groups eliminate or avoid obstructions.

Of course, it does no good to empower individuals to do something in unpleasant situations if they are neither skilled nor trained in conflict management, windbag deflation, or data analysis. If we truly believe there is no such thing as natural-born leadership, then we must accept the fact that we all need opportunities to learn leadership. In this chapter and in the two that follow, the goal is to help you learn to maneuver through the "falling-rock zones." The site for such learning is the ubiquitous meeting.

A CHAOTIC MEETING

3:00 p.m.: Members of a team file into a large meeting room with a large oblong table and chairs as well as chairs arranged around the walls. None choose to sit at the table. No leader exists because their former leader was promoted out of the team and has not been replaced. (This organization does not train all members in leadership skills, nor does it authorize all to lead when necessary.) All talk at once.

3:05: A member waves several sheets of paper and shouts, "Shut up!" He then makes a typical productivity report and moves on to the night's goal for the second-shift employees (the number of pallets of the product that must show up on their inventory report the next morning). One person at the opposite end of the room says, "Why us?" in a quiet voice amid general murmuring.

3:15: Another member begins handing out copies of a "complaint list" from a member of management. The meeting breaks into groups of people who look at the list together and make comments, such as "He's got to go," "This is not true," and "I don't believe that," while pointing to specific items.

3:20: Meeting does not adjourn but breaks up. Members file out.

In Chapter 2 we learned about dialogue and the ideal speech situation, in which we treat each other as respected equals. In the tug-of-war that meetings sometimes turn into, we may forget our ideals. In the very worst meetings, chaos reigns. No one is willing to tackle disruptive member behaviors. Side conversations among small groups take the place of whole-group discussion, so shouting seems necessary. Members deny responsibility, become defensive, and struggle for control. Because the only thing that matters is getting the meeting over with, discussion, if any, is cut off prematurely; no information is shared. "A Chaotic Meeting" illustrates such an incident.

In the case of bad meetings featuring extreme control rather than chaos, authority figures may talk down to members, interrupt them, or actually hoard information to gain or keep power. They may also attempt to reach their goals by use of a **hidden agenda,** by which the leader tries to manipulate members by seeking sympathy, perhaps, or using other emotional appeals. The others eventually do what the leader wishes, and if the hidden agenda has been successful, these members think it was their own idea. The case study you read in Chapter 7 was characterized by such a hidden agenda.

A GOOD FIVE-MINUTE MEETING

3:35 p.m. Staff Meeting:

Member A: Reports on pounds produced

Member B: Asks about roll changes

Member C: Responds

Member B: Asks about progress on getting one production process restarted after planned shutdown

Member D: Says, "Things are still in a mess down there," [laughter] and elaborates on the problems

Two others: Elaborate on problems

Member A: Asks about safety issue that arose during the day

Member D: Reports accident and describes cause and actions taken

Visitor from management: Announces important meeting next week

Member E: Reports how team will handle representation

Member F: Makes announcement

Member A: Says, "Anything else?"

Member A: Says, "Meeting adjourned," at 3:40

Appropriate Meeting Communication

The best meetings feature attention to and genuine discussion of agenda items, balanced participation, openness to the positions of others, and a preponderance of **information sharing.** This latter element of communication consists of informing or describing, elaborating or amplifying, comparing or contrasting, and giving examples or statistics. Once information has been presented in these ways, attention shifts to clarification and analysis, then to assertions and suggestions or proposals, and to praise and support for people and ideas. Humor in such settings is not hostile or mocking but often self-deprecating. Rather than using humor at the expense of others, members find ways to laugh at situations or at "the joke of the day."

"A Good Five-Minute Meeting" illustrates the content of a successful meeting.

Of course, most meetings last more than five minutes. You may keep the features of this short meeting in mind as a model, however, as we now apply them to a longer business meeting, as shown in "An Effective Thirty-Minute Meeting."

AN EFFECTIVE THIRTY-MINUTE MEETING

2:00 p.m. Safety Meeting: The designated meeting leader opens with the comment, "Let's get started; we have a lot to cover." The leader begins with a number of items under "Old Business":

Where We Stand in Regard to Safety Standards

Goal: The group wants only one Occupational Health and Safety Administration (OSHA) recordable (lost-time accident) per quarter. They are currently on goal. The leader uses overhead transparencies to inform members.

Specific Safety Issues: The leader seeks input from members about specific issues, solutions attempted, progress made, and problems remaining.

Consensus Seeking: The leader asks for members' agreement on a plan of action to solve one problem, then another.

Where Are the New Problems or Potential Problems Going to Arise?   The group discusses new equipment and processes with no safety record to rely on.

There are several suggestions from members and a request from the leader to "write that up."

Announcement of Safety Award   The leader asks who can attend. A member volunteers.

Meeting adjourns at 2:30 p.m.

WHAT ARE THE PRINCIPLES OF EFFECTIVE MEETINGS?

Face-to-Face Meetings

The first principle of good meetings is that those attending need to see a purpose being fulfilled. Each person attending needs to have a legitimate role and understand that individual role. All must have a real stake in the outcome. If team-meeting success is actually a part of one's formal performance appraisal, then the stake is clear. If team decisions affect the quality of the members' work life, then the stake is clear. However, if meetings are perceived as mere formalities, as sham, or false, efforts at employee involvement, the personal connection become murky. Likewise, in voluntary associations, if members feel that only the officers actually have any influence over the organization, they will probably lose enthusiasm for the cause or issue that originally brought them to the group.

A second principle concerns the essential structure and focus for meetings. Well-constructed agendas can provide both. Recurring items give members a sense of continuity and enable them to predict the course of a meeting. Because many people feel somewhat inhibited at the thought of speaking aloud in public, at least at first, knowing agenda topics and their order in advance gives them a chance to think about what they may want to say and thus relieves some of the tension.

Third, individuals must be educated in small group communication processes and practices if they are to have good team meetings. They must be taught how and why to follow the rules for brainstorming, for example, in order that the process can fulfill its purpose. Part of that education should include methods for dealing with conflict, over- or under-participation, dominance, or interruptions. Team members must also fully understand how to complete decision-making procedures through consensus or other resolution methods so that they can solve problems systematically. They must have been shown the differences between traditional views of leadership and newer, shared-leadership practices.

In an article in *Business Communication Quarterly,* Thomas Clark (1998, pp. 42–43) summarizes well the qualities of good meetings. First, they must have a "clear vision," that is, they must be important, necessary, and planned with clear goals and objectives in mind. Second, they must consist of the "right people," or those "importantly affected," who have the blend of "expertise" needed. Third, they must feature "good preparation" in that those who attend "know in advance where their expertise can be used." Fourth, they follow a "clearly articulated plan" with no interruptions and with sufficient time allotted. Fifth, once decisions have been made, "appropriate follow through" will be completed through clear "take home objectives" and distribution of minutes. "Issues That Determine Meeting Effectiveness" summarizes good meeting characteristics that relate to issues of purpose, people, preparation, and procedures.

ISSUES THAT DETERMINE MEETING EFFECTIVENESS

Purpose

An effective meeting occurs only in order to reach a specific purpose or goal that requires the completion of specific objectives.

People

An effective meeting is attended by those who have an actual role to play in reaching that goal, understand that role, and have the necessary knowledge in both task completion and meeting skills.

Preparation

An effective meeting is preceded by creation and distribution of its own concrete agenda so that those attending can come prepared with useful and relevant thinking and information.

Procedures

An effective meeting features orderliness; structure; leadership; well-distributed participation without dominance or excessive disruption; sufficiency of time allotment per agenda item; systematic decision making, problem solving, or conflict management processes; and clear follow-through.

Virtual Meetings

Many of the principles explained above certainly apply as well to electronic meetings. However, some consideration must be given to adapting principles and characteristics to virtual meetings. It would seem merely common sense to say that all members must have equal access to the technology for such meetings or communiques to be effective. However, in voluntary associations, not all members may have e-mail at home, for instance, or may not be equally skilled in its use. If, however, the association's elected officers choose to use e-mail as a primary method of contacting members because of its ease of use, equality may be sacrificed for convenience.

In business groups, all members of a team might not agree on the usefulness of electronic meetings and so would not fully support such efforts. For others, the novelty of such meetings could preoccupy participants to such a degree that meeting structure and focus are lost. Confusion could result that would prevent understanding of who should do what by when. As our earlier research studies indicated, electronic anonymity could result in more ideas produced with little

---

ADDITIONAL ISSUES THAT DETERMINE VIRTUAL-MEETING EFFECTIVENESS

- Purpose: Actual meeting goal must be reachable by means of electronic communication technology.

- People: All members support using the technology and are equally or adequately skilled and comfortable in using the technology.

- Preparation: All members have equal access to the technology. Preparation and advance distribution of agenda allows participants to bring needed data to workstation, telephone, or teleconference setting.

- Procedures: Meeting focus is maintained by structuring processes that could be chaotic, as in use of a chat room, for instance, in place of face-to-face discussion. Timeline is clarified from a global time zone perspective, if necessary.

---

personal risk but with less personal responsibility attached. "Additional Issues That Determine Virtual-Meeting Effectiveness" adapts characteristics of effective meetings to computer-mediated meetings.

Use of Delphi Technique in Virtual Settings   In earlier chapters we learned about the various techniques groups can use to stimulate creative thinking, such as brainstorming. Again, as we have seen in this chapter, the virtual team presents special opportunities in idea generation, but conversely it also presents problems. One process, the Delphi technique, which is a variation of the nominal group technique that we studied in Chapter 5, eliminates pressure for conformity and provides anonymity but does not require synchronous meetings. Using the Delphi technique requires a facilitator, or any trusted person, whose job it is to compile all the responses sent electronically by the members. The facilitator then sends out all of the responses and asks for feedback. This time-consuming process would need to be repeated a number of times if decision making were the goal, but it can be quite useful for the simpler process of brainstorming to generate ideas (Thompson and Brajkovich, 2003).

Before we leave the topic of virtual meetings, an exploration of their use by student groups is in order. If your class has an electronic bulletin board, forum, or chat room, you may have already experienced the problems and promise of virtual meetings. In a live chat, because some members think or type faster than others, questions and answers will not necessarily follow each other in an orderly sequence, and soon the messages may seem merely random. A **threaded discussion board** can solve that problem but loses the qualities of face-to-face or at-the-same-time electronic interaction so important to teamwork. With a predetermined agenda and diligent attention to it during a chat meeting, the randomness can be overcome or at least minimized. Good meetings online take practice. In Appendix B and C you will find selected transcripts of such meetings held by both my graduate and undergraduate students in small group process courses.

CONCLUSION

Thousands of meetings are going on in American business and industry while you read this chapter—in the morning, at noon, night, and on the weekend. According to one estimate, U.S. businesses lost $37 billion in 1990 "because of poor meeting management" (Kayser, 1990); think what that figure must be by now. Think also of the number of meetings that are held for "no good reason," that is, there is no real purpose to be served. Determining the purpose and then organizing an agenda to satisfy that purpose must be the first steps. Then, of course, arranging for time, space, and comfort variables in face-to-face as well as virtual settings comes next. All of those factors can be perfect, and the meeting can still fail, however, if the "talk" that goes on there prevents the participants from sharing their knowledge and expertise.

The key differences between productive and destructive meetings lie in the "common sense" principles discussed in this chapter and summarized in "Issues That Determine Meeting Effectiveness" and "Additional Issues That Determine Virtual-Meeting Effectiveness." In the next two chapters we continue our focus on overcoming obstacles that stand in the way of following even the "most" commonsense standards.

COLLABORATIVE LEARNING ACTIVITIES

1. Brainstorm a list of obstacles your team might encounter if you were located in different parts of the world and had to meet via the Internet. Decide on the meeting purpose through a class discussion and then construct an agenda for a virtual, twenty-minute meeting of such a global team to be held on a computer chat room.

2. If your class has access to its own chat room or electronic forum or bulletin board, hold the virtual meeting for which you wrote the agenda in the previous activity. When the class reconvenes, discuss the problems you encountered. Did your meeting accomplish its purpose?

Chapter 9

Obstacles and Challenges to Teamwork

JFK Library, Boston, MA

Human and Situational Problems

KEY WORDS AND CONCEPTS

affective cognitive style

argumentativeness

assertiveness

belief in group morality

centralization-of-authority theory

cohesiveness

collective rationalizations

communication apprehension (CA)
    state anxiety
    trait anxiety

concertive control

direct pressure on dissenters

groupthink

illusion of unanimity

illusion of invulnerability

logical cognitive style

pressure to conform

receptiveness to feedback

self-appointed mind guards

self-censorship

self-disclosure

stereotyping of out-groups

task-irrelevant communication

unwillingness to participate

values-based control systems

verbal aggressiveness

To find out more about the Key Words and Concepts discussed in this chapter, use InfoTrac College Edition. Type in the keywords and subject terms. You can access InfoTrac College Edition from Wadsworth/Communication homepage: http://communication.wadsworth.com.

CAREER APPLICATION

Corporate hiring practices today require skill in both problem analysis and decision making regardless of the sort of work one seeks. At Toyota, for instance, all potential employees, whether in information systems, accounting, or manufacturing, participate in a four-and-one-half-hour group simulation. Here as in other pre-hire simulations, potential employees are screened for their willingness to participate, their communication styles, their approaches to problem solving, and their interpersonal and small group communication skills (Embry, 1994, p. E1).

Most large organizations also administer standardized tests to potential employees. These tests measure personality traits, personal style tendencies, intelligence (or perhaps different kinds of intelligence), aptitudes, and the ability to reason and make critical judgments. Some employers even attempt to put together teams of people who they think can work in harmony based on the results of these tests.

In this chapter we investigate the barriers to teamwork from the standpoint of two major factors. First, the human communication characteristics that hinder working together are explored. Then organizations themselves come under scrutiny for their failures to provide tangible support for teamwork or for their own long-standing cultural features that may be destructive to the equality necessary for teamwork.

HUMAN COMMUNICATION CHALLENGES

Individual Preferences

People problems, like people, come in many shapes and sizes. We live in a society that prides itself on individualism; we are taught from our earliest days to "be yourself." Even our legal system, however, insists that my right to swing my arm extends only to the tip of your nose. Once I begin to invade your space, my freedom of choice has ended. In a teamwork environment you must be concerned with not only the space rights of your teammates but also with their choice rights, their opinion rights, and their decision-making rights as well.

Major problems arise, especially in traditional workplaces that are transitioning to teamwork, when some individuals prefer to work alone and cannot or will not try to adapt. An engineer interviewed for this book insisted that teamwork only got in the way of his progress. As Dumaine (1994, p. 86) notes in *Fortune* magazine, "Workers who are lone wolves or creative types aren't necessarily better off in teams."

Some have a strong need for personal, singular achievement. Others have no patience with the additional time needed for teams to make decisions. A strong preference for doing things quickly and efficiently often precludes doing them methodically and effectively. Thus individuals with these different approaches to work find themselves engrossed in conflict when forced together (Boyle, 1992).

In order to understand the problem of differences in communication-style preferences, America West Airline conducted a study of decision-making-style preferences of their employees. They found those in the "male-dominated . . . highly skilled profession" of pilot "to be task-oriented, preferring a **logical cognitive style** of problem solving." Among those in the "female-dominated . . . service occupation" of the flight attendant, employees "preferred an **affective cognitive style** and orientation to decision making" (Chute and Wiener, 1995, p. 260).

Other challenges persist because of personal communication styles, preferences, or simple differences, some of which may be culturally based. For example, our culture seems to require males to speak more aggressively and argumentatively than females, an expectation that does not seem to have declined significantly even as sex-role boundaries have blurred (Eakins and Eakins, 1978; Infante, 1982; Burgoon et al., 1983; Nicotera and Rancer, 1994). Violations of those cultural expectations will have consequences, especially when groups or teams are in formative stages. As people get to know each other, they can create their own norms and idiosyncrasies.

Although stereotypical cultural expectations for communication styles persist, feminist thinkers have begun challenging not only cultural, gender-based expectations such as these but even the foundations of small group communication studies. Meyers and Brashers (1994, p. 69), for instance, suggest that "connection and cooperation" should be valued as "alternatives . . . to influence and competition" that permeate small group communication research. As they point out, most of the work on cohesion, or the degree to which the group sticks together, has been conducted from a negative point of view, that of **groupthink.** They urge, instead, that we study "nonhierarchical, consensual decision-making" groups "where women traditionally congregate or gather" that "value social relations among members" and "privilege cooperation over competition, and shared responsibility over autonomy" (p. 77). Value and style preferences such as these have the potential to clash within mixed-gender groups in the workplace or the community.

Certainly style differences exist among men and women and not always in the stereotypical ways indicated in the airline study above. Style differences relate, of course, to culture, age, status, ethnicity, situational context, and a host of additional variables. Learning about communication-style options by trying them out in the classroom can enhance each student's repertoire of skills available. Practice in both logical-cognitive and affective-cognitive styles is needed by both male and female students.

Many other communication-style differences exist among team members. One set, based on differences in levels of **self-disclosure** and **receptiveness to feedback,** consists of four types of communicators: open, blind, hidden, and closed (Luft, 1970). Another set of styles, consisting of such variables as dominance, drama, contentiousness, friendliness, and animation accompany our content messages and signal how such a message should be received, for instance, as serious or as a joke. Yet another set of communication-style possibilities includes **assertiveness, argumentativeness,** hostility, and **verbal aggressiveness** (Infante, Rancer, and Womack, 1990). See Tables 9.1 and 9.2 for explanations of specific styles.

In the college classroom, quiet or nonassertive students may find themselves facing highly dominant and even contentious or aggressive teammates. As we learned in Chapter 2, the ideal speech situation requires that members treat each other with mutual respect. As we learned in Chapter 7, shared leadership requires that all members take responsibility for ensuring that respect. The significance of these two norms, respect and shared leadership, cannot be overstated. The classroom is the place where individuals who have been rewarded for dominance can learn to share control and where those who have been rewarded for submissiveness can learn to lead.

Preferred-style differences can become obstacles to teamwork if one style comes to be perceived as the right style or the powerful style and the other comes to be perceived as the wrong or weak one. However, an appreciation for differences can turn them into team resource advantages.

TABLE 9.1	OPENNESS VARIABLES AND COMMUNICATOR STYLE
Communicator Style	**Characteristics**
Open	Is able to disclose her or his personal self to others and to take in information about her or his personal self from others
Hidden	Does not choose to disclose but does take in feedback from others
Blind	Does disclose his or her self to others but fails to take in adequate feedback to understand how he or she "comes across" to others
Closed	Discloses and receives feedback as little as possible so is not known well to her- or himself or to others

Adapted from Luft, 1970.

TABLE 9.2	ASSERTIVENESS VARIABLES AND COMMUNICATOR STYLE
Communicator Style	**Characteristics**
Assertive	The tendency to stand up for one's own interests while not harming others' interests; perceived as positive
Argumentative	The tendency to express one's point of view and to contend with others' points of view; perceived as positive
Hostile	The tendency to express anger toward others; perceived as negative
Verbally Aggressive	The tendency to try to harm another by attacking the person rather than the person's point of view; perceived as negative

Adapted from Infante, Rancer, and Womack, 1990.

Fear of Speaking

Fear of speaking, a characteristic that can incapacitate individuals, relates either to the topic under discussion or the other person; "the less familiar the topic or the other person, the greater the fear" (Lederman, 1982, pp. 287–288). For fearful persons, "preferring to listen [is] associated for them with the label 'shy,' a label that they [see] as negative. That is, shy to them [means] being overpowered by others, something they would rather not be." Although early writers in psychology and in speech communication attempted to differentiate between reticence, fear of negative evaluation, social avoidance and distress, shyness, communication apprehension, and **unwillingness to communicate,** more recent analysts characterize them as overlapping in their symptoms and similar in their

---

EARLIER PERCEPTIONS OF SHYNESS

Social Avoidance and Distress (SAD)

Those Who Suffer from SAD

- Avoid social interactions
- Prefer to work alone
- Report that they talk less
- Are more worried and less confident about social relationships
- Are more likely to appear for appointments

Fear of Negative Evaluation (FNE)

Those who suffer from FNE

- Are nervous in evaluative situations
- Work harder either to avoid disapproval or gain approval

Data from Watson and Friend, 1969, p. 448.

---

consequences (Phillips, 1968; Watson and Friend, 1969; Zimbardo, Pilkonis, and Norwood, 1975; McCroskey, 1976; Zimbardo, 1977; Crozier, 1979; Kelly, 1982; Breidenstein-Cutspec and Goering, 1988, 1989; Hawkins and Stewart, 1991). "Earlier Perceptions of Shyness" and "Zimbardo's Concept of Shyness as a 'Social Disease'" summarize a number of such findings.

Phillips's descriptions (1968, p. 40) of the reticent person, or one "for whom anxiety about participation in oral communication outweighs his [or her] projection of gain from the situation," provide ample evidence of the problems inherent in the condition. Reticent people Phillips observed experienced, he said, "shakiness" and other "physical symptoms" such as "'butterflies in the stomach,' loud or rapid heartbeat, headache, throbbing temples, nausea, excessive perspiration, and inability to see the audience" if they attempted to speak publicly. They sometimes "found it necessary to break off communication . . . abruptly"; they were unable to "communicate with 'important' people." Others had called their "communication inadequacies to [their] attention," and, not surprisingly, they felt "themselves consistently on the fringes of social gatherings." They became "unnaturally apologetic when their ideas were challenged, and they interpreted questions about content of communication as personal criticisms." They preferred written to oral communication (p. 41). Because his subjects were students, Phillips noted that most "expressed singular inability to talk with their parents" (p. 42).

McCroskey and a number of coauthors published articles during the 1970s and 1980s defining and refining the concept of **communication apprehension (CA),** comparing and contrasting it with shyness and reticence, and developing

ZIMBARDO'S CONCEPT OF SHYNESS AS A "SOCIAL DISEASE"

- Characterized by social problems
- Negative emotional correlates
  - depression
  - isolation
  - loneliness
  - difficulty in being appropriately assertive
  - confusing others
- Poor self-projection; seems to be
  - snobbish
  - bored
  - unfriendly or weak
- Deficiency in thinking clearly
- Self-consciousness
- Caused by cultural norms that overemphasize competition, individual success, and personal responsibility for failure

Zimbardo et al., 1975, pp. 69–72.

the personal report of communication apprehension (PRCA) which now includes four contexts: group, meeting, interpersonal, and public (McCroskey et al., 1975; McCroskey and Richmond, 1976; McCroskey, 1978; McCroskey, 1982; McCroskey, 1984). Rather than seeing CA as a permanent and pervasive condition, McCroskey and many others began to divide the concept into **trait,** or "a relatively enduring, personality-type orientation," and **state,** or situational, CA. With the concept of apprehension opened and perceived in this latter way, as a "transitory orientation toward communication with a given person or group of people," context mattered more than originally thought (McCroskey, 1982, p. 149). You will find the PRCA self-test in Appendix D.

Two studies from the 1990s have special significance to the field of small group communication. Hawkins and Stewart (1990) sought the relationship between leadership style and state or situational communication apprehension in small, task-oriented groups. They concluded that leaders who balanced "task structuring behaviors and consideration behaviors create group environments in which group members experience lower levels of state anxiety" (p. 6; see also Bass, 1981, for explanations of structuring and consideration behaviors). What does that mean to us?

As we have noted before, structure improves performance. Anxiety is provoked in some group members by ambiguity about what they should be doing to accomplish the group's task. A leader or shared leadership that structures the task reduces that ambiguity and thus relieves the apprehension. Anxiety is also produced in situations of inequality and in situations likely to exhibit negative evaluation. Consideration behavior means "treatment of fellow group members as equals, seeking input from fellow group members, making efforts to build fellow group members' self-esteem" (Hawkins and Stewart, 1990, p. 6). Again, it would seem merely common sense that genuine efforts to reduce inequality and to enhance members' self-concepts could reduce anxiety. Unfortunately, common sense does not always prevail in the sometimes heated environment of a meeting.

Continuing their studies of communication apprehension, Hawkins and Stewart (1991) reported findings that should provide comfort to those of us who have found our hearts pounding at the thought of communicating in public about something important. Noting as others had done before them that anxiety in the small group setting tends to decrease over time, they moved beyond that to show that perceptions of actual performance by apprehensives were inaccurate. Although other members thought that apprehensive people "missed group meetings, didn't offer original input, lacked interest, and generally, were not helpful," the only actual differences in participation came in the fact that apprehensive people engaged in less **"task-irrelevant communication,"** such as "small talk" or "chit chat" (p. 8).

These research findings are important for two major reasons. First, the inclusion of apprehensive people in a group or team does not automatically detract from the team's progress in completing their work; indeed, their inclusion simply reinforces the already vital need for structure. Second, apprehensive people will likely miss out on the relationship- or community-building aspects of the team's activities unless efforts are made to relieve their anxiety through consideration behavior.

ORGANIZATIONAL OR SITUATIONAL COMMUNICATION BARRIERS

Unwillingness to Participate

Employees differ in their willingness to participate or to show open enthusiasm about their work for fear of ridicule by co-workers. Especially among established workforces, negative attitudes about us versus them only serve to harden the separation between hourly and salaried staff or between management and labor. An absence of clear role distinctions causes misunderstandings about the real power of teams to make decisions that will "stick." If no team decisions are ever implemented, it is little wonder that disillusionment and frustration result in even less participation in the future.

Fear of Losing Control

One daunting organizational barrier to teamwork is the fear of losing power and control on the part of middle managers or former supervisors (Song, 1994; Webb, 1988; Stewart, 1991; "Employees . . .", 1994; Verespej, 1990). In his review of teamwork in four manufacturing plants, Vallas (2003, p. 244) found that "mid-level

A Mail-Order and Retail Firm

In the fall of 1994, the human-resources director of this firm and the director of its mail-order department launched a teamwork initiative. At that time, the employees in mail-order were divided into three groups, the largest being telemarketers, who responded to customer-initiated calls, which resulted from catalog direct marketing. The second largest group was customer-service representatives, who responded to calls about products sold either through mail order or through the company's retail stores. The smallest group was technical-service representatives, who helped customers install products or otherwise assisted customers in using the products.

The Teamwork Initiative

The mail-order director saw teamwork as an opportunity to eliminate a rather chaotic system, in which calls were routed from telemarketing, to customer service, to technical service, and then perhaps around again before being resolved. Her vision, a one-number call center, required that all three groups of employees be trained in all three functions: sales, customer service, and technical service. That training, she thought, could be best accomplished gradually through placement of individuals from all three groups into teams that sat together and listened to and learned from each other. Two such teams were created, along with a management team, made up of five mail-order supervisors. The remaining employees continued to function as usual but were, in the next year, called upon often to fill in for the team members while they attended teamwork training sessions and team meetings.

In the fall of 1995, a second implementation phase began in mail order with the creation of additional teams. At the same time, the distribution center director decided to create teams among employees involved in picking, packing, and shipping of products, both to mail-order customers and to the firm's retail stores. He began by forming one team made up of hourly employees from those three functional areas as well as a management team of warehouse supervisors. Teamwork training began for all new team members.

Management Concept

This firm maintained its "old-style" supervisory practices. For those in the call center, the only difference now lay in not knowing for sure who "the boss" was. Although the hourly employee teams met together and tried to share information, management still treated them in a clearly top-down, hierarchical style. For example, management team members, who ironically named themselves

"ETC" to stand for an Empowering Team of Coaches, carefully monitored their teams' meetings and training times and sternly warned that it was "time to get back on the phone," regardless of the issue under discussion.

The situation in the warehouse was infinitely worse. The director deliberately made himself a member of the management team. Nothing could convince him that with him always present and answering all of the questions before anyone else had a chance to speak, his "team" still functioned merely as his staff. The management team then took the same approach to their hourly employee team, even to the point of insisting that all members of the management team could never attend one of their own meetings or one of their training sessions at the same time because someone had to be on the warehouse floor to watch the employees. The management team claimed that their employees were different from the mail-order team members because they were uneducated, unmotivated, seasonal, unable to work hard, and unwilling to work hard unless someone made them.

Discussion Questions for Case Study

1. Is teamwork possible in an environment such as this one?

2. What strategies could be implemented to improve the environment for teamwork in this company?

3. What are the barriers that could prevent any strategies from being put into place?

managerial and engineering employees did not merely resist organizational change or defend their traditional authority; rather, they used selective features of the new work practices to expand their authority." Among those Vallas studied, "most achieved only limited gains and were generally unable to transcend the traditional boundary between salaried and hourly employees." The key factor that hindered progress was the inability of "corporate executives to demonstrate the very capacity for flexibility that they often demand of their hourly employees" (p. 223). For an understanding of day-to-day struggles over issues of power and trust, consider the case study beginning on p. 154.

Lack of Trust

The case study shows the interrelationships between individual and organizational barriers to teamwork. Indeed, they are so woven together and so invisible to the members themselves, outside consultants must often be brought in to sort out one from the other. The case demonstrates management reluctance and fear of change, but it also shows an organizational climate that perpetuates status differences that engender distrust on all sides. Indeed, the lack of trust of employees by management and of management by employees may be the greatest barrier of all to teamwork. As Dumaine (1994, p. 90) states bluntly in *Fortune,* "You can't have teams without trust."

The history of American economic institutions, whether in manufacturing, finance, sales, service, or the public sector, has, of course, been influenced by the fluctuations of the business cycle. As the economy flourishes, business booms and employees are hired; as the economy languishes, layoffs, shutdowns, downsizing, and the transfer of operations and jobs out of the country result. An earlier management philosophy, Theory X, taught that employees would not do their work unless forced to do so. That this combination of factors has resulted in distrust is not surprising. Unfortunately, trust can be further endangered when teams are created across functional lines, which stirs up "turf" battles (Stewart, 1991; "Employees . . . ", 1994).

Lack of Coordination and Commitment

Cross-functional teams have been created specifically to help alleviate another organizational barrier, lack of coordination between shifts, departments, functions, or staffs. In the case-study organization mentioned above, the only internal employee who could see the need for coordination between the warehouse teams and the mail-order teams was a training facilitator from the human-resources department. Her plea for mutual meetings went unheeded as "too expensive and time consuming."

A serious organizational barrier, lack of commitment, manifests itself in inadequate time, effort, and money spent on teamwork training; in failure to clarify the roles and goals of teams; and in abandonment of the project under stressful conditions. As one General Electric executive was quoted as saying in *Fortune* magazine, "If you teach a bear to dance, you'd better be prepared to keep dancing till the bear wants to stop" (Stewart, 1991, p. 49). We might add, if the bear has not had good dancing lessons, all potential dancing partners are in jeopardy.

Inequality

An almost overwhelming organizational barrier, status differences among the members, permeates the lives of all who live in an individualistic culture such as ours, and perhaps in all other societies as well. Kenneth Burke (1945, 1950, 1966) has said that not only do people seek perfection, they also seek order, and they strive for both by conceiving of and placing things and individuals into hierarchies, or pyramidal structures. The large mass remains at the "bottom of the heap" as fewer and fewer rise through the layers to the top. In organizational terms, the largest group of employees remains in the lowest pay grades and possesses the least power or control over their own work. Fewer and fewer rise to a second, to a third, and to a fourth level. At the executive level, a very few earn the most and possess the most power. In human terms, even children can understand concepts like "good, better, best."

The effects of these status differences on teamwork can be enormous. For example, suppose those high in the pyramid take an inflated sense of self-importance outside the workplace and make a practice of failing to speak to those lower in the hierarchy when they pass each other in the grocery aisle or at the local school's ballgames. How can lower-level people be expected then to feel comfortable taking suggestions, innovations, or proposals up the chain of command?

This comfort-level problem goes far beyond the failure to receive simple but useful information. Some have suggested that during crises, or even merely stressful situations, people tend to defer to the leader—the so-called **"centralization-of-authority" theory.** Because of contradictory findings, Driskell and Salas (1991) tested the theory and found that, indeed, low-status members become more deferential or respectful of authority when the group is under stress. However, they found that high-status members—the designated leader or manager, for example—become more receptive to inputs from low-status members when under stress. They suggest two possible reasons: to enable the high-status member to evaluate his or her own thinking by comparing it with that of others or to share or diffuse his or her own responsibility.

Although some have suggested that low-status members be given assertiveness training, Driskell and Salas (1991) maintain that both high- and low-status members must be given training that intervenes in their behavior. Otherwise the high-status people would probably react with hostility after viewing the low-status individuals "behaving inappropriately" (p. 477). This tendency to dismiss or even resent suggestions by lower-level employees may be seen again in the period leading up to the disintegration of the space shuttle *Columbia.* As one of the engineers tried to make his grave misgivings about the mission known to those higher up, one manager said that he, for one, "refused to be a 'Chicken Little'" while another sent an e-mail message calling his concern "a dead issue" (Glanz and Schwartz, 2003). The implication in the first response was that the engineer was like the misguided chicken in an old children's story who went around telling everyone that the sky was falling simply because an acorn had fallen on his head. The implication in the second response was that if someone above you in rank says that something has been discussed enough, then your expertise doesn't count.

Examples of Status-Difference Barriers   To understand the everyday importance of this problem, we need only look at two real-life disasters from the airline industry. In one example, passengers and flight attendants saw "debris, fire, and smoke coming from the left engine." However, the flight crew in the cockpit thought the right engine was on fire and shut it down, "causing the airplane to crash just short of the runway and break apart, leading to nearly fifty fatalities" (King, Murray, and Blocher, 1996, p. 21). In another example, passengers and flight attendants saw snow and ice building up on the wings while the plane was parked at the ramp, but the cockpit crew only saw snow melting as it hit the ground. As a result, "the airplane crashed soon after takeoff, breaking into three major sections. More than twenty people died" (p. 22).

One obstacle that prevented the vital flow of intra-crew communication in both cases has long kept such valuable input from being offered: status differences.

According to one flight attendant who survived such a crash, "You have a front-end crew and a back-end crew, and we are looked upon as serving coffee and lunch and things like that. Certain captains are not disposed to seriously consider information from flight attendants" (p. 25).

This fragmentation of an airline crew into two separate crews who do not see themselves as a team "contributes to misunderstandings and problems in coordination and communication on the part of airline crews in the performance of their duties. These issues can become even more apparent in abnormal situations when the two crews must unite and act as a cohesive team" (Chute and Wiener, 1995, p. 258). If they fail to understand each other's duties and usefulness, their consequent "lack of trust can endanger lives" (p. 259).

Organizational barriers erected both by the airline industry and the Federal Aviation Administration (FAA) further complicate the scene. Pilots generally work "under flight operations in which safety is stressed, whereas the cabin crews are typically part of the marketing department in which the emphasis is service." In addition, the two types of crews receive "segregated training," which leaves "gaps in the instructions crews receive" (Chute and Wiener, 1995, pp. 260–261). Because of the ambiguity of FAA regulations, communication between pilots and cabin crews is "risky business" (Chute and Wiener, 1996, p. 213).

The risk arises because of the so-called sterile cockpit concept. The goal is "reducing non-essential communication in the flight deck for all phases of flight below 10,000 feet—including ground movement" (King, Murray, and Blocher, 1996, p. 22). If, in the deadly instances described above, flight attendants had contaminated the sterile cockpit by communicating what they saw happening outside, they would have been taking a chance on violating the FAA rule and thus becoming "vulnerable to sanction" (Chute and Wiener, 1996, p. 213).

Another obstacle is terminology. For example, on a plane with several engines, which is engine number one? Which side is port; which engine on the port side is inboard? Which side is starboard; which engine on the starboard side is outboard? Which side is the "captain side," which is the "first officer side," which part of the plane is fore, and which is aft? In the commercial aviation industry, understandings of the ways these words work together are called "mental models," or "situational awareness" (King, Murray, and Blocher, 1996, p. 24).

In the first crash example described above, the cockpit flight crew's mental model was affected by previous problems with the right engine. In the second example, the situational awareness of snow melting on the ground caused the cockpit flight crew to conclude that it would also melt on the wing. Only by being receptive to input from the cabin crews could the two cockpit crews have avoided these fatal accidents, but, as we just learned, the two crews do not receive comparable training, nor do they see each other as equals.

Chute and Wiener (1996) give numerous instances in which the cabin crew reported noises or observations that concerned them and that, when checked out by the flight crew, sometimes reluctantly, turned out to be life threatening. These include thumps or other "funny sounds" that were the result of engine failures, tire and rim destruction, or broken oil lines or fuel cells. However, because flight attendants have no technical training and are perceived as incompetent to speak about such matters, their warnings often go unheeded.

They conclude that "it would be seen as appropriate for a flight attendant to talk about a piece of cabin equipment, but unacceptable to comment on an operational matter, such as the possibility of too much snow on the wings" (p. 223; Moshansky, 1992).

These problems of divided authority and expertise among groups can also be problematic in student groups. For example, university science departments often apply for grants to fund student research projects. Students from different majors are chosen to participate, and a variety of faculty members likewise serve as advisors. If the professional advisors start with the assumption that students cannot understand the project's goals, objectives, processes, and outcomes adequately, little collaboration will occur. Schools that highly value undergraduate student research must find ways to incorporate student perspectives into the projects' leadership structures.

Social Cohesiveness

Overcohesiveness Resulting in Groupthink

The term groupthink, coined by Irving Janis (1972), was defined as "a mode of thinking that people engage in when they are deeply involved in a cohesive in-group, when the members' strivings for unanimity override their motivation to realistically appraise alternative courses of action" (p. 9). Because of the complexity and vagueness of this definition, Janis (1982) later revised it as simply "concurrence seeking." Although some writers have deleted items from Janis's list of symptoms of groupthink, all eight deserve consideration here. They are outlined in "Symptoms of Groupthink."

The symptoms—the **illusion of unanimity,** the **illusion of invulnerability, collective rationalizations, direct pressure on dissenters, self-appointed mind guards, self-censorship, belief in the inherent morality of the group,** and **stereotyping of out-groups**—certainly can be observed working among organizational teams. The development of an us-versus-them environment certainly provides fertile ground for collective rationalizations and for in-group and out-group stereotyping.

The human need to belong sometimes overwhelms our sense that the group is wrong, so we just don't speak up. The expertise of those at the top of the hierarchy not only contributes to the illusion of invulnerability on their own part but even induces others to have unquestioning faith in their rightness. Had the cabin crews of the two planes that crashed had less faith that the pilots knew what they were doing, they might have spoken up more forcefully. However, even an off-duty pilot riding in the cabin of the snow-covered plane refused to intervene, perhaps because of his in-group position as a pilot.

Many strategies have been devised to prevent groupthink from replacing effective group decision making. Janis (1971) suggested that groups actively seek opinions and data contrary to their own knowledge and that members try to put aside their opinions in order to be "critical evaluators." His advice to leaders suggested that they withhold their views until others have spoken, that they occasionally allow others to lead, and that they encourage consideration of

SYMPTOMS OF GROUPTHINK

The Illusion of Unanimity   Because no one openly disagrees, we must all be in harmony.

The Illusion of Invulnerability   Because we all know what we are doing, nothing we do can be wrong.

Collective Rationalizations   We find ways to convince ourselves that our course of action must be correct, or we would not have chosen it.

Direct Pressure on Dissenters   Surely you would not be so foolish as to disagree with such an obvious course of action.

Self-Appointed Mind Guards   We can't let that piece of information reach those who have worked so hard to come to this decision.

Self-Censorship   This does not seem "right" to me, but who am I to say so?

Belief in the Inherent Morality of the Group   This group has been so carefully chosen and is made up of such "good" people, how could we be in error?

Stereotyping of Out-Groups   Those who disagree with us are, no doubt, misinformed, at least, and evil, at worst.

Adapted from Janis, 1982.

diverse options. Then, before it is too late, the group should revisit its decision and subject it to a final scrutiny (p. 76; Janis, 1979; Janis and Mann, 1977). A philosophy of shared emergent-leadership could help alleviate some of the leader issues noted by Janis.

Overcohesiveness Leading to Concertive Control   Another concept related to cohesiveness bears careful consideration, that is, **concertive control.** As in the case of groupthink, the group's insistence on conformity is more than simple peer pressure. A number of writers in communication have explored the concept (Tompkins and Cheney, 1985; Barker, 1993; Barker and Cheney, 1994). Barker (1993), for instance, says that groups who work in concert develop **values-based control systems.** Instead of freeing the members from controls imposed by either supervisors or bureaucracies, these systems control the members even more strictly (p. 408). Individuals within the "iron cage" that the team becomes "must invest a part of themselves in the team: they must identify strongly with their team's values and goals, its norms and rules. If they want to resist their team's control, they must be willing to risk their human dignity, being made to feel unworthy as a 'teammate.' Entrapment in the cage is the cost of concertive control" (p. 438).

Although the research studies on concertive control have been conducted using corporate work teams, this concept can be a problem even in short-term student groups. If you have formed into decision-making or project teams in your small group communication class, think about the ways in which the group controls the members' behaviors. If you belong to a social organization on campus or if you participate in clubs organized around majors, take special note of the values and perceptions of "who we are" that set each group apart from the others.

Cohesiveness as Advantage

Too much group cohesiveness, in the instances of groupthink and concertive control, can become a problem; however, an appropriate level of cohesiveness can also be an advantage. In experimental research studies of effectiveness, groups that spent their early time together getting to know one another, reaching consensus on group goals, and building a real team environment had more success, at least in business game performance, than those who concentrated on getting the task accomplished (Jaffe and Nebenzahl, 1990, p. 144). The task for this computerized game consisted of making five business decisions in order "to maximize profits and to manage an efficient organization" (p. 136). Once they had become a cohesive group, however, "teams that continued to emphasize the social aspects . . . at the expense of the task eventually performed relatively poorly" (p. 144). Just the right amount of cohesiveness can enhance commitment, job satisfaction, and motivation while helping relieve job-related stress (Bartkus et al., 1997).

The norms of behavior that develop in a team make a significant difference to the team's potential for success. In the same way, the norms of behavior in an organization will have a major impact on the communication practiced there. If rudeness starts the day, hostility cannot be far behind. If high-status members do all of the talking, others will retreat into silence. Everyone loses in such a world.

Fortunately, efforts are underway to intervene in these problematic situations. For example, a relatively new system, cockpit resource management (CRM), originally devised to encourage others among the cockpit crew besides the pilot to participate more often in decision making, has been extended to cabin crews. Thus some communication barriers to teamwork are being lifted.

CONCLUSION

In this chapter we have looked at challenges to teamwork that arise from two communication sources: people and organizations. Some challenges defy classification because both factors contribute to their construction. In the personal realm, we found that individuals' attitudes, preferences, style differences, degrees of openness to feedback, willingness to self-disclose, and levels of fear of communicating all function as potential barriers to effective team communication. Organizational hierarchies confer status differences that may result in power struggles, obviously hindering teamwork. Moreover, teams that manage to avoid these divisive factors may become overcohesive and fall prey to group-think or concertive control.

All of these obstacles are capable of creating conflict within a group; thus, all may be destructive or constructive, depending on how they are perceived. In the next chapter we will find that conflict—something most of us view as harmful and so try to avoid—may actually be beneficial to a team, depending especially on how it is handled. The spirit of collaboration, so necessary for teamwork, guides our thinking in the next chapter where we explore ways of evaluating and managing conflict.

COLLABORATIVE LEARNING ACTIVITIES

1. Complete the PRCA self-test found in Appendix D. Turn in your four individual scores as well as your overall scores with only your group identity (if you have formed into class teams), not with your name. Your teacher or a designated person can list the scores for each team for comparison. Talk about how these differences in communication apprehension can affect your team's communication patterns. Use your personal scores to set some individual goals in the course.

2. Analyze the personal preference differences in your team. How could they hinder your group? How can they be accommodated without taking away any important elements of "free choice" from any members?

Chapter 10

Managing Team Conflict

Superstock

Causes and Effects Both Positive and Negative

KEY WORDS AND CONCEPTS

accommodation

affective conflict

argument culture

attribution theory

avoidance

collaboration

competition v. cooperation

compromise

conflict

conflict metaphors

denial and equivocation

false consensus

four-phase model of decision emergence

force

incompatible goals

interdependence

linguistic diversity

nonfluencies

passive aggression

procedural conflict

substantive conflict

wants v. needs

withdrawal

 To find out more about the Key Words and Concepts discussed in this chapter, use InfoTrac College Edition. Type in the keywords and subject terms. You can access InfoTrac College Edition from Wadsworth/Communication homepage: http://communication.wadsworth.com.

CAREER APPLICATION

"It was the worst three days of our lives."

This description of a work situation comes from a member of the team you first saw in the Career Application in Chapter 3. The group fired a member who could not work with women and minorities. The conflict over what to do took three difficult days of collaboration before their decision was finalized. Below you will see one member's description of the ways the team worked through it.

"We have ninety days to assess a member's performance while he or she is on probation, and at the end of this guy's ninety days, we decided that maybe we hadn't been as helpful to him as we could, so we gave him thirty more days. At the end of that time we reevaluated him and decided that though he knew what we wanted from him, he didn't give it, and so we took that decision on up to personnel.

We trained him on a job, and he couldn't do it. So we put somebody with him for a week, and he still couldn't do it. Even if he didn't know something, he would argue for his opinion on it to the end. As far as the people part, he would sit in the break room and call the women on our team neo-Nazis, and he would put down black people, and we didn't need any of that. We were afraid it would tear the team apart. We kid and carry on, but we pick on everybody equally. We couldn't let his attitudes hurt the team."

Conflict may be one of our least understood communication concepts. When we hear that individuals, teams, organizations, or nations are engaged in conflict, we worry about the outcome and its impact on future relationships. We may have grown up in households where the only outward conflicts were explosive and destructive, so we learned early to try to avoid them at all cost. However, researchers and writers in the field of conflict management stress that, like most things, conflict can be good or bad, can be productive *or* destructive, and can actually lead to growth of both persons and relationships.

Two leading writers in the area of communication and conflict, Joyce Hocker and William Wilmot (1991, p. 12), define **conflict** as "an expressed struggle between at least two interdependent parties who perceive incompatible goals, scarce resources, and interference from the other party in achieving their goals." In deriving their definition, they point to the work of earlier theorists, many of whom focused on conflict's war-like or harmful aspects (Fink, 1968; Coser, 1967; Deutsch, 1973; Mack and Snyder, 1973). Still others have written in less-ominous terms about conflict (Simons, 1972; Schmidt and Kochan, 1972) or in prescriptive terms about peacemaking (Boulding, 1987; Keltner, 1987). Note that in their definition, Hocker and Wilmot acknowledge that the parties to the struggle not only recognize their difficulty but also speculate on possible reasons for the conflict.

Putnam and Poole (1987, p. 552) have adapted earlier conflict definitions to the small group context; they define conflict as "the interaction of interdependent people who perceive opposition of goals, aims, and values, and who see the other party as potentially interfering with the realization of these goals." They summarize conflict's three characteristics as **interaction, interdependence,** and **incompatible goals.** In a group, then, five or more members who depend on each other to accomplish incompatible goals with limited resources come to the realization that their membership or their participation in the team may limit their potential individual goal accomplishment. At that point, they may be said to be "in conflict" (see Putnam and Poole, 1987, pp. 549–599, and Hocker and Wilmot, 1991, pp. 12–14, for further elaboration of this process).

According to Hocker and Wilmot (1991), communication fills a number of functions in regard to conflict, including its creation. Communication may also reflect conflict, as well as serve as a "vehicle for the productive or destructive management of conflict" (p. 13). According to Putnam and Poole (1987, p. 552), communication "constitutes the essence of conflict." In this chapter we look at conflict types, how and why conflict occurs, its normal and essential nature, its potential positive and negative effects, and suggestions for its management, all the while focusing on team or group communication practices.

CONFLICT TYPES

In an early study, Guetzkow and Gyr (1954, p. 55) identified two general types of conflict in decision-making groups: "**substantive,** or conflict rooted in the substance of the task; and **affective,** or conflict found in the group's interpersonal relations." Knutson and Kowitz (1977) refined the descriptions of these types. Substantive conflict consists of "an opposition, resistance to, or disagreement with a suggestion, solution, or interpretation pertaining to the group's task-oriented activities." Affective conflict consists of "statements that relate to the personal characteristics of group members" such as "motives, . . . ability, . . . undesirable personal traits, or offensive interpersonal behavior in the group" (p. 57). Finally, Knutson and Kowitz developed a three-category conflict system that included **procedural conflict** as well as the previously mentioned substantive and affective conflict. Procedural conflict may include disagreement over leadership in terms of goals, tasks, roles, or communication networks (pp. 61–62).

CONFLICT'S CAUSES AND FUNCTIONS

Language Itself

Deborah Tannen (1998, p. 4) says we live in an **"argument culture,"** where opposition, debate, polarization, litigation, attacks, and criticism are perceived as "the best way to get anything done." Our talk is filled, she says, with "war metaphors," and "everything is framed as a battle or game in which winning or losing is the main concern." As a result we "distort facts," we "waste valuable time," we "limit . . . our thinking," and we are encouraged "to lie," all in the interest of winning a contest over issues that seem to have only "two sides—no more, no less" (pp. 4–5).

We certainly see conflict in negative **conflict metaphors.** McCorkle and Mills (1992) conducted a study of ways in which the language choices we make both illustrate and shape our perceptions of our own roles in conflict situations. They present Crum's (1987) "five mind sets, which people assume in conflict situations that include destruction, decay, survival, success, and artistry." How do these mindsets affect one's reactions to conflict? Destruction, decay, and survival "are negative, diminish energy, invoke fear, . . . and require struggle." Success and artistry "are positive, invoke love, . . . and are effortless and joyful" (McCorkle and Mills, p. 59). McCorkle and Mills's research subjects generated only negative metaphors in their conflict descriptions. Some of the most common ones had to do with animals, "two rams butting heads," or natural processes, "a tornado." Others related to one-way communication, "talking to a brick wall"; confinement, "tied up in chains"; violence, "stabbed in the back"; struggle, "rocky road"; or parenting, "being treated like a child" (pp. 61–62).

Competitive Culture

Stewart Stokes (1994, p. 43) claims that our work life causes interpersonal conflict because "[o]rganizations have typically rewarded individual performance, and competition among people and departments has been a preferred organizational style." Certainly we are influenced by broad societal habits and by organizational reward systems, but we can also bring causes down to the personal level. For that we look at the application of communication theory to a psychological theory, that is, to Alan Sillars's adaptation (1980) of Fritz Heider's attribution theory (1958).

Attribution Theory

Heider called his theory naive psychology, and he generally said that human beings normally try to figure out why people do the things they do. Is it because of the situation or because of the person him- or herself? Just because we attribute or attach a behavior to a particular cause, that does not mean we have found the cause. However, we often behave as if we actually had found the cause. Not only do we conclude that we know the cause of another person's behavior, but then we assign our own meaning to that behavior, as if it were our own behavior. For example, if two friends are engaged in a conflict, both may blame the other and see themselves as completely innocent. They will attribute the disruption of their relationship to stubbornness, jealousy, or pettiness on the part of the other person, though an action that they themselves have taken may be the true "cause." In the case of a student group, the cause of one member's absence from a meeting may be attributed by others to lack of commitment until they learn about the twenty-four-hour virus that has afflicted their teammate.

Sillars applied this human tendency to his studies of conflict and arrived at three general strategies of conflict resolution: passive or indirect actions that have **avoidance** as a goal, distributive actions that seek winning at the expense of the other party, and integrative actions that aim for winning on both sides. Littlejohn (1992) explains the usefulness of Sillars's theories in understanding conflict management. "First," he says, "individuals' attributions in a conflict determine what sorts of strategies they will choose to deal with the conflict" (p. 289). If one person sees herself or himself to blame, this attribution "may lead to the use of cooperative strategies, but when a person thinks the other communicator is responsible, a more competitive approach may be taken" (p. 289).

Littlejohn says that "biases in the attribution process discourage the use of integrative strategies. These include a tendency to see others as personally responsible for negative events and to see oneself as merely responding to circumstances." If we think others have "bad intentions," or if we see them as "inconsiderat[e], competitive, . . . or inadequate," we blame them instead of ourselves. If, as he claims, "both partners in a conflict tend to believe that the other person caused it," and that they are "merely responding to the provocations of others," think of the complexity of potential attributions of blame in a team environment (p. 289). Littlejohn's third insight into the usefulness of Sillars's work is perhaps the most important. He shows that our choice of strategy based on our attribution of blame results in either **cooperation** or **competition.** If we choose "cooperative strategies," we "encourage integrative solutions and information exchange." If we choose "competitive strategies," we "escalate the conflict," which "may lead to less satisfying solutions" (p. 289). See "Sillars's Conflict Categories" and imagine them operating in a group discussion or team decision-making session.

SILLARS'S CONFLICT CATEGORIES

Avoidance Behaviors

Denial and Equivocation
   direct denial
   implicit denial
   evasive remark

Topic Management
   topic shifts
   topic avoidance

Noncommittal Remarks
   abstract remarks
   noncommittal statements
   noncommittal questions
   procedural remarks

Irreverent Remarks
   nonhostile joking

Cooperative Behaviors

Analytic Remarks
   description
   qualification
   disclosure
   soliciting disclosure
   soliciting criticism

Conciliatory Remarks
   empathy or support
   concessions
   accepting responsibility

Competitive Behaviors

Confrontative Remarks
   personal criticism
   rejection
   hostile imperatives
   hostile questioning
   hostile joking or sarcasm
   presumptive attribution
   denial of responsibility (Littlejohn, 1992, p. 288)

Sillars, 1986.

A Decision-Making Phase

Fisher (1980) adapted the work of Robert K. Merton (1957) to his work on conflict as a process important in group decision making. Merton classified what he called "deviance" into four groups, three of which—"ritualism," or "blind conformity"; "retreatism," or withdrawal; and "rebellion"—Fisher described as harmful to group processes. The fourth, "innovation," in Fisher's terms, "innovative deviance," should be considered "normal to the process of group decision making" because it is "part of the normal communication performed by all group members who are committed to the group goals" (Merton, pp. 247–250).

Fisher's work (1970), developing a **four-phase model of "decision emergence,"** features conflict as the second phase. In the first phase, orientation, members are getting to know each other or getting comfortable in their interactions, and they tend not to disagree but to speak ambiguously. In the second phase, conflict, they begin to disagree about ideas, proposals, opinions, information, and so forth, and to polarize into those who support and those who oppose options. In the third phase, emergence, meaning that decisions begin to emerge out of the discussion, members do not disagree as often, and they return to ambiguity to provide an avenue for eventual agreement or consensus. In the last phase, reinforcement, members reach consensus through a process of adding reasons for agreement to the suggestions of others, thus reinforcing the unity of the group (pp. 145–149).

A number of earlier researchers had developed models of group processes based on the length of time groups worked together on problem solving or decision making (Bales, 1950; Bales and Strodtbeck, 1951; Bennis and Shepard, 1956, 1961; Dunphy, 1964). Tuckman's model (1965) of group stages described the same processes but named them, especially the second stage, more colorfully. His four stages—forming, storming, norming, and performing—correspond directly with orientation, conflict, emergence, and reinforcement.

CONFLICT'S EFFECTS

Potential Positive Effects

As you saw earlier, conflict can have both negative and positive effects. It is certainly uncomfortable to go to a meeting knowing that difficult times are ahead because the team is in disagreement on a particular issue. However, among the positive effects of conflict we can certainly list the avoidance of groupthink, a harmful, potentially disastrous process we learned about in Chapter 9. Healthy conflict does not guarantee against groupthink, but the absence of conflict is in itself a danger sign. Conflict management may provide the additional "thinking time" needed to prevent premature or poorly thought-out decisions. Full discussion of areas of disagreement may allow previously unknown perspectives to emerge. Knutson and Kowitz (1977) cite early studies that show that "the presence of conflict during . . . deliberations results in higher quality solutions" among problem-solving groups (Hall and Watson, 1970; Bower, 1965). The stresses and strains of conflict situations may shift the balance of power in a team toward greater equality.

Fisher (1980, pp. 235–236) found that conflict "breeds not only social interaction but also increased involvement. The member who is apathetic toward the group and toward the worth of the group task has little reason to engage in the painful process of social conflict. Moreover, the virtual absence of social conflict in group interaction is a trustworthy indication of the low involvement or commitment of group members." In cohesive groups, meetings will involve "rather frequent, though not extended, periods of social conflict. Thus, the natural development of group cohesiveness presupposes social conflict" (p. 237).

Fisher suggests that conflict is a necessary component of consensus decision making "owing to increased involvement of group members with their task performance" (p. 238). He reasons that the conflict itself "serves as a stimulus to critical thinking and stimulates members to test their ideas" (p. 239). Not only does conflict assist groups in reaching consensus, it also helps prevent what Fisher refers to as "one of the problems that haunts every real-life decision-making group," that is, "the possibility of superficial or **false consensus.**" In that case, agreements are reached for the sake of agreement, but the members "remain uncommitted to them"; they are "never put into effect or are implemented only halfheartedly and consequently fail." Fisher claims that such agreements are "more likely to result from suppressed conflict than from expressed conflict" (p. 239).

Recalling our discussion of individualist and collectivist cultures in Chapter 3, we might assume that teams in a collectivist country such as China would seek to maintain harmony at any cost. However, in a recent study, Tjosvold and his colleagues (2003) investigated the relationship between team members' "conflict values and relationships" and team effectiveness. Surprisingly, they found that among employee teams at state-owned enterprises in Shanghai and Nanjing, "positive conflict attitudes" and a willingness to engage in conflict "can contribute to strong relationships, which in turn strengthen team effectiveness and employee citizenship" (p. 69).

Potential Negative Effects

Besides the general unpleasantness stirred up in a group, conflict also seems to affect members' ability to communicate generally. Prentice's study (1975) of purposeful "trust-destroying communication" in a laboratory setting illustrated the power of conflict to reduce verbal fluency. In his analysis of tape-recorded discussions, Prentice categorized conversational elements into message fluency, or "the degree to which verbal behavior consists of a continuous flow of words, phrases, or sentences grouped into meaningful units, with a minimum of purposeless interruptions," and **nonfluencies,** or "sounds, words, or phrases in verbal behavior which are unnecessary for understanding the meaning of the oral message" (p. 265).

Prentice's list of nonfluencies, adapted from Zimbardo and colleagues (1963), included "word repetition, stutter, sentence change/incompletion, omission, intruding/incoherent sound, 'you know,' and 'I mean,' all of which significantly increased during the experiment" (p. 265). Prentice concluded that "if the communication of just one group member lacks clarity, the value of his [or her] contribution to the group is diminished." As a result, "the reduction in the effectiveness of one member may also reduce the effectiveness of the entire group" (p. 270).

Bell (1983) studied the relationship between conflict and **linguistic diversity** and cited Osgood (1960) for his conclusion that "as people become more anxious, they will repeat themselves." This repetition occurs because they "simply cannot think of additional words to reflect what [they are] thinking, so use . . . the same words." They may also use "simple, shorter sentences with minimal elaboration" (Bell, p. 128). Then, because "people devalue low diversity," according to Bradac and others (1977), the language used by those in conflict tends to "reinforce . . . the negative reactions which initially prompted the exchange" (Bell, p. 132). As conflict escalates, people seem less able to take the perspective of others and less likely to think about the possible impact of their words on others or to adapt to the needs of others (Bell, pp. 132–133).

McCorkle and Mills (1992) concluded from their conflict metaphor study that those who used disaster metaphors in their descriptions cast themselves as "the passive and innocent victim of a sudden and overwhelming force" against which they became "powerless" (p. 64). The result may be that the victim takes "little or no responsibility for [his or her] own actions that sustain the conflict." This person may feel either that the other party or parties to the conflict have "all the choices" or that "no one involved has any choices." The most likely response will be avoidance (p. 64).

CONFLICT MANAGEMENT

If we can accept both the inevitability of conflict as a normal phase of group processes and the positive role it can play in decision making, perhaps we can come to fear it less and thus avoid the tendency to sweep our differences under the carpet. Still, we cannot afford to lull ourselves into a false sense that team conflicts can be easily worked out. Both positive and negative methods have been devised in the course of human history to try to resolve differences. I have chosen the word *management* as a goal in preference to the word *resolution* because conflicts are rarely eliminated altogether. Some conflicts, as we have seen above, are too beneficial to eliminate. Still, they must all be managed, or recognized and dealt with in some way.

Business organizations recognize the need to educate their employees in conflict management, especially in "collaborative and contentious teamwork environments" (Stokes, 1994, p. 44). For one thing, self-directed teams have "no manager there to help them sort out their grievances." At Saturn, item number four of the company's "Thirty Work Unit Functions" says that "a work unit that resolves its own conflict recognizes a problem as an opportunity for a 'win-win' situation within the work unit prior to seeking intervention from the outside" (Saturn Corporation, 1990). Win-win methods will be explained in more depth later in this chapter.

Negative Strategies

Traditional methods of dealing with conflict range from simple **denial** that it exists to command and control strategies, **passive aggression,** and other sorts of pressure to conform. We have all, no doubt, found ourselves in a position where no one forced us to agree, yet we somehow knew we had to conform to the will of the group. Others may have just stopped looking at us or talking to us; cutting off communication works quite powerfully. Or we may have been urged to "go along and get along" or urged not to rock the boat. Or someone may have looked hurt or may have actually shed tears—sometimes thought of as passive-aggressive weapons that work quite well. Remembering our cautions above regarding false consensus, we need methods of reaching agreement that do more than just work.

More Positive Strategies

Newer methods have developed as we have tried to avoid both overt and covert force in our interactions among nations, economic groups, or team members. Negotiation involves a process of bargaining, perhaps between a labor union and a group of employers, in which each side begins with a long list of wants and both move inevitably toward some middle ground they can agree upon (see Putnam, Van Hoeven, and Bullis, 1991, for an interesting case study of teachers' bargaining sessions analyzed through Bormann's [1983, 1985, 1986] symbolic convergence theory). If the parties to the conflict cannot agree, then perhaps an outsider is consulted through a process of arbitration, which may be binding in the sense that both sides must agree in advance to submit to the agreement worked out by the arbitrator. Mediation, yet a third conflict-management alternative, also requires the input of an outside party, but one who helps those in conflict to change their own positions and thus reach agreement.

Both negotiation and arbitration typically work toward **compromise,** which requires that both sides give in on some aspect of the conflict in order to gain on a different aspect. Mediation may involve compromise, or it may seek an arrangement whereby both sides can perceive that they have won, or at least gained more than they lost. This notion of winning and losing may be applied to one of our most useful models of conflict management, derived from Blake and Mouton's "Managerial Grid" (1966, 1970, 1985). The keyword here is **"collaboration,"** which appears at the upper right corner of the model shown in Figure 10.1.

According to this model, individuals in groups have a range of five behaviors to use during group conflict, based on their level of concern either for people or for task results. At the level of low concern for both people and the task, the choice would be **withdrawal;** with high concern for people and low concern for the task, the choice would be smoothing, also referred to as **"accommodation"** (Thomas, 1976). With the combination of low concern for people and high

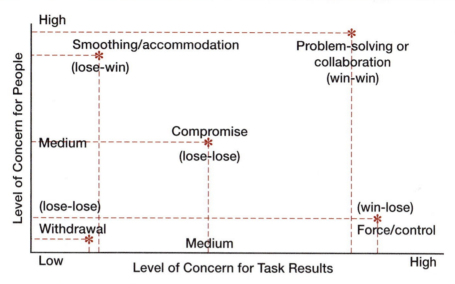

FIGURE 10.1 CONFLICT-MANAGEMENT MODEL

Adapted from Blake and Mouton, 1985, and Thomas, 1976.

concern for the task, **force** would be chosen. If individuals in a group were in the mid-range of concern for others and for the task, they might choose to compromise. If, finally, they operated at a high level of concern for both each other and the job they had to do, they would work beyond compromise to what Blake and Mouton call "problem solving" and what Thomas calls "collaboration."

Collaboration: The Most Positive, Yet Most Difficult Strategy If withdrawal is chosen, everyone loses (a lose-lose method). If either smoothing or force is chosen, some win, and some lose. If compromise is chosen, all parties both gain and lose. The only win-win method of resolving conflict is collaboration, and this is true only if all members actually believe that everyone should win. Collaboration also comes at the price of time spent (Conrad, 1990; Weaver, 1984). Figure 10.2 adapts this grid model to a five-person team and shows the real complexity of team conflict. "Collaborative Problem Solving" provides an example of collaboration among members of student groups. The case study on page 174 illustrates the power of collaboration on a global scale.

For managing conflict overall, Fisher (1980) suggests that groups should always confront their differences rather than denying they exist. Similarly, he shows that compromise should be a last-resort solution to conflict. The problem with compromise, other than that all must give up something to achieve it, is that it seems an easy first choice, and so groups often move to compromise too early. Then, though most or all of the members realize that they have as a group

**GLOBAL COLLABORATION IN THE
RACE AGAINST SARS**

*I*n an article in *Technology Review,* Seth Shulman (2003, p. 74) asks this
question: "Why did it take less than two weeks to find the mutant coro-
navirus responsible for Severe Acute Respiratory Syndrome, or SARS, while
it took the better part of three years to find HIV?" His answer includes "better
technology and a less elusive viral target," but he urges us not to "discount
the unprecedented level of worldwide communication among SARS researchers." Shulman notes that "collaboration was not exactly a strong point
in the search for the virus that causes AIDS. That effort, while marked by
some remarkable scientific work, was conducted mostly by individual labs
working in secret. Pride, prestige, and profit were all very much on the line."

Worldwide collaboration in the battle against the SARS virus was achieved through the work of a team made up of scientists in eleven labs in nine
countries that had previously been established by the World Health Organization to combat the next potential influenza pandemic (worldwide epi-
demic). They communicated through "secure Web sites" that "could display
patient samples and electron microscope pictures in real time to colleagues
continents away. Details of each lab's analysis and testing of samples were
posted online so researchers could instantly act upon relevant information."
Such collaboration helped "prevent the messy kind of patent battle that occurred over the HIV test. In this regard, the research team at the University of
Hong Kong that first isolated the SARS virus . . . deserves special credit for
openly sharing its results. The researchers could easily have delayed things
by seeking patent rights or public acclaim, but instead, . . . 'They thought
about it for about an hour' and thankfully kept their eyes on the big picture
instead."

Discussion Questions for Case Study

1. Technology had improved during the period between the outbreaks
   of AIDS and SARS, but how do you account for the change in attitudes toward collaboration when money and prestige were still to be
   gained by keeping information secret?

2. How might our lives be different if more such collaboration could
   occur?

given up too much, outwardly they speak of having achieved consensus when
actually it was false consensus, if consensus in any sense (pp. 252–255).

Another way of looking at conflict management based on this concept of
winning and losing would be to try to separate our mere **wants** from our real
needs. Teams want peace and harmony, but they need members who hold no

COLLABORATIVE PROBLEM SOLVING

The Situation   A student group must find one hour per week for the next eight weeks to work together on a project.

The Problem   Their schedules are quite different, and it seems impossible to work them out.

The Members

- Mary, who commutes one hour each way, has classes from 11:00 a.m. to 12:00 p.m. and 2:00 to 4:00 p.m. daily and is a single mother with two children in elementary school.

- George, who has classes from 9:00 a.m. to 12:00 p.m. and from 1:00 to 4:00 p.m. three days per week, works some weekends and is married with no children.

- Barbara, who has classes from 9:00 a.m. to 12:00 p.m. and 3:00 to 4:00 p.m. three days per week, works three evenings per week.

- Nasuhiro has classes from 9:00 to 10:00 a.m. daily and three night classes from 5:15 to 8:00.

- Kerry has classes from 1:00 to 4:00 p.m. three days per week and two night classes from 5:15 to 8:00.

Two of the members hold part-time jobs, one has child-care concerns, and the fifth is president of a campus organization. Those with night classes and those who work after school prefer not to meet early in the morning. All have been accustomed to having lunch with their individual friends and family members.

Solutions

- **Withdrawal:** The group decides to meet at 8:00 a.m., and the commuting student never attends.

- **Accommodation:** The group decides to meet at 8:00 a.m., and the commuting student reluctantly attends.

- **Force:** The commuting student, who is perceived to be a real expert at completing projects like the one the group has been assigned, says, "I simply will not come at 8:00, and if you want my help, you won't meet at that time."

- **Compromise:** The group decides on two possible meeting times, 8:00 a.m. and noon. They alternate times each week.

(Continued)

COLLABORATIVE PROBLEM SOLVING (CONTINUED)

■ **Collaboration:** The group lists all possible meeting times of one-hour duration. Then they think of ways to complete the eight-hour project using other blocks of time. They agree that the commuter and those who work evenings or have night classes all would prefer not to meet early in the morning. They discuss getting together for longer time periods on two weekends, if George can switch his work schedule. They seek times when the commuting student plans to come to campus on week-ends. They offer to come to a restaurant halfway between the campus and the commuter's home for a weekend meal and meeting. By continuing to work through their schedule conflicts, they come to appreciate each other's efforts and manage to complete the project.

FIGURE 10.2 CONFLICT-MANAGEMENT MODEL, FIVE PERSON TEAM

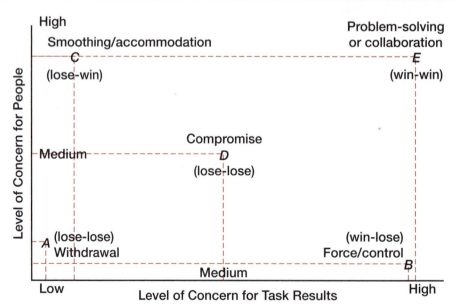

Person A:	Apathetic, may be overwhelmed with many personal problems
Person B:	Has strong need to determine the outcome
Person C:	Friend of B, has seen this controlling behavior often
Person D:	Always seeks "middle ground," refuses to confront A, B, or C
Person E:	Task oriented but recognizes and perceives as normal the needs and fears of team mates, continues to work, seeks their input

Adapted from Blake and Mouton, 1985, and Thomas, 1976.

deep-seated animosity against each other (or anyone) based on race, gender, age, ethnicity, or any other differences. These sorts of wants and needs can become irreconcilable. However, most conflict situations are not nearly so difficult as long as members can separate the decisions they actually need from those they simply would prefer.

Ellis and Fisher (1975) sought to determine the role of conflict in the development of "groupness." They found that decision making is often characterized by three **phases of conflict** interaction. The first is interpersonal conflict centered on personal differences; the second is confrontation, which involves testing ideas and choosing sides; and the third is substantive conflict that deals with issue differences (pp. 250–251).

Management of conflict in these three phases calls for differing behaviors. Because interpersonal conflict often results when groups have not presented enough data over which to disagree, their disagreements become personal. Thus, generating more data would be helpful in the first phase. In the second phase, conflict results often from too much data, so the tactic needed there would be integrating existing information. In the third phase, of course, the information that has been gathered and integrated must then be applied to the issues in dispute (Fisher, 1980, p. 251).

COMMUNICATING DURING CONFLICT

All of the attributes of good communication that we learned in Chapter 2 are necessary for communicating during conflict situations, perhaps doubly necessary. Openness, in both its verbal and nonverbal forms, is essential but often difficult. Fear of the consequences of speaking one's opinion may silence that opinion. Fear of confronting others we perceive to be powerful and unpredictable may cause us to stifle our disagreements with them.

Keeping criticisms focused on ideas, rather than on people, helps get the conversation started. To accomplish that ideal, we must first try to keep ideas from being equated with individuals and avoid labeling a particular proposal as "Jane's idea" as opposed to "Joe's idea." Indeed, all of our word choices always matter, and their importance escalates during conflict. Recall the discussion of loaded words, for example, in Chapter 2 and the distinctions made between communication climates that help us feel supported as compared to those in which we become defensive. Evaluation, control, strategy, neutrality, superiority, and certainty arouse our defenses regardless of our level of trust.

Even if the team conflict seems not to affect you personally, taking sides can fuel disagreement among the other members. A better choice of communication would consist of attempting to refocus the discussion on the substance under consideration in all its complexity. Most issues involve far more than "yes or no" or "this or that." If your class team always seems to struggle over just those sorts of closed questions, you will need to rephrase your research or decision-making questions so that they are open ended. Tannen (1998, p. 5) suggests that we stop

THE VIRTUES OF OPEN QUESTIONS VERSUS CLOSED QUESTIONS

Two-Sided, Closed Questions That Promote Debate

Is the current grading policy fair?

Should we ban the use of cell phones by automobile drivers?

Has freedom of speech been abused?

Whose interests should be protected—loggers or environmentalists?

Open Questions That Promote Discussion

How should our school's grading policy be structured?

What sort of regulations could be applied to the use of cell phones in moving automobiles?

How has the First Amendment been interpreted to apply to television broadcasting?

What are the issues at stake in the controversy between the timber industry and environmental groups?

turning all of our discussions into debates with only two sides and instead seek out all of the "other sides." "The Virtues of Open Questions Versus Closed Questions" illustrates ways of turning two-sided debates that contain only closed questions into more productive discussions based on open questions.

Teams must address the potential consequences of continuing their disagreements. At Saturn, the process for handling conflict involves "putting aside hoped-for outcomes, political posturing, and hidden agendas and focusing on the stakes, equities, and needs in each position" (Saturn Corporation, 1990, p. 6). To think about what is at stake if conflict persists to the point of diminishing returns, how conflict affects the equality of the members, or how it might detract from the genuine needs of members puts the conflict in a different light. On a daily basis, managing conflict may be as seemingly simple as this example from a successful organizational team: "We agreed at the start that if we had a problem with one another, we would hash it out, talk it out, and then we'd probably go to lunch together."

Virtual teams bring an added dimension to the need to communicate in ways that manage conflict appropriately. Joinson (2002) quotes an Illinois software company president whose teams operate online as saying, "The written word can be so much more harsh than the spoken word; even a critique needs to be phrased positively" (under "Team Challenges"). Add to that the frustration of waiting for a response from a teammate who may work in a different time zone or even in a different part of the world. Patience and a resolve to think responses through carefully before clicking on the "send" button can, potentially, prevent negative, nonproductive conflict from occurring.

CONCLUSION

In this chapter we have looked at conflict from a number of perspectives ranging from definitions, types, and causes to effects both positive and negative. Recognition of our own part in creating conflict can help in its management much better than denying that we have contributed in any way. Recognition that conflict is a naturally occurring phase of group work and that "it, too, shall pass" and may even be "good for us" can help alleviate its unpleasantness. Knowing, also, that there are better ways of managing conflict than simply ignoring it in hopes it will go away can give teams strategies useful in overcoming or benefiting from conflict's obstacles. Dominance, accommodation, withdrawal, and even compromise may give short-term relief to those in conflict, but collaborative efforts to actually work through differences provide the greatest long-term satisfaction.

The willingness and ability to talk it out in either a face-to-face or virtual environment are found in highly responsible and committed team members. But once they have resolved their differences, what then? First, you must prepare to agree to disagree. No resolution lasts very long. Indeed, conflict is a naturally recurring phenomenon. In addition, as we noted earlier, most conflicts are not resolved but managed. Second, if you have achieved your goal at the expense, unfortunately, of a teammate's goal, celebrate but avoid rubbing it in. Third, focus on "where we go from here." If you are to continue working together, you must move beyond this point. The high road is always open, but the path taken is up to you.

COLLABORATIVE LEARNING ACTIVITIES

1. Divide into groups of five members and hold a discussion about the relevance of Heider's attribution theory to your own experiences with conflict. Concentrate on the explanation of ways we attach causes to behaviors that may or may not be the actual causes.

2. Choose related questions from "The Virtues of Open Questions Versus Closed Questions" and have a short discussion focusing first on the closed question and then on the open version. Explore which type of question yields the most insights and why.

Chapter 11

Team Outcomes

Superstock

Oral Presentations and Written Reports and Proposals

KEY WORDS AND CONCEPTS

Aristotle	need-satisfaction step
arrangement of data	needs of the occasion
attention step	need step
audience analysis	objectivity
call-for-action step	pathos
competence	presentations to inform
conclusion	presentations to persuade
constraints	proposals
credibility	recency
criteria for information	rehearsal
data types and sources	reports
demographic analysis	rhetorical
dynamism	target audience
ethos	transitions
introduction	trustworthiness
logos	visual aids
motivated sequence	visualization step

To find out more about the Key Words and Concepts discussed in this chapter, use InfoTrac College Edition. Type in the keywords and subject terms. You can access InfoTrac College Edition from Wadsworth/Communication homepage: http://communication.wadsworth.com.

CAREER APPLICATION

In a retail and mail-order sales organization, a customer-service team learned from numerous customer complaints that shipping methods had resulted in damage to a specific line of custom-ordered products, window blinds in particular. Because the products were cut to size and thus could not be replaced, repaired, and reshipped to other customers, their return was costing the company a sizeable amount of money each month. The team made a comprehensive oral presentation to a comparable team in the shipping department in which they showed costs in both dollars and customer goodwill. Together the two teams researched ways to eliminate the problem and wrote a proposal to the shipping department management team outlining changes they recommended that would cost more initially but would provide long-term benefits to the organization.

The completion of processes such as decision making and problem solving does not necessarily mark the end of a team's activities regarding those issues. Each process may be extended into a presentation phase in which the team must prepare and provide information to an audience that describes their findings or the reasons for their decisions. In the organizational world, teams may also make budget and project proposals, or they may present descriptions of their projects. They may seek policy changes or request that actions be taken. Regardless of the purpose, a presentation must contain accurate and timely information that is well organized. Only then can the team's message be conveyed clearly to the intended audience. Although presentations may be in either oral or written form, typically an oral message will be accompanied by written support and graphic displays. This chapter explores all these means by which teams or groups can **inform** or **persuade,** or even accomplish both purposes at once.

PREPARING FOR THE PRESENTATION

Determining and Satisfying the Needs of the Occasion

Adequate planning well in advance is vital to the success of any individual or group presentation, and a good first step in that planning process consists of determining the needs required by the occasion. "Preparation Steps that Satisfy the Needs of the Occasion" outlines the preparation steps for presentations.

PREPARATION STEPS THAT SATISFY THE NEEDS OF THE OCCASION

1. Clarify your purpose: Do you wish to inform or persuade?

2. Analyze your audience: Is it a general or a target audience?

3. Determine the information types and sources available: How will you go about gathering data?

4. Organize your materials: Which items are vital, and which are actually expendable?

5. Prioritize presentation elements to fit your time limit: Will it need to be structured to fit into five, ten, or thirty minutes?

6. Adapt your presentation to the constraints of the physical space available to you: Is it small or large, dark or light, quiet or noisy? Will it accommodate your technical equipment needs?

Purpose   Perhaps the most important consideration would be whether the purpose is to inform, such as in a student organization's opening meeting of the school year, in which the group's purposes and interests are presented to potential new members. Alternatively, the purpose might be to persuade, as in the case of an appeal to the group's members later on in the year to participate in

---

CASE STUDY   **A WORKSHOP TO PREPARE EMPLOYEES FOR TEAMWORK**

*O*ne of the first steps companies often take when implementing teamwork is to develop a set of workshops to assist employees in understanding the management concepts and practices of the new system. The workshop, whether it lasts three hours or three days, may be considered a "presentation to inform" because employees will want to understand why and how their lives will change. It is also, of course, designed to persuade because it is in the company's interest to encourage participation and enthusiasm about the teamwork initiative. Partlow and Wynes (2002) provide a description of a "Project Jumpstart Workshop" created by a communication consulting firm. It includes the following agenda items for the first day.

- Consider business drivers, key stakeholders, and political and cultural sensitivities from the project sponsor's perspective.

- Candidly explore make-or-break success factors.

- Validate project scope, major milestones, and organizational interfaces.

- Clarify roles, responsibilities, reporting relationships, and handoffs.

- Create a communications plan for team members and for other stakeholders.

Partlow and Wynes, 2002, p. 15.

Discussion Questions for Case Study

1. If you were in charge of putting together a thirty-minute informative presentation for the first item above, how would you start? How would you determine your target audience? What sources of information would you be likely to use?

2. Using your knowledge of virtual team communication, what would your "communications plan" consist of if you knew that the company preparing for teamwork has branches around the globe? What would be the benefit of presenting this information graphically? How would you go about creating graphics?

the annual fundraising campaign. Although some theorists claim that all communication is really an attempt at persuasion, we can generally separate persuasive from informative efforts and prepare accordingly. You might think about the two purposes in the following way: If you want your audience to learn or understand something, your purpose is to inform; if you want your audience to favor, support, or actually *do* something, your purpose is to persuade. Of course, one can build upon the other; the process of informing can result in persuasion. Conversely, you will rarely persuade anyone to change without also providing some sort of additional information. The case study on page 183 illustrates how a blending of the processes of informing and persuading may be used in a business-workshop setting.

Audience   Once the purpose has been clarified, the next need to arise will be **audience analysis.** Who will be listening and watching? We often think in terms of a **target audience** for our messages, meaning those individuals or groups who can best help us accomplish our goals for communicating. Convincing peers that your team could do great things if you just had a little more money may result in some organizational support, but the target audience would be those who hold the purse strings, typically found higher up the organizational ladder. The question for a business team to answer might be, "On whose agenda can we be scheduled to make this presentation?" Indeed, one such success often leads to another, as lower-level managers persuade others higher up to hear the message.

Once the target audience is designated, it may be analyzed in various ways, for example, **demographically.** Does it consist entirely of white, male middle managers ages forty to forty-five who have been with the company at least ten years? Or is it a city council made up of women and men representing constituencies from all income groups and a wide range of ethnicities from whom your neighborhood association is requesting a zoning change? Are they likely to be hostile to your presentation, friendly and helpful, or neutral? What do they need? In our profit-driven American culture, audiences are often concerned with costs—how much something will cost, or how much it will save. However, as we know from our earlier study of Maslow's hierarchy of needs (1954), individuals are motivated by much more than money.

Data   Once audience features have been considered, the need for appropriate information takes priority as groups begin to investigate available **data types and sources.** The early Greek philosopher **Aristotle** (384–322 BC) defined the art of rhetoric as "finding the available means of persuasion," (1954, section 1335b) and good information is one of those means. Certainly good information must be accurate; it must also be relevant, clear, and compelling. It can come in the form of examples, cases, or anecdotes. If your audience believes only what can be measured, provide statistical proofs of your claims or appeals.

Once gathered, the data next need to be **arranged,** or organized. Classroom groups invariably complain that "there's so much out there" that they have a hard time managing it all. The group must develop some system of categorization so that the information can be placed in a rational order, that is, one that makes sense both to the presenters and the listeners. If groups have gathered data for use in a meeting, then the meeting agenda can be constructed around a logical ordering of the data, for example, possible causes, then effects, then potential solutions. If, on the other hand, information has been gathered to inform a decision-making group about a situation or problem, then a chronological arrangement of the material might be beneficial.

Every meeting where presentations are made has (or should have) a finite duration. In some cases, meeting rooms are very tightly scheduled so that if the 8:00 a.m. meeting goes overtime, it throws off the whole day. The point here is the need for groups to prioritize valuable data and delete unnecessary details so that when their twenty-minute presentation must be squeezed into a five-minute window of opportunity, they will know what to say and what to omit. Here is a good place to develop useful **criteria for information.** For instance, if your topic under consideration is time-bound, that is, if decades-old information would be useless to decision makers, then **recency** could be used as a standard. The question, of course, would be "how recent is recent enough," which would require a judgment call.

Environment   A final situational need that should be explored relates to the physical environment in which the presentation will be given. On the one hand, a beautifully appointed conference room complete with a walnut table and comfortable chairs would not work for a large meeting where most participants or listeners would be forced to stand along the walls. Still, you may find yourselves in that sort of situation. On the other hand, groups sometimes prepare for a small audience in a small room and only at the last minute learn that others have been invited and the meeting has been moved to an auditorium. Their small **visual aids** become useless. Their voices require amplification. They grow nervous and make a bad showing. All of the **constraints** of the physical space available for meetings must be considered in advance and planned for.

Constructing the Oral Message

As you have seen above, thinking through and responding to situational needs are preliminary steps toward making effective team presentations. Once these needs have been considered, and, to the extent possible, satisfied, the group can begin constructing the informative or persuasive message. The actual arrangement of that message depends upon its purpose. "Constructing the Group Presentation to Inform" provides possibilities for developing an informative presentation.

Purpose: To Inform

Introduction   One of the most used, but least effective, ways people start to speak publicly is to say, "We're here today to talk about . . ." But how else should you start? Presentations, like speeches, should begin with interesting introductions that invite the listeners into the topic, that help them focus their attention, and that stimulate their interest in what will happen next. Rather than simply introducing the team members to the audience as an opening activity, a

CONSTRUCTING THE GROUP PRESENTATION TO INFORM

Thinking Through a Brief Introduction

Although it comes first, it may need to be developed last.

- Tell a (short) story.
- Describe a scene.
- Give a quote.
- Provide a context or setting.
- Paint a visual image.

Introducing the Team

- You may introduce yourself.
- One person may introduce all members.
- Tie each person into the project to personalize.

Weaving Together the Message Elements

- Place your main points in an appropriate order.
- Show causes and effects.
- Present problems and solutions.
- Lead the audience through space or time.

Connecting the Parts with Transitions

- Use "Once we have . . ., then we can . . . ."
- Use "On the other hand, ..."
- Use "Now that we understand . . ., we can compare it with . . . ."
- Use "The second item in this series, . . ., functions as . . . ."

Concluding Well

- Use a final summarizing transition, such as, "Let us reiterate that . . . ."
- Return to your introductory image, quote, or description and thus unite the beginning with the ending.

more creative approach may feature an anecdote, a short narrative description, an example, or a quotation that reveals an important aspect of your topic and purpose. Then it may be advisable to present the members, a necessary part of the presentation, in a way that connects them individually to the introduction and the topic and purpose. Actual development of the introduction is often best left until last because you will, by then, know the exact content of the entire program.

Body   In planning the body of the presentation, groups have a variety of arrangement possibilities for their major points of information. In the case of team certification meetings, the topical order is known ahead of time, and certifying boards come to expect arrangements that conform to a pattern. They may be checking off items as they listen in order to judge the merits of the groups. The same would be true of evaluators of classroom groups perhaps working with a grading criteria checklist. However, if the group is providing information for information's sake, and not according to a prescribed format, the simplest arrangement would be topical, such as three types of computer software or the four parts of a public school system. Information about the history of a problem could be arranged chronologically, whereas problem analysis might require a problem/solution or problem/cause/solution format. Data that compare results of a practice or procedure in different company locations could be arranged geographically. These message elements must be woven together with transitional sentences, phrases, or short paragraphs that allow the presentation to flow. Without these **transitions,** the presentation or speech appears to the listener to jump from one topic to another, making it difficult to follow.

Conclusion   The same mistake mentioned above in regard to introductions often applies equally to conclusions. Speakers and groups should never say, "in conclusion," but instead should end their speeches or presentations by providing a comforting sense of closure for the listeners. Novice speakers or presenters may fail to plan for this significant "wrapping up." It may be especially important to plan for ways of ending well if time runs short. Your planned conclusion, if brief enough, could be stated quickly and effectively even if the bell rings, the whistle blows, the camera fades to black, or the next meeting is due to start. The conclusion allows the team to make its final effort at promoting understanding, and that, of course, is the purpose.

Purpose: To Persuade

If you or your team wants your listeners to agree with your point of view, to support your cause or your proposal, to provide funding for your projects, to change company or university policy, to help you build Habitat for Humanity houses, or to vote for your candidate, then you have entered the **rhetorical** realm, the world of persuasion. To accomplish these purposes, you must generally provide reasons and evidence. Once again, we turn to Aristotle (1954, section 1356a), who said that you must "state the case and prove it," using **ethos,** or your (or your team's) own credibility or believability; **pathos,** or appeals to the audience's emotions; or **logos,** or logic, the convincing rational approach.

Speaker (or presenter) ethos, or **credibility,** derives from several sources: **trustworthiness, competence, dynamism,** and **objectivity** (Hovland and Weiss, 1951; Whitehead, 1968; Smith, 1973; Wilcox, 1987). It may be difficult to isolate the deeper sources of perceived trustworthiness of one individual compared with another. Knowing the people, having a history of dealings with them, and talking with others about their experiences with the two individuals affect your willingness to trust their statements and judgments. However, such seemingly simple things as being willing to make eye contact with the listeners affect perceived trustworthiness. Perceived competence again comes from knowing whether the speaker has actually had the experiences he or she is describing and is thus qualified to speak about them accurately. Those who speak with confidence appear to be more competent than those who speak tentatively or timidly. "Sources of Credibility" summarizes these four roots of ethos.

Dynamism, or enthusiasm, must be balanced with reason and genuineness in order to improve credibility. Too much zeal can be counterproductive. Objectivity, or the ability to see both or all sides of issues, must also be balanced with actual commitment to avoid being seen as "wishy-washy." If you or your team can present counter-arguments to your proposals yet follow them up with reasons yours should be adopted, you will gain in credibility.

Pathos, or the use of emotional appeals, is controversial in that it may be used to "short-circuit" the ability of the audience to think logically. Some even question the ethical nature of such appeals because they may reduce audience members' freedom to make their own choices (DeVito, 1989). Team efforts to frighten, disgust, or anger audiences are likely doomed to failure, regardless of the ubiquity of such strategies in the popular media. However, teams will stand a better chance of persuasion if they attempt to phrase their appeals to coincide with the "feelings, attitudes, or state of mind of the audience" (Campbell, 1982, p. 174).

Logos, or the use of reasoning and proofs, may well be a critical factor in the persuasive presentations of teams. If you are making a proposal based on the

SOURCES OF CREDIBILITY

Trustworthiness: "He maintains good eye contact and doesn't show nervous mannerisms."

Competence: "The members of this student team are always prepared for class discussions."

Dynamism: "She's so enthusiastic about this project; it must be quite important to her."

Objectivity: "I know he's the kind of person who always tries to see all sides of an issue."

Adapted from Hovland and Weiss, 1951; Smith, 1973; and Whitehead, 1968.

kind of decision-making or problem-solving processes you learned about in Chapter 6, you will have gathered enough information to convince yourselves of the rightness of your decisions. This information can serve you well as you construct your presentation arguments, choose your best materials, and arrange them for the best effect.

Just as informative presentations may need to follow a prescribed format, so may persuasive appeals. However, if you are free to arrange the materials as you see fit, you may want to choose from among some "tried and true" arrangements, such as the motivated sequence. In developing this sequence, Alan Monroe (1975) used the same sort of information we have previously studied in regard to problem solving from John Dewey's (1910) influential book *How We Think*. If people "naturally" think through and solve problems in a particular manner, then that manner can be adapted toward persuading them to solve problems in the ways we would prefer. As illustrated in "Monroe's Motivated Sequence," the steps are as follows: getting attention, showing a need, showing satisfaction of that need, presenting a visualization of the results, and calling for action (Monroe and Ehninger, 1975, pp. 241–262).

MONROE'S MOTIVATED SEQUENCE

Meeting Purpose* To persuade university administration to provide funding for additional space for housing the communication department

Those Attending College dean, academic vice president, chairs of university academic council and faculty senate, college curriculum committee chair, university budget director, budget committee chair, and other college department heads

Those Presenting Communication department faculty and staff

Attention Step

A thirty-second video montage of student activities associated with the communication department: debate, radio and television production classes, public speaking, and small group interactions, for example

Need Step

Problem "As you can see, our students are always busy doing the things that help them learn . . . ."

Illustration "Our increasing enrollment, however, is resulting in crowded classrooms, studios, and places to practice the skills so vital to their success."

(Continued)

MONROE'S MOTIVATED SEQUENCE (CONTINUED)

Ramifications   "We may be forced to cap enrollments or limit the number who can become involved in forensics and other extracurricular activities, which would put an end to the excellent period of growth we have experienced in the past ten years."

Pointing   "Of course, we recognize the importance of tuition dollars not only to our department but to the college and the operation of the university as a whole."

Satisfaction Step

Solution   "The Scott residence on the northwest edge of campus, near our current offices and classrooms, was recently willed to the university and would make an excellent addition to our facilities."

Solution Meets Needs   "It is a large enough structure to both accommodate our forensics team's practice-room needs and provide office spaces for our adjunct faculty and graduate assistants, who currently have nowhere to meet individually with students to work on outlines or speech topics or to talk about how to conquer speech fright."

Answer to Objections   "We are aware that others have made requests for use of this property. Our growth as a university has strained all of our facilities. However, though some programs can exist without student activities, our students thrive on interaction and practice. How else can they learn to communicate?"

Visualization Step

Negative Future   "We dread the day we must begin limiting our numbers simply because we can't fit them all in."

Positive Future   "We look forward to the day when senior students coming to campus for the high-school speech tournament visit our new home to see where they will spend their next four years."

Call for Action Step

"We hope you will help us continue to welcome these excellent, well-motivated students to our university by providing us with the physical facilities we must have."

* This illustration represents the basic skeleton of the whole presentation. You would, of course, provide numerical data, quotes from students, additional video showing trophies and championships, group and individual speech activities, meetings between faculty and students, and so forth.

The **attention step** can be approached in the manner described above related to introducing the presentation. The importance of this step cannot be overemphasized because without the attention of the listener, all else is futile. According to Monroe (1975, p. 250), the **need step** requires four elements: a statement of the problem, an illustration of the problem, the ramifications or seriousness of the problem, and pointing out or clarifying how the problem affects the listeners (p. 250). In the **need-satisfaction step** you would state and explain your solution to the problem, show how your solution meets the need and works in actual experience, and answer "any objections which might be raised against the proposal" (p. 251). In the **visualization step** you could describe the happy future resulting from your plan, the dismal future if the audience fails to support it, or a contrast of the two with the negative image placed first. In the **call-for-action step** you confidently ask for support, funding, approval, a policy decision, or whatever else you seek (pp. 251–253).

Constructing the Written or Visual Message

Oral presentations are often accompanied by brief reports in the form of handouts for the audience. This would be especially useful if the listeners need access to highly technical or very detailed data. However, we can be virtually certain that with the information overload most of us suffer today, listeners do not want and would not read lengthy documents. Unless you plan to lead the listeners through charts or other items in the handouts, it would be less distracting to give out the information after the presentation has been concluded.

More relevant to group presentations would be considerations of the technical visual elements to be incorporated into the presentation. Where once we might have spoken of hand-constructed visual aids mounted on poster board or drawn on flip charts, today we ponder the intricacies of high-quality, computer-generated graphics. However, some of the same rules still apply. Any visual presentation must be not only clearly visible but completely legible to all members of the audience. The use of a small, seemingly normal-sized font that works well enough on paper printouts will not be readable even by those close to the screen for a computerized presentation or for an overhead projection. Each "page" shown should contain a single major point, surrounded by well-balanced blank space, or what we once referred to as "white space" (now it may be red, blue, or most any color we choose). Even if you have no access to presentation software, excellent visuals can be made from transparencies overlaid in various colors and projected on a screen.

Your specific "best use" of technology may also feature videotapes to illustrate process improvements; objects or models that represent your products, interests, or values; and demonstrations or depictions that enhance the needs step or the visualization step outlined above. Regardless of your delivery systems, limit the quantity of data presented at one time. Listeners and viewers can absorb only so much before tuning out. The coordinated presentation of visual images that reinforce the spoken words will have greater effects and remain with audience members longer than jumbled items that overwhelm the senses (see, for example, Hamilton and Parker, 2001, pp. 395–434, for an excellent chapter that summarizes suggestions for the use of visual aids).

REHEARSING AND DELIVERING THE ORAL PRESENTATION

Once your team has determined its purpose, chosen the content and arrangement of its verbal material, taped and edited its video segments, created its computer slides or overhead transparencies, and made the all-important decisions about who will do and say what, it's time for a run-through. Your **rehearsal** should mimic the "real thing" in every way possible. Try to use the same physical space under the same lighting conditions. If you must dim the lights to enable the audience to see your visuals, find ways to continue to see your materials in the darkened room. Although you must be able to see the visuals, find ways not to turn away from the audience. Perhaps, with adequate rehearsal, team members could coordinate the handling of the technical aspects throughout the presentation. You should practice using all of the equipment starting from the point at which it is all turned off. Learn how to proceed from turning on the power buttons on the VCR and monitor, the overhead projector, the laptop computer, LCD panel, or proxima. Know how to troubleshoot for loose connector wires. Plan around a blown-out projector bulb. Create backups such as hard copies or overhead transparencies of your computer materials. Be able to make your presentation even if all technology fails.

When the technical aspects have been brought under control, rehearse the entire oral presentation with, if possible, a neutral audience who will react to what they see and hear. You must become aware of the way audience laughter in unexpected places can disrupt your train of thought. Ask for feedback. Are your word choices inappropriate, confusing, or boring? Are your nonverbal expressions mismatched to your words or otherwise perplexing or distracting? If speaking to an audience is not feasible, videotape or audiotape your presentation, view or listen critically, and then revise. In whatever ways you can, practice, practice, practice!

WRITTEN PROPOSALS AND REPORTS

As we saw earlier, oral presentations may be accompanied by written materials and graphics. Such materials may even replace oral presentations. Although our major concern in this text is with oral communication, some further explanations and suggestions should be useful to those who also submit supplemental written reports or proposals or to those who submit only written materials.

Definitions and Purposes

As Thomas and Fryar (1984, p. 300) explain, a **report** is a "written update on some project or job." Reports and proposals are sometimes closely tied together. For instance, a report may "follow the acceptance of a proposal and be a part of the evaluation process described in that proposal," or a report could "precede the proposal and be an extensive report on the nature of the problem," thus forming a "background for the proposal." A **proposal** is typically a "call for action by individuals or by a group" that may "precede an oral presentation, be distributed during an oral presentation, or be a follow-up to an oral presentation" (p. 313).

In the same way we divided oral presentations into informative and persuasive types, we may likewise categorize reports and proposals. The goal of any group preparing a written report is to inform the organization about a situation or decision process. On the other hand, the goal of those preparing proposals is to persuade the organization to accept the call for action.

Constructing the Written Message

Reports   The same principles outlined earlier in this chapter for preparing oral presentations—determining your purpose, analyzing the target audience, and gathering and organizing data—also apply to written reporting. In the business world, reports may follow a specific format adopted by the organization. In the college classroom, reports may follow a specific format provided by the teacher. If none is available, however, the following suggestions may be used as general guidelines.

Report writers, like oral presenters, must carefully think through the same issues mentioned previously, that is, how to introduce the topic, how to best arrange the data, and how to conclude. Reports should begin with a title page that clarifies such things as who, what, when, and where. The "why" could be found in a purpose statement or in an authorization statement, in the case of a business report requested by the organization. Lengthy reports would also include in the introduction a table of contents that outlines the order of issues or

---

CHECKLIST FOR THE CONTENTS OF A REPORT

If your purpose in a report is to inform or analyze, you should

- Cover the main ideas or points.
- Discuss the facts that support each idea.
- Briefly restate the main points, together with any important conclusions you have drawn about them, especially if your report is an analysis.

Adapted from Sitzmann, 1983, p. 39.

CHECKLIST FOR REVISIONS

- Did we accomplish our purpose?
- Did we adequately cover the subject?
- Have we included all necessary items and eliminated all unnecessary ones?
- Does the body of the report give a logical and complete discussion of the material?
- Is the conclusion logically drawn from the information presented?
- Is the report unified and coherent?
- Are all terms and references clear?
- Is the draft free of spelling, grammar, and punctuation errors?
- Is the report easy to read and to understand?

Adapted from Thomas and Fryar, 1984, p. 313.

---

topics, supporting data, conclusions and recommendations, references, and possible appendices or graphics.

The body of the report should be divided into logical parts labeled by headings and sub-headings. For instance, in a small group communication class report, students who have researched and analyzed questions of fact, value, or policy could write final reports on their findings. The reports would differ depending on the question type.

In the case of a fact question, such as "What is the relationship between book prices and profit margin at the university book store?" the body of the report might contain the following headings: current mission of the university bookstore; markup on bookstore items, subdivided into categories such as books, notebooks, writing instruments, clothing, computers, toiletries, snacks, and so forth; financial data from the university budget; and other financial data available. For a question of value, such as "Is it desirable for university bookstores to operate as profit centers?" the body of the report could contain headings such as the following: historical context of the bookstore; comparison of historical and current context; and attitudes, subdivided into public, student, faculty, staff, and administration. For a question of policy, such as "What should the university bookstore's mission be?" the body of the report could contain headings such as the following: financial need by university for bookstore as profit center; student need for bookstore as service institution; comparison of attitudes as determined through value analysis above; and comparison with benchmark universities.

Once the relevant information has been provided in the body of the report, the writers then present their conclusions based on their research. In some situations, especially if they have been asked to prepare the report in order that

---

ORGANIZING PLAN FOR A TEAM PROPOSAL

- Background: Present the history of the situation that caused the team to suggest a change.

- Problem Description: Identify the problem and the criteria for a solution.

- Program Objectives: Describe the proposed change and the objectives it will accomplish.

- Evaluation Design: State the methods that will be used to determine whether the solution is working.

- Budget: Specify the money and the time needed to implement the solution.

Adapted from Thomas and Fryar, 1984, p. 315.

---

some sort of action can be taken, they would also present their recommendations to the organization. The recommendations would be followed by an alphabetized reference list or bibliography detailing the sources of information used in the report. If decision makers need much more detailed information, then an appendix can be attached containing charts, graphs, illustrations, interview or survey questions used to determine the attitudes mentioned above, or other data.

Sitzmann (1983) summarizes the necessary components of a report in three suggested activities, found in "Checklist for the Contents of a Report."

Once a draft report has been prepared, the group will need to reread it carefully and give themselves adequate time for revision. Remember this rule: There is no such thing as a good first draft! Thomas and Fryar (1984) provide several questions, found in "Checklist for Revisions," that can help you find what still needs to be done.

Proposals   As noted, the purpose of a proposal is to suggest action. In an organizational context, whether a business organization, voluntary association, or college student group, the recommendations mentioned above could set the stage for a proposal. As you can see from examples given throughout this text, students can propose real solutions to campus or community problems if they have fully researched the problems for their causes and effects, for the values threatened if the problems persist, and for reasonable policy alternatives.

Careful arrangement is needed to write a persuasive proposal. If the intended reader has not requested a proposal, the writer has even more reason to write a compelling introduction to draw the reader in. One method for setting up a proposal, provided by Thomas and Fryar (1984), is shown in "Organizing Plan for a Team Proposal."

As you can see, much of the same kind of information needed for a presentation or report is also needed for writing a proposal. John Dewey's (1910) problem/solution format, mentioned often in this text, would serve well as a model for proposal writing. Sitzmann (1983, p. 39) adds another element you might find useful; he suggests that proposal writers give "examples and details of how a similar solution to the problem worked in the past (testimony of experts, facts, figures, statistics) or is working in the present."

CONCLUSION

All teams engage in making decisions and solving problems, whether for themselves or for their organizations. Once they have decided what needs to be done, they generally must either inform others about their plans or convince others of the need to help accomplish their plans. Although some teams promote community projects, and others run emergency rooms, most business teams find themselves making presentations and writing proposals and reports. In this chapter we have considered both the presentation purposes and the processes likely to accomplish those purposes. Often oral presentations are accompanied by written reports designed to inform or written proposals designed to persuade. Regardless of the purpose, oral and written presentations must meet professional requirements such as adequacy, relevance, logic, coherence, clarity, readability, and compliance with the rules of spelling and grammar.

In a real-world proposal to an organization, methods of evaluation for the proposed solutions, as well as budget estimates, would be crucial to whether the proposal would stand a chance of acceptance. This issue of evaluation brings us to the close of this chapter and creates the context for Chapter 12, in which methods of performance evaluation are explored.

COLLABORATIVE LEARNING ACTIVITIES

1. Develop a proposal presentation that a group of interested students could present orally to college or university officials regarding the implementation (or elimination) of plus/minus grading.

   A. Write a one-sentence purpose statement that begins with "We want our listeners to . . ."

   B. Analyze your audience using your school officials as listeners.

   C. Develop brainstorming lists of possible information sources for use in this presentation.

   D. Choose the "best" place on campus to make the presentation and describe it in detail.

2. Develop a list of technical equipment actually available to you for use in this proposal presentation. Choose the kinds of information you would present in visual form. Sketch out a plan for the visuals.

Chapter 12

Team Assessment and Evaluation

Brownie Harris/Corbis

Members, Processes, Skills, Relationships, and Ethical Considerations

KEY WORDS AND CONCEPTS

attainable goals

clarity

collaboration

coordination

commitment

communication skills

concrete objectives

conflict resolution

emotional intelligence

ethical evaluation

evaluation

forum format

goal setting

group efficacy

interpersonal evaluation

knowledge, skill, and ability
(KSA)
   interpersonal
   self-management

legibility

listening

open communication

panel discussion format

performance evaluations

procedural evaluation

professional language

self-assessment

skepticism

substantive evaluation

symposium format

team-effectiveness criteria

trust

 To find out more about the Key Words and Concepts discussed in this chapter, use InfoTrac College Edition. Type in the keywords and subject terms. You can access InfoTrac College Edition from Wadsworth/Communication homepage: http://communication.wadsworth.com.

CAREER APPLICATION

One of the most difficult tasks teams have taken on is that of completing an **evaluation** of their own work. This job, once the prerogative of management, now requires not only that judgments be made about individual members' performances but also that the team's performance be measured as well. According to leading management writers Peter Senge, Stephen Covey, and Tom Peters, self-evaluation through the use of agreed-upon standards is the best way to evaluate performance because it results from a combination of both individual and team efforts. Although self-evaluation might seem, at first, to be simple and self-serving, teams must grow into the process because of its inherent difficulty.

Mahoney, 1997, p. 66.

> ## REQUIREMENTS FOR EFFECTIVE ORAL PRESENTATIONS
>
> ### An Effective Oral Team Presentation Must
>
> - Inform and/or persuade its audience
> - Entertain, or at least interest, its audience
> - Be well organized, with a beginning, a middle, and an end
> - Incorporate relevant and appropriate visual enhancements, such as computer graphics, overhead transparencies, videotapes, or models
> - Fit into a reasonable time frame
> - Be the collaborative effort of all team members

For the same reasons and in the same ways teams learn to evaluate their own work performance, they can learn to assess their strengths and weaknesses in presenting themselves or their proposals or decisions to others. Check sheets or other instruments they develop should logically include evaluation criteria for all of the presentation elements described in Chapter 11. Thus, a criterion of thoroughness may be applied to aspects of the planning process or the preparation stages. Scaled items could be prepared for evaluating how thoroughly audience analysis has been accomplished, for judging how well agenda items have been prioritized, or how well extraneous materials have been eliminated. **Clarity** could serve as a criterion for aspects of the oral presentation as well as for drawings, charts, or other visual data. **Legibility** could be used to judge the graphics featuring words. Chapter 11 contains additional evaluation criteria for longer written reports and proposals.

The warning in Chapter 11 that the first draft of a piece of written work is never good enough applies equally to a mere plan for an oral presentation. The presentation itself must be rehearsed, critiqued, and revised. After completion of the team's self-evaluation of the rehearsal, an immediate action plan is called for to correct problems that have appeared. Remember that though the dress rehearsal may have been a disaster, the show must go on, and it will go on because you will have made your mistakes in private rather than in public. "Requirements for Effective Oral Presentations" summarizes the key components of successful presentations.

TEAM EFFECTIVENESS EVALUATION

Whereas concrete events such as team presentations can be measured in fairly straightforward ways, the same may not be said for the qualities of the team *as a team*. The underlying small-group or team-effectiveness criteria that allow groups to make outstanding presentations do not readily translate into simple checklists. Still, it is vital that groups learn to differentiate between the behaviors that help them succeed and those that hold them back. Barker, Melville, and Pacanowsky (1993), in their classic study of teams, concluded that, sadly, the groups they studied did not learn from their mistakes.

Hundreds, perhaps thousands, of research studies have been conducted over the years in communication, management, and psychology to determine what makes groups effective. Once each decade or so, a report will be made summing up the conclusions from those studies. Although most find that a combination of task and maintenance successes are necessary to determine that a group has been effective, it has been stated time and again that "there is no singular, uniform measure of performance effectiveness for groups" (Guzzo and Dickson, 1996, p. 309). Cohen and Bailey (1997, p. 243) reviewed hundreds of effectiveness studies and found that "effectiveness at one level of analysis," that is at the individual or group level, "can interfere with effectiveness at another level," perhaps at the "business unit or organizational level."

Goodman, Ravlin, and Schminke (1987, p. 138) assert that our understanding of effectiveness "depends on how we delineate the concept" in terms of its "dimensional structure," its "temporal nature," and "the perspective of different constituencies." They outline a number of problems associated with the concept. First, no clear definition exists because effectiveness can only be understood in relation to other factors. The second problem is one of point of view: whose should be considered, the team's, the organization's, the leader's, those of other groups, or clients? A third problem is "temporal." When does effectiveness occur? How long does it persist? Yet another problem lies in the attempts to apply measures of organizational effectiveness to the group or team level

---

EFFECTIVENESS CRITERIA FOR HEALTH-CARE TEAMS

Team Member Characteristics

- Commitment to high-quality health care
- Responsibility to evidence-based practice, learning, and follow-up
- Communication skills such as confidence, listening, clarity, and adaptability
- Ability to lead but flexibility to "shift into the background"
- Expertise as a practitioner
- Advocacy for one's own profession but high respect for all others
- Ability to work with others to create shared values
- Consideration for others that creates a "culture of caring"

Adapted from Coppola et al., 2002, p. 26.

(pp. 136–137). A further complication arises in the case of "multi-professional" teams, such as health-care teams, such as the one we studied earlier in Chapter 1, made up of a doctor, a nurse, a social worker, an occupational therapist, and a physical therapist. "Effectiveness Criteria for Health-Care Teams" suggests ways to think about success in such a diverse group.

Richard Hackman (1990), a leading writer in the field of teamwork, describes the difficulty of determining effectiveness in an organizational context. "Few organizational tasks have clear right and wrong answers," he says, and even those that do cannot be judged well in terms of effectiveness as compared with efficiency, or in terms of the cost of that efficiency, human and otherwise. Hackman proposes the following three dimensions of effectiveness: "the degree to which the group's productive output . . . meets the standards of quantity, quality, and timeliness of the people who receive, review, and/or use that output"; "the degree to which the process of carrying out the work enhances the capability of members to work together interdependently in the future"; and "the degree to which the group experience contributes to the growth and personal well-being of team members" (pp. 6–7).

As a follow-up to Hackman's work (1990), Pescosolido (2003, p. 21) sought an understanding of the role of **"group efficacy,"** defined as "the group's collective estimate of its ability to perform a task," in ensuring effectiveness. After studying twenty-six teams of master of business administration (MBA) students, he found "significant relationships between early group efficacy perceptions and group member willingness to continue as a member of the group, perception of learning, and ability to work independently within the group." Indeed, it was the "early perceptions" that they could accomplish the task that provided the strongest relationships. He concluded that "group efficacy plays a large role in the establishment of group processes and procedures, which in turn affect how group members work and interact over the lifetime of the group" (p. 41).

Varney (1989) provides a set of symptoms of poor teamwork, the opposites of which could serve as criteria for effective teamwork. These include both cautious and overly formal communication, as well as a lack of disagreement; all of these symptoms may represent fear. The failure to share information or to provide feedback, the use of punishing criticism or a combative, competitive conflict style destroy trust or confidence and create tension. Poorly structured meetings, low commitment to unclear or unrealistic goals, and misunderstanding of roles lead to misuse or nonuse of members' talents. Performance appraisal based on opinion rather than "concrete results" undermines real participation. Finally, if real decisions are not made by teams, or if all decisions come down to teams for their approval only, they will have no sense of responsibility for implementation (pp. 14–18).

Parker's model (1990, p. 33) of effective teamwork proposes that the following twelve items set the good teams apart from the rest: clear purpose, informality, participation, **listening,** civilized disagreement, consensus decisions, **open communication,** clear roles and work assignments, shared leadership, external relations, style diversity, and **self-assessment.** To this list Glover (2002) would add **"emotional intelligence,"** or "the ability to understand the emotional make-up of others and empathise" (p. 40). Likewise, Kiffin-Petersen and Cordery (2003, p. 93) would add members' "dispositional variables," such as the propensity to "**trust** co-workers" as influencing their "preference for working in a team" and ultimately affecting the team's performance.

As a result of their study of thirty-two management teams, 80 percent in manufacturing and 20 percent in service organizations, Larson and LaFasto (1989, pp. 133–134) concluded that common strengths of successful teams consisted of a clear elevating goal or performance objective that justified the team's existence, competent team members who were "capable of collaborating," and standards of excellence that provided a "clear visualization" of achievement. The most common team problems included lack of unified commitment, lack of external support and recognition, and lack of **collaboration** among the members (pp. 134–135).

Larson and LaFasto (1989) focus on team-member competence as a prominent factor governing team effectiveness. Of course, the members need technical and **communication skills** and abilities. For management teams, however, basic competencies are not enough. These teams need not only bright persons who can work well with others but also those with high standards, maturity, a sense of urgency, and "presence" (pp. 62–65).

Effective teams consist of individuals who are committed to the success of their team. The importance of that **commitment** cannot be overstated, but finding evidence of it may be difficult. How do you measure caring? Its outward manifestations would likely include attendance, participation, interest, and effort. It would require a spirit of cooperation and a loyalty that finds expression in the words one uses about the team—is it "me and them" or is it "us"? On the other hand, effective members do not exhibit unquestioning loyalty, group-think, or pressure toward mere conformity; they retain a healthy **skepticism** about the right course of action.

Effective team members are interesting people because they have interests; they are not apathetic or "bored with it all." They have opinions, and they can acquire information, both of which are needed to help the team move forward. They are knowledgeable without being know-it-alls. They have room to learn and grow. They consider the wants and needs of their teammates, and they are willing to work to meet those wants and needs through collaboration. The case study on page 203 gives you an example of serving your own needs while serving those of your teammates.

Effective teams understand and practice processes that are both formalized and flexible. For example, meetings should always be run according to an agenda that all members have had access to, both in terms of possessing it and shaping its content. However, not all meetings should follow the same agenda; agendas should be tailored to the purposes of the individual meetings. Effective teams have clearly understood missions, or reasons for their existence, accompanied by realistic and **attainable goals** to be accomplished by meeting **concrete objectives.** Each member of an effective team understands where he or she fits into that mission and those goals and objectives, and how he or she will be evaluated for performance. "Qualities of Effective Teams" summarizes the characteristics of a successful organizational team.

DEVELOPING RESPONSIBILITY

*C*hristopher Avery (2002, p. 47) poses this dilemma: "Nowadays, all work is teamwork, and the challenge is to perform well when having to share the responsibility to get something done with other people over whom you have no authority." The team you will see in this case study struggled without success to solve the problem of responsibility without authority.

A group of retail managers in a large department store was put together into a "team" of managers and told that their jobs now would consist not only of supervising others but also of "working together" to supervise others. They received customary training in interpersonal communication, team communication, and "working with difficult people." Corporate executives assured them, through memos, that the creation of a management team would be "challenging" but would put them "at the cutting edge" of management practices in retail sales. However, when they began to coordinate the "supervision" tasks related to their large sales force, they began to notice differences in their styles of communicating with employees.

At first these style differences were masked by a screen of "niceness" that everyone displayed as often as possible. Because teamwork had been introduced during the "slack season" in retailing, no one felt pressured to "control" outcomes. Training sessions were pleasant, much camaraderie was established, and team members felt good about their jobs and about each other. However, that was all about to change drastically. As they built up to the holiday buying season, tension increased, and "niceness" vanished. Although the management team met weekly with a consultant hired by the corporation to work specifically with them, they began to disengage from the team and from each other.

A number of factors were responsible for this change. Certainly the busy season contributed, but the overwhelming differences in the ways each of them treated the employees split the team apart. One member, a laid-back young man who was well-liked by all, came into the team with an outstanding record of performance evaluations. A second member, a woman known for her perfectionism, also came with strong credentials. A third member, a man who appeared simply hardworking, but who treated employees with great disrespect and had a poor record as a supervisor, had been put into the team so that he could learn from the others. A fourth member, a woman thought to be a "rising star," had asked to be assigned to the team to forward her own career goals. The fifth member, a woman who had been hired away from a successful teamwork environment, was a "true believer" in the team concept.

(Continued)

Whereas once each manager had been supervisor of a specific group of employees, now the management team had responsibility for them all. Employees began to take their questions about their work and their complaints about their treatment to the more congenial managers, thus sidestepping the need for interaction with the disrespectful manager mentioned above, if at all possible. They also began to avoid working with the "careerist" and the "perfectionist" if they could and took their instructions, instead, from the "nice guy" and the "true believer."

As the workload shifted, the team members began to complain to each other. The management team felt squeezed between the executives' demands for teamwork and the employees' demands for consideration. Excuses were made for postponing or canceling meetings. None of the members were willing to discuss the issue of "good supervisory communication," nor were they willing to set any standards for their own conduct as managers. They felt truly caught in the dilemma presented by "responsibility without authority."

Avery (2002) provides the following guidelines for responsibility in a team:

- Instead of seeing yourself as the effect and something else as the cause, responsibility means seeing yourself as both cause and effect. Accept that your past choices placed you in your current situation.

- Commit to exercising your responsibility every day.

- Retain your personal power by treating every action and decision that affects you as one to which you consent. Speak up when you disagree with your team's purpose and direction.

- Choose among the annoyances that you've been wishing someone on your team would take care of, such as confronting a teammate's difficult behavior, and take care of it yourself.

Adapted from Avery, 2002, pp. 48–49.

Discussion Questions for Case Study

1. Using any of the theoretical effectiveness criteria suggested in this chapter, evaluate this group's performance. If you were a communication consultant to this company, what interventions would you suggest?

2. How realistic do you find this team? How realistic do you find Avery's suggestions? How responsible are you?

QUALITIES OF EFFECTIVE TEAMS

Regardless of their locations—college classroom, health-care facility, accounting firm, auto manufacturing plant, service-sector call center—and regardless of their contexts—social group, city council, Habitat for Humanity board, support group, classroom task group—effective teams possess the following characteristics.

1. They meet their goals by achieving their objectives.

2. They accomplish their missions and become their visions.

3. They meet their organizations' requirements.

4. They can give and receive feedback to monitor results.

5. They can present their own achievements to their organizations.

Two recent studies help clarify the sorts of skills needed for team effectiveness. Hawkins and Fillion (1999) interviewed and surveyed personnel managers from both the corporate and public sectors and sought the specific communication skills needed among work-group members. They found support for thirteen skills, arranged in "Communication Skills of Successful Teams" from most to least supportive.

Stevens and Campion (1999) have developed a set of **knowledge, skill, and ability (KSA)** requirements for teamwork that may be applied to team self-evaluation processes. These requirements are divided into two general sets, **interpersonal KSAs** and **self-management KSAs**. The interpersonal category is further divided into **conflict resolution,** collaborative problem solving, and communication skills. The self-management category is divided into **goal setting** and performance management and planning and task **coordination** skills. "Knowledge, Skill, and Ability Team Requirements" illustrates these KSAs in more detail.

In a comprehensive study, Mattson, Mumford, and Sintay (1999) have synthesized the work of many others in regard to **team-effectiveness criteria** to produce their own model. They take into account the ways work characteristics and team structures fit together to enhance team effectiveness in three areas: performance, satisfaction, and viability, or the ability to work together in the future. They divide work characteristics in two ways, types of tasks and task interdependence. For instance, in regard to types, team tasks may involve creativity or decision making. Those tasks may require that actions be taken by individuals independently or by various group members in a particular sequence. On the other hand, the tasks may be such that all members must work together continuously and constantly.

Mattson, Mumford, and Sintay (1999, p. 3) suggest that team structures can range along a continuum from nonteams of people who merely work for the same organization to self-led teams of people who are "long-term, autonomous

COMMUNICATION SKILLS OF SUCCESSFUL TEAMS

Team Members Must Be Able to

1. Listen effectively
2. Understand their roles and responsibilities
3. Be active, contributing members
4. Ask clear questions
5. Establish and maintain good professional rapport
6. Communicate effectively with people with different cultural backgrounds
7. Use clear, concise, accurate, and **professional language**
8. Communicate effectively with people with different professional backgrounds
9. Give clear and accurate instructions
10. Nonverbally convey a professional image
11. Recognize and aid in the resolution of conflicts
12. Receive information and transmit an accurate summary
13. Give a brief, clear, coherent, well-organized, and informative presentation

Adapted from Hawkins and Fillion, 1999.

groups that possess both managerial and leadership responsibilities." In between lie teams that possess a variety of responsibilities. Effectiveness thus depends on the types of tasks, the interdependence of the tasks, and the level of responsibility in terms of management and leadership regarding those tasks possessed by the team. Figure 12.1 illustrates this model.

Evaluation Criteria and Methods for Student Groups

Dennis Gouran (1990) asks group members to evaluate themselves in four general areas: **substantive, procedural, interpersonal,** and **ethical.** Even though, as he notes, groups rarely take the time for self-evaluation, such a process has value in two ways. First, it gives the group "a basis for improving their future performance." Second, it "serves as a final check on the wisdom of the decision the group has just reached" (p. 221). "Questions to Ask Yourselves about Your Group's Work" presents sample questions to help group members think through their procedures in each of these four general areas.

KNOWLEDGE, SKILL, AND ABILITY TEAM REQUIREMENTS

Interpersonal Knowledge, Skill, and Abilities

Conflict Resolution

- Recognize and encourage desirable team conflict, discourage undesirable team conflict
- Recognize type and source of conflict, implement appropriate strategy
- Employ integrative (win-win) strategy

Collaborative Problem Solving

- Identify and use participative situations
- Recognize and correct obstacles to collaboration

Communication

- Understand communication networks
- Communicate openly and supportively
- Listen nonevaluatively and actively
- Coordinate verbal and nonverbal messages
- Engage in and recognize importance of small talk and ritual greetings

Self-Management Knowledge, Skill, and Abilities

Goal Setting and Performance Management

- Establish specific, challenging, and accepted goals
- Monitor, evaluate, and provide feedback on individual and team performance

Planning and Task Coordination

- Coordinate activities, information, and tasks
- Establish task and role assignments, balance workload

Adapted from Stevens and Campion, 1999.

FIGURE 12.1 **A TEAM STRUCTURE–WORK FIT MODEL OF TEAM EFFECTIVENESS**

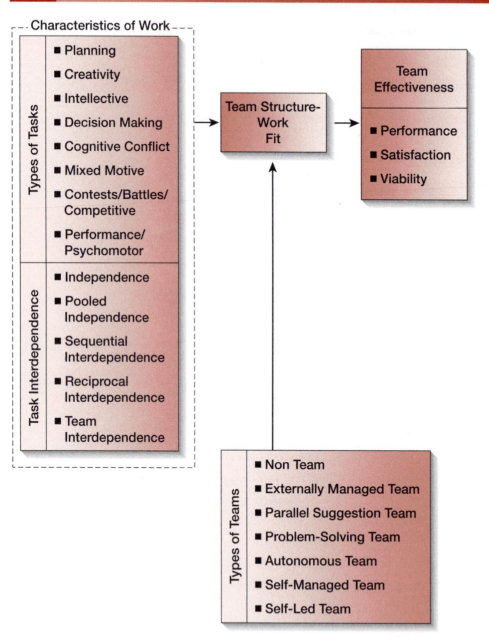

From Matteson et al., "Taking teams to task: A normative model for designing or recalibrating work teams," 1990, p. 3. In S. J. Havlovic, *Academy of Management Best Papers Proceedings*.

QUESTIONS TO ASK YOURSELVES ABOUT YOUR GROUP'S WORK

Substantive

- Did we have enough information?
- Did we understand it well enough?
- Were there gaps in our knowledge?
- Were our sources reliable and appropriate?
- Did we apply appropriate criteria to resolve information conflicts?
- Did we limit our alternatives?
- Did we rethink positions if we found new information?
- Did we apply appropriate criteria to each alternative?
- Did we agree on how we would make decisions—would they all have to be consensus decisions, for example?
- Did we make our final decision based on information, criteria, and sufficient alternatives?

Procedural

- Did we state our research question clearly?
- Did we define our terms sufficiently?
- Did we use an effectively organized agenda?
- Did we assess where we stood before moving on to the next step?
- Were the members goal directed?

Interpersonal

- Did we focus conflict on issues rather than people?
- Did we attempt to manage conflict appropriately?
- Did personal feelings about others unduly affect the outcome of our decision-making process?
- Did group maintenance needs override task performance?
- Did pressure to conform override task performance?
- Did the members willingly accept the group's decision?

(Continued)

QUESTIONS TO ASK YOURSELVES ABOUT YOUR GROUP'S WORK (CONTINUED)

Ethical

- Did we show concern for those whom our decision would affect?
- Did we act responsibly throughout?
- Did we misrepresent or misuse any information?
- Did we harm anyone's sense of self-worth?
- Was everyone shown due respect?

Adapted from Gouran, 1990.

Group performances may be designed in the familiar **panel discussion format,** in which groups present information to an audience in a formal and perhaps even scripted way. Groups may also engage in holding a **symposium,** in which each member would specialize in a particular aspect of the topic, or in a **forum,** in which questions may be asked by an audience. Evaluation criteria could focus on whether they met their goals for such performances.

In the organizational world, individuals and teams are subject to periodic **performance evaluations.** In some places, as you have seen, team members are evaluated by their immediate supervisors and by each other. Performance successes are then used as a basis for pay raises or other rewards. In your future careers, you will likely be expected to evaluate others. The ability to complete that task well may have an impact on your career success. In college classrooms students rarely grade themselves or each other, though some do, but knowing good performance from bad could certainly improve your chances of success. The knowledge gained here should carry over into other aspects of your school or work performance.

CONCLUSION

As we learned early in this chapter, no one method of evaluation for team performance will suffice for all teams. Thus, we have provided several sets of criteria, some of which overlap, from among the abundant standards in use around the world today. The common denominator among the sets is, of course, communication. To work alone takes little effort in that regard, but to work with others requires not just an understanding of how to communicate, but an attitude that supports its importance.

In this chapter we have considered the meaning of effectiveness itself and focused not just on productivity, or getting the task accomplished, but also on the interpersonal elements that affect the members themselves in important ways. Considering the two realms together, the tasks and the relationships, we can come to an understanding of team viability, or whether the members can continue to work together. We end the chapter with some very practical suggestions for your student teams as you move toward the end of the course. Perhaps you can use the suggestions in "Questions to Ask Yourselves about Your Group's Work" to guide your thinking as you evaluate yourself and your team's performance in the class. Although we have thought about ethics a number of times along the way, this last look at the ethical dimension of your performance may give you additional insights about yourself as a student and a team member.

COLLABORATIVE LEARNING ACTIVITIES

1. If your groups are evaluated on oral presentations such as proposals, construct a checklist of evaluation criteria you would find appropriate. Think carefully about what you would like to be held accountable for and then graded on.

2. If your groups are evaluated on written reports, design an evaluation form to use as a checklist in the preparation stage that you could propose and be willing to accept as potential grading criteria for the final report. Think carefully about how you would overcome the problems inherent in the process of writing together, such as achieving coherence in the report though you each have different writing styles.

Appendices

APPENDIX A   INVENTORY OF TEAM-MEMBER CHARACTERISTICS

Please fill out the following questionnaire with accurate information but do not identify yourself by name or in any other way. You may leave any or all questions or items blank if you wish.

- Gender:
  Female____   Male____

- Age:
  18–23____   24–29____   30–35____   35–40____   over 40____

- Year in college:
  1st____   2nd____   3rd____   4th____

- Region you consider "home" (if U.S.):
  Northeast____   Atlantic Coast____   Southeast____   Midwest____   Mountain West____
  South____   Southwest____   Northwest____   Pacific Coast____   Alaska____
  Hawaii____   Puerto Rico____   Other (please specify)____

- Region you consider "home" (if international):
  Canada____   Mexico____   Caribbean____   South America____   Central America____
  British Isles____   Western Europe____   Eastern Europe (including Russia)____
  Asian continent____   Indian subcontinent____   Southeast Asia____   Pacific Islands____
  Africa____   Australia/New Zealand____   Other (please specify)____

- Nationality: _____

- First language: _____

- Second language: _____

- Degree of computer competence:
  Expert____   Moderately skilled____   Beginner____

- Work preference:
  Competitive environment____   Cooperative environment____

- I am: introverted____   extroverted____   neither____   both____

- In terms of communication, I am likely to be:
  open____   closed____   somewhere in between____

- In terms of speaking in public, I am:
  fearful____   not fearful____   fearful in some situations but not in others____

- In terms of working in groups, I:
  enjoy such work____   dread such work____   have had more good than bad experiences____
  have had more bad than good experiences____

- In terms of leadership, I prefer:
  a strong leader____   a democratic leader____   no leader____   shared leadership____

- I am:
  assertive_____   not assertive_____   aggressive_____
- I: enjoy_____   do not enjoy_____   helping others.
- Please add any other diversities you think matter:

  _____

  _____

  _____

APPENDIX B   TRANSCRIPT OF A VIRTUAL MEETING

Graduate course in small group communication processes, Western Kentucky University

In this transcript you will see a number of events occurring that are common to electronic or Internet-based meetings. An activity based on this transcript may be found in the Instructor's Manual.

Meeting purpose   To finalize the group's policy question, a process they began in a face-to-face class meeting, then discussed on their class asynchronous discussion board, and now need to complete.

Participants   Judith is the instructor. Claude, Tonissa, Amy, Lori, Margaret, and James are the team members. One member, Shelly, a restaurant manager, had to deal with a sudden problem at work and could not participate.

Judith: I'm going to simply observe unless you need something from me. Where would you like to start?
Claude: I think we need to address Lori's original concern from the discussion page.
Tonissa: I think that we should first start with our question of policy. Lori's question about our policy being broad is a concern of mine as well. What does anyone else think about our question of policy?
Amy: I was concerned about how broad the topic could be. I believe that Claude had mentioned limiting the question more directly to hand gun violence by students against teachers in schools. Is this correct? I can't recall and didn't print out the earlier discussion.
Claude: It appears as if our scope is too broad and we need to think of a policy that covers a specific violence in schools; violence covers too much material for a 30 min discussion.
Claude: Could the policy read as follows: How should we deal with handguns in the secondary schools in the U.S. ?
Tonissa: My thoughts exactly. Now we have to agree on a specific topic of violence in schools. However, James and Shelly are missing. How will we do this because we may need to do new research?
Lori: I suggested a definition of violence. Do you guys think it's too broad?
Judith: Are you thinking about a policy for a specific school? Are you thinking about prevention or punishments?
Lori: All of my research centers on prevention.
Claude: I was thinking about US school systems and prevention
Amy: I would rather focus on prevention.
Tonissa: I would rather focus on prevention as well
Claude: Almost consensus
Judith: Can you phrase a question based on this discussion so far?
Lori: Who are we aiming this policy to?
Claude: If prevention, the target would be the public?
Judith: At the end do you want every high school in the US to have a policy that states . . .?

Claude: Is that unreasonable Dr. H?

Judith: Do you want to act as a local school board?

Judith: Schools are a state and local matter.

Claude: Local policy may help us because of the trends of our area

Beth: How about Bowling Green High School?

Lori: What does a local school board govern? One school? A county?

Judith: It governs its school district, whatever that may be.

Beth: I think there is only one city HS in BG

Tonissa: You're correct, Beth. The other schools are county schools (3 of them)

Beth: Yeah! James is here.

Judith: Welcome, James.

Tonissa: Hi James

James: Hey, guys. Sorry I'm late.

Judith: Amy, are you still here?

Claude: We could be the reps from the Warren County district proposing a policy for the four area high schools?

Judith: Yes, you could. Someone catch James up on what's what.

Lori: I like Claude's idea

Tonissa: Would we be able to include Bowling Green High School since it is a city school?

Judith: No

Amy: Yes, I'm still here. I keeping getting beat to the keyboard when making a comment about the topic. I would rather make our decision from the local school board point of view.

Claude: James, our focus was originally too broad so we have been talking or writing in this case about a re-focus of the policy

Tonissa: Then there would be only 3 high schools.

Judith: So, what should the question say?

Tonissa: What about: What can be done to reduce/prevent violence in secondary schools in Warren County?

Claude: How should we deal with the prevention of handguns in WC, WE, and GW high?

Judith: I like Tonissa's version.

Amy: What can be done to reduce the possibly of hand gun violence in Warren County High Schools?

Amy: I also like Tonissa's reduce/prevent suggestion.

Claude: I'm on board.

Judith: Lori, does this help with the problem you raised originally?

James: I'm sorry I'm so far behind. Have we discussed if we're going to talk about only one type of violence?

Beth: Someone had suggested we deal with only handgun violence so Amy's suggestion sounds good to me.

Claude: Yeah James—we are talking about handguns instead of the term "violence"

Judith: Is it big enough since as Claude pointed out, handguns in school are already illegal?

Beth: Hm.

Lori: Yes, I like Tonissa's question, but I think I disagree with eliminating other deadly weapons from our violence definition.

Judith: Is it only kids shooting someone we're interested in?

James: Beth, what do you mean by Hm? You obviously are thinking something.

Tonissa: I think that since we have narrowed our focus to a specific area, we will have time to cover school violence as a whole.

Claude: They are illegal, but the law is not preventing them from being in the schools.

Beth: I'm showing thoughtful respect to Dr. Hoover's opinion!

Judith: After metal detectors, what?

Lori: This is going really fast. What are we talking about?

Claude: Violence prevention programs maybe . . .

James: That's what I would think.

Judith: We're still trying to phrase the question.

James: So, aren't we getting ahead of ourselves?

Tonissa: We need to decide on exactly what our question of policy is going to be at this point.

James: I liked your question a few minutes ago, Tonissa

Lori: I like Tonissa's question with no changes.

Beth: Write it again, Tonissa

Tonissa: The question was: What can be done to reduce/prevent violence in secondary schools in Warren County?

James: Is everyone in agreement?

Claude: Are we going with the violence definition on the discussion board?

Amy: I don't recall all of Lori's definition of violence from earlier, but maybe we could define violence a bit more in the terms. I like Tonissa's suggestion and specifying what types of violence might be a way to make it work.

Tonissa: I like Lori's definition of violence that was posted on the discussion page.

James: I also seem to remember liking it

Lori: I could go get it and paste in, if you want . . .

Amy: Yes, please.

Claude: Technology is wonderful.

Judith: Has everyone written down the question Tonissa suggested?

Lori: Here's what I said: This is not a complete definition, but I would like to limit "violence" to: situations occurring within or on the grounds of a high school involving a student bearing a deadly weapon (gun, knife, grenade, etc.) and threatening or inflicting harm upon other students and/or faculty/staff. This would exclude such things as fist fights and gang violence.

James: How about if Tonissa posts it in the forum?

Tonissa: I will post it on the discussion page for everyone to see. This will also enable Shelly to see the question.

Judith: The definition would need to say "or otherwise threatening . . ." to include violence without weapons, if that's what you want to include.

Claude: Does this include grenade launchers or just grenades?

James: You can hit someone over the head with a launcher

Beth: You can hit someone over the head with your fist.

Judith: Do you want to exclude fist fights and gang violence?

Tonissa: I think Lori's definition suggested that we exclude gang violence and fist fights.

Lori: I guess I was thinking of weapon bearing exclusively.

James: I think it would be difficult to separate the gangs from the guns.

Amy: Gang violence would make our topic rather broad again. Gang violence is a topic in itself

Judith: Will keeping weapons off school grounds stop violence?

Claude: Is a pencil a weapon?

Beth: The policy statement might be more helpful if it encompassed "or otherwise threatening." Who knows, if we do a good job Warren County might be grateful and implement our policy.

Lori: Dr. Hoover, if we use the above definition, then yes it would.

Claude: No—Dr. H, only help deter serious acts of violence

Judith: Have you read any research that says it's a climate of violence or hatred that causes these incidents rather than the presence of weapons?

Lori: There's not much media coverage on violence that doesn't involve a deadly weapon. Fist fights don't generally kill people

Claude: My hands are registered as a deadly weapon, but that is in China.

Beth: In China?

Judith: My screen is flickering. I may get tossed off. If so, I'll be back.

Judith: Where are we?

James: -0

Beth: If Dr. Hoover is off line, maybe we could cheat and take a vote?

James: I think she's on—you're busted!!

Judith: Gotcha

Beth: Yikes!

Amy: Back to our debate. Do we want to limit our policy to only deadly weapons?

Tonissa: Does everyone agree with the question of policy? If so, I think we are at the point of defining terms, for example "violence."

Claude: We are looking at the term violence- what to include or exclude

James: I'm for excluding fist fights

James: I know y'all are still there!

Tonissa: I'm here. Just waiting for a response.

Claude: If we exclude fighting we can't use the term violence; in my opinion we need to be specific about the kinds of violence

Amy: I'm trying to read the violence definition again and kept getting returned to the bottom. Please give me a second.

Tonissa: Dr. Hoover, what do you think about using the term violence in the question as long as we define violence in the definition part of our agenda?

Judith: It works.

Claude: That works for me

Amy: I agree.

James: I'm in

Judith: Lori?

Lori: Me too. But what's the definition?

Claude: I think the one you proposed.

James: With modifications, or as is?

Amy: I like Lori's definition. And, still want to eliminate gangs and fist fights.

Judith: With weapons only?

Tonissa: I like Lori's definition too.

James: According to the definition, they just have to bear the arms. Lori is that how you meant it?

Lori: Yes, I think so. Do you all agree?

Tonissa: Yes

James: So I'm violent if I take a gun to school but don't use it? I'm not arguing, I'm just asking.

Amy: Question. Do we create this policy on violence with the understanding that gangs, fighting would be addressed elsewhere?

Judith: What about a pocket knife? I have one in my purse.

Lori: James, well, the definition said "and threatened or actually inflicted harm on others."

James: We already know you're violent!

Claude: Can you still carry a knife to school with a certain inch blade? You could in my high school

Lori: Dr. Hoover, if you threatened or hurt someone with it, that would be violence.

James: you're right. It takes both to be "violent." I should have read more closely.

Tonissa: Amy, to answer your question, I think we would address that in the definition of violence.

Lori: I could paste it in again, and we could make modifications to it, yes?

Judith: You could try to prevent violence, excepting gang violence, and still try to prevent "otherwise harm" to someone.

Amy: So, we're briefly addressing gangs/fighting, but focusing on deadly weapons. I am staying rather lost in all of this discussion.

Beth: But simply having a weapon in one's possession is illegal—whether it is used or not—right?

James: Do you guys want to do Title IX instead (a joke!)?

Lori: Okay, here it is.

Lori: Situations occurring within or on the grounds of a high school involving a student bearing a deadly weapon (gun, knife, grenade, etc.) and threatening or inflicting harm upon other students and/or faculty/staff. This would exclude such things as fist fights and gang violence.

James: I'm still of the opinion that we should leave gangs in

Beth: The definition implies that simply having a weapon would not be a problem—only using it (as in "and")?

Tonissa: I like Lori's definition

James: To address Beth's comment, Dr. Hoover has a knife, but she hasn't used it on anyone (that we know of)

Judith: Here's my problem with the definition as stated: If you can use metal detectors and eliminate metal weapons of all sorts, is that all there will be to your policy?

Amy: Could we add something like "or acting in a physical manner to threaten or inflict" and then carry on with Lori's definition?

Claude: Yes, but the policy is aimed directly at weapons violence prevention.

Beth: So, James, its OK to have a gun as long as you don't use it?

James: Yep!

Beth: But it is already illegal to have a gun in school

Claude: Dr.H, I see your point

Lori: I see your concern, Dr. H, but the research I've found doesn't necessarily indicate the need for metal detectors in all schools. There are many other recommendations we could make, especially if we take cost into consideration.

James: Dr. Hoover, I think we could promise to offer more than metal detectors. Beth, I'm not ignoring you. I just don't have a rebuttal

Lori: To add to that, students come in and out of many doors. Putting a detector at every door would be cost prohibitive.

Judith: Yes, and would add to a bunker mentality.

Claude: Clear bookbags, for instance

James: No bookbags

Claude: gun trade-in programs for schools

Judith: It looks like the group has decided on its definition. What's next?

James: Do we have other terms to define?

Tonissa: Lori, would you post the exact definition on the discussion page so that everyone is together

Lori: Okay

James: And put FINAL DRAFT, or something

Lori: Okay

James: Do we have other terms?

Claude: Before we can continue, we need to gather research based on the refocused policy question.

James: Can't we do a little more of the agenda? I think we agreed to keep the same criteria for judging info, too, yes?

Tonissa: I don't think that there are any other technical terms to define within the policy. Am I wrong?

Amy: Question. What about bomb threats? Do we consider this in our definition of violence?

Tonissa: I think that we can keep the same criteria for judging information.

James: To answer Amy's question, I think we should exclude bomb threats. That doesn't have to be a student, and they don't have to bring anything to school, so I don't think it fits our definition.

Amy: I know that there have been bomb threats, but I don't know if they were ever made by students.

Tonissa: I agree with James. Bomb threats creates a new thread to the subject.

Amy: Ok. Just needed clarification.

Claude: Bomb threats are tough because anyone can call one in.

Tonissa: Does anyone think that we have any other terms to define?

Amy: I cannot think of any and have been trying.

James: I don't think so.

Lori: Do we need to define "secondary schools"?

James: I think the 3 schools in question all have 9–12

Lori: Right!

Tonissa: You're right James.

Lori: What about categorizing our data. Is it too early for that?

Amy: Are we ready to move on?

James: Okay, without research, I think we'll be hard pressed to offer alternative answers at this point. Are we agreed that we're also going to keep the same criteria for choice of alternative?

Tonissa: I think we are ready to agree on criteria for judging information. Does everyone want to keep the same criteria?

Lori: I agree.

Amy: Yes, that seems to be the same as last time.

James: Are we agreeing on both criteria for judging information (III) and criteria for choice of alternatives (V)?

Judith: Policy choice criteria would be quite different from those you had for your fact discussion.

James: Okay

Amy: Is Friday's class work session an effort to prepare for our discussion or a completely different topic?

Judith: Friday's work session is definitely for this discussion.

James: I'll bring the laptop!

Tonissa: Will we have to come up with alternative answers to the question before we come up with criteria for choice of alternatives?

Judith: Laptop . . . good idea all around.

Judith: Yes, Tonissa, your alternative answers should come out of the research data.

Judith: And your criteria, such as cost effectiveness, should come out of your collective wisdom.

Tonissa: At this point, will anyone have to do additional research since we have changed our question of policy? If so, we may not be able to move to the next step in the agenda.

James: Okay guys, is there any more we can do?

Lori: I've gotta do more research.

Judith: How much more research will you have to do?

Lori: Not much, but I quit researching when the scope question came up.

Amy: I need to do additional research.

Tonissa: What about you James? Claude?

Judith: Where are we?

James: Yes ma'am, a little more research.

Tonissa: What is our next step?

Lori: Why don't we wrap this up, go do our research and talk on Friday.

Tonissa: I agree with Lori

Amy: I agree with Lori.

Judith: Works for me

Judith: You are such a good group. I think you accomplished quite a bit tonight.

Lori: Okay, I'm going to run. See ya'll Friday.

Tonissa: Me too.

Beth: Have a good night.

James: Happy Researching!

Amy: Bye

APPENDIX C   CHAT SESSION: GROUP DECISION MAKING

This group met online to try to finalize the topic for their question of value for their first major graded discussion. In the previous practice round, rather than staying with the question of fact as assigned, they moved into a discussion of solutions. They had also divided up the topic for research purposes. The result was that some members lacked information on the topics they actually discussed and had information only on items they never got to with the limited time available. You'll see that the teacher's (Judith) participation in the chat session was limited to clarifying, reminding, and asking questions when they seemed to need help. One member, Kyle, signed on late but was able to participate even though he was several hundred miles away for a job interview.

Courtney: Should we get started or wait for Kyle?
Greg: Let's give Kyle a few more
Judith: He said he would be here. I don't know where he was accessing the internet from.
Greg: He could be running late
Courtney: Should we clarify our purpose?
Greg: What are you talking about courtney
Lisa: I suppose we should go ahead and begin
Greg: Just joking
Courtney: Ha ha
Greg: Clarifying . . .
Hope: I think we need to address our topic and discuss how we want to go about our project
Greg: Just as well
Courtney: Sounds good. Our purpose is to brainstorm for ideas for the question of value, right?
Lisa: Have we completely decided on a q of value, or are we undecided
Courtney: I guess we're still open for debate
Greg: Let's address the?
Judith: You need to have your question nailed down by the end of this session.
Greg: OK
Courtney: Stick with on-line music or explore other topics?
Courtney: I think we'll find plenty of sources on music.
Lisa: If we go w/online music how many benefits and detriments will we be able to explore
Greg: I like the scope of doing online music
Lisa: I like the idea a lot, but will we have enough to discuss.
Greg: There are a lot of developments in the news about major labels opening their own type of Napster
Judith: Has anyone done any research?
Greg: But those co. would be restricted to the labels they record
Courtney: I think there are a lot of detriments and benefits from many different points of view.
Greg: I agree
Courtney: I have a few articles from MSNBC.com
Kyle: Logged in
Courtney: Howdy Kyle.
Lisa: Hi Kyle
Greg: WHAT'S UP KYLE
Greg: Kyle are you ok??
Kyle: Yes it just took me forever to sign on
Kyle: So what is up?
Courtney: Do we have a consensus for online music?

Lisa: Then what else should we do? Should we think of some of the detriments and benefits to different people?

Hope: I think we need to focus on how it affects different audiences i.e. the music industry and the public

Greg: Dr. hoover said we need to have the? of value nailed before the end, kyle

Kyle: Did we decide not to do online music?

Lisa: No, we are doing it

Kyle: OK OK . . . sorry for my late arrival

Hope: Kyle, we are talking about our q of value: what are the benefits and detriments of online music services for example Napster

Courtney: I have descriptions of 4 other online music sources.

Kyle: Isn't that our question of value?

Hope: Yes

Kyle: Ok

Lisa: Should we outline what the benefits are first

Hope: How should we approach the subject

Kyle: For who? Have we indentified the audience?

Courtney: For everyone

Greg: Benefits to consumer vs. benefits to company

Kyle: I mean benefits for the buyers, or the artists

Courtney: Recorders, industry people, consumers

Courtney: What do you think?

Greg: That's good

Kyle: Benefits for all those, or just a particular group?

Hope: All of them for now, let

Courtney: That way we can get lots of info. we have to take up 30 minutes

Lisa: Are we supposed to pick one point of view

Hope: Sorry, lets explore all options first

Greg: Yes there are several angles we can come from, will we do all or limit to one

Lisa: I thought we were

Kyle: I thought we were doing benefits for consumers, and detriments for the artists?

Hope: Kyle's suggestion sounds good

Greg: I don't know if we can divide it up like that

Greg: Can we dr.-hoover

Courtney: We could possibly find some benefits for artists like free publicity

Lisa: I was under the impression that we have to stick to one viewpoint

Judith: Aren't there benefits and detriments to both artists and consumers?

Courtney: I think we should just say "benefits and detriments"

Kyle: Yes there are

Greg: Yes so we should cover all aspects??

Kyle: So for both

Hope: Maybe we can take a problem solution stand point and find a compromise for both artists and consumers

Kyle: That is cool

Lisa: So, we can discover the ben and det from all viewpoints

Kyle: Yeah

Courtney: We're not looking for solutions though

Kyle: True

Judith: What is the task for this assignment?

Kyle: We are just showing both sides

Courtney: We got in trouble for that last time
Lisa: To find the value of something
Hope: I don't think we know
Courtney: I think we just look at the benefits and detriments
Kyle: I agree . . .
Hope: I agree
Courtney: To anyone involved
Judith: You look for benefits and detriments in order to figure out the value of something.
Hope: Maybe we should be more specific
Greg: Can each take an angle to research
Judith: No, no, no
Kyle: Without giving a solution
Greg: Sorry
Judith: Eek!!!
Courtney: I found opinions of some particular artists like limp bizkit and green day
Kyle: What is wrong why all the eeks, and sorries?
Courtney: We said we could divide research
Greg: It's you kyle, IT'S ALL YOUR FAULT!
Judith: Remember that you absolutely should not divide up the research.
Hope: Are we doing the same thing we did in the practice round just with a diff topic (current situation on campus parking/ben and det of free online music services)?
Kyle: Slow down we are jumping ahead
Kyle: Dr. Hoover just said do not divide the research
Judith: Let's start over. What is the task for this assignment?
Kyle: Question of value
Courtney: Question of value
Judith: How should the question be worded?
Kyle: We determine the value from the benefits and detrements to free online music
Lisa: What are the benefits and detriments of using online music services?
Courtney: We can examine the detriments and benefits of free online music services WITHOUT dividing up research
Greg: Yes from all aspects!!!
Judith: Is it free online music or is it online music?
Courtney: Sounds like a plan
Hope: Free online music
Judith: How will you conclude your discussion?
Kyle: GOOD QUESTION Dr. Hoover
Hope: Is our topic worded correctly?
Judith: Lisa's version above is well worded.
Courtney: This has been a great discussion. We'll get to work on researching!
Greg: OK so that's it?!?!?!
Hope: Sounds good
Greg: Thanks for joining everyone
Lisa: Let's conclude w/knowing our topic is decided, and let's all do some research this weekend between weekend things, and share our newfound knowledge on Mon
Judith: Just remember not to move to solutions.
Kyle: Right!!! Not good
Lisa: NO solutions . . . got it
Courtney: Can we log off?
Judith: Yes, see you Monday

APPENDIX D   PERSONAL REPORT OF COMMUNICATION APPREHENSION (PRCA-24)*

Directions: This instrument is composed of twenty-four statements concerning your feelings about communication with other people. Please indicate in the space provided the degree to which each statement applies to you by marking whether you (1) Strongly Agree, (2) Agree, (3) are Undecided, (4) Disagree, or (5) Strongly Disagree with each statement. There are no right or wrong answers. Many of the statements are similar to other statements. Do not be concerned about this. Work quickly; just record your first impression.

_____   1. I dislike participating in group discussions.

_____   2. Generally, I am comfortable while participating in group discussions.

_____   3. I am tense and nervous while participating in group discussions.

_____   4. I like to get involved in group discussions.

_____   5. Engaging in a group discussion with new people makes me tense and nervous.

_____   6. I am calm and relaxed while participating in group discussions.

_____   7. Generally, I am nervous when I have to participate in a meeting.

_____   8. Usually I am calm and relaxed when I am called upon to express an opinion at a meeting.

_____   9. I am very calm and relaxed when I am called upon to express an opinion at a meeting.

_____   10. I am afraid to express myself at meetings.

_____   11. Communicating at meetings usually makes me uncomfortable.

_____   12. I am very relaxed when answering questions at a meeting.

_____   13. While participating in a conversation with a new acquaintance, I feel very nervous.

_____   14. I have no fear of speaking up in conversations.

_____   15. Ordinarily I am very tense and nervous in conversations.

_____   16. Ordinarily I am very calm and relaxed in conversations.

_____   17. While conversing with a new acquaintance, I feel very relaxed.

_____   18. I'm afraid to speak up in conversations.

_____   19. I have no fear of giving a speech.

_____   20. Certain parts of my body feel very tense and rigid while giving a speech.

_____   21. I feel relaxed while giving a speech.

_____   22. My thoughts become confused and jumbled when I am giving a speech.

_____   23. I face the prospect of giving a speech with confidence.

_____   24. While giving a speech, I get so nervous, I forget facts I really know.

* This instrument is written by James C. McCroskey. James C. McCroskey, *An Introduction to Rhetorical Communications,* 4th ed. (Englewood Cliffs, NJ: Prentice-Hall, 1982). The instrument may be reprinted and used for research and instructional purposes without additional authorization of the copyright holder. Uses for which there is expectation of profit, including publication or instruction outside the normal college or school environment, are prohibited without permission of James C. McCroskey.

SCORING

Group = 18 − (1) + (2) − (3) + (4) − (5) + (6)
Meeting = 18 − (7) + (8) + (9) − (10) − (11) + (12)
Interpersonal = 18 − (13) + (14) − (15) + (16) + (17) − (18)
Public = 18 + (19) − (20) + (21) − (22) + (23) − (24)
Overall Comprehension Apprehension = Group + Meeting + Dyadic + Public

References

Chapter 1

Ardrey, Robert. *The Social Contract*. New York: Atheneum, 1970.

Burningham, Caroline and Michael A. West. "Individual, Climate, and Group Interaction Processes as Predictors of Work Team Innovation." *Small Group Research*, v. 26, #1, February 1995, pp. 106–17.

Chadwick, Alex. "Employees Make Success Story of Running Steel Plant." National Public Radio. *Morning Edition*. March 23, 1994.

"Children Learn About Teamwork at Camp." *New Straits Times-Management Times*, July 16, 2003.

Coppola, Susan, Cherie A. Rosemond, Nansi Greger-Holt, Florence G. Soltys, Laura C. Hanson, Melinda A. Snider, Jan Busby-Whitehead. "Arena Assessment: Evolution of Teamwork for Frail Older Adults." *Topics in Geriatric Rehabilitation*, v. 17, #3, 2002, pp. 13–28.

D'Antoni, Helen. "Behind the Numbers Teamwork is Key to Tech Improvements." *Informationweek.com*. September 16, 2002, p. 56. http://www.informationweek.com/story/showArticle.jhtml?articleID= 6503504.

Desivilya, Helena Syna. "Jewish-Arab Coexistence in Israel: The Role of Joint Professional Teams." *Journal of Peace Research*, v. 35, #4, July, 1998, pp. 429– 53.

Dumaine, Brian. "The Bureaucracy Busters." *Fortune*, June 17, 1991, pp. 36–38, 42–50.

Embry, Mike. "Center Opens a New Window on Automobile Production." *Louisville (KY) Courier-Journal*, June 22, 1994, pp. E1–E2.

Friedman, Will and Jill Casner-Lotto. *Teams Work: Lessons from Successful Organizations*. Work in America Institute. Quoted in "The Power of Teamwork." *Worklife*, v. 14, #1, 2002, pp. 8–9.

"Fueling Productivity with Trust and Teamwork." *Broker Magazine*, v. 5, #3, June/July 2003, p. 12.

Hall, John R. "ACCA Contractor Epitomizes Teamwork." *Air Conditioning, Heating & Refrigeration News*, June 10, 2002, p. 10.

Hamilton, Barton H., Jack A. Nickerson, and Hideo Owan. "Team Incentives and Worker Heterogeneity: An Empirical Analysis of the Impact of Teams on Productivity and Participation." *Journal of Political Economy*, v. 111, #3, June 2003, pp. 465–98.

"High-Performance Workplace Increases Efficiency." National Public Radio. *Morning Edition*. May 3, 1994.

Hospital Consortium Presentation, Louisville, KY, 1994.

Hospital Group Employee. Interview with author. 1994.

Johnson, D. W., R. T. Johnson, and K. A. Smith. "Cooperative Learning Returns to College: What Evidence Is There That It Works?" *Change*, v. 30, July/August 1998, pp. 27–35. Quoted in Pfaff, Elizabeth and Patricia Huddleston. "Does It Matter if I Hate Teamwork? What Impacts Student Attitudes Toward Teamwork." *Journal of Marketing Education*, v. 25, #1, April 2003, pp. 37–45.

Lewandowski, Jim and Jack O'Toole. "Forming the Future: The Marriage of People and Technology at Saturn." Presentation to Stanford University, Industrial Engineering and Engineering Management. March 29, 1990. Quoted in Saturn Corporation. News Release. Spring Hill, TN, September 18, 1990.

Maslow, Abraham H. *Motivation and Personality*. New York: Harper & Row, 1954.

McGregor, Douglas. *The Human Side of Enterprise*. New York: McGraw-Hill, 1960.

Nelson, Bob. "Making Teamwork Work." *Bank Marketing*, v. 34, #6, July/August 2002, p. 10.

Ouchi, William G. *Theory Z: How American Business Can Meet the Japanese Challenge*. Reading, MA: Addison-Wesley, 1981.

Panepinto, Joe. "Maximize Teamwork." *Computerworld*, v. 28, #12, March 21, 1994, p. 119.

Pearson, C. A. L. "An Assessment of Extrinsic Feedback on Participation, Role Perceptions, Motivation, and Job Satisfaction in a Self-Managed System for Monitoring Group Achievement." *Human Relations,* v. 44, #5, 1991, pp. 517–37.

"People Power Pays Off." *CMA: The Management Accounting Magazine,* v. 61, May/June 1987, pp. 18–23.

Peterson, Christopher and Martin E. P. Seligman. "Character Strengths Before and After September 11." *Psychological Science,* v. 14, #4, July 2003, p. 381.

Plant Manager. Interview with author. August 10, 1994. Danville, KY.

"Project Managers Learn Teamwork at Adults' Space Camp." *CNN Future Watch.* May 21, 1994.

Rider, Allen. "Nine Keys to Getting Hired." *Resource: Engineering and Technology for a Sustainable World,* v. 6, #e, March 1999, pp. 23–25.

Rorrer, Ronald A. L. "Credentials for the Job." *Mechanical Engineering,* v. 125, #8, August 2003, p. 50.

Samovar, Larry A., Linda D. Henman, and Stephen W. King. "Small Group Process." In *Small Group Communication: Theory and Practice,* 7th ed. Eds. Robert S. Cathcart, Larry A. Samovar, and Linda D. Henman. Dubuque, IA: Brown & Benchmark, 1996, pp. 7–11.

Schutz, William C. *The Interpersonal Underworld.* Palo Alto, CA: Science & Behavior Books, Inc., 1966, pp. 18–25.

Shields, Jean. "Community Building Checklist." *Curriculum Administrator,* v. 35, #8, August 1999, p. 9.

Song, Kyung M. "Alliant's Teams Are Forging a World Without Bosses." *Louisville (KY) Courier-Journal,* July 20, 1994, p. 10B.

Spiro, Melford E. *Kibbutz, Venture in Utopia.* Cambridge, MA: Harvard Univ. Press, 1956.

Stayer, Ralph. "How I Learned to Let My Workers Lead." *Harvard Business Review,* November/December 1990, pp. 66–83.

Steel Employee. Interview with author. Tennessee. January 26, 1994.

Stewart, Thomas A. "GE Keeps Those Ideas Coming." *Fortune,* August 12, 1991, pp. 41–49.

Stinson, Sonya. "A Workplace Where Differences Are Second Nature: An interview with George David, President and CEO of United Technologies, Inc." *The Black Collegian,* February 1995, v. 25, #2, pp. 56–60.

Stokes, Stewart L. "Moving Toward Self-Direction." *Information Systems Management,* v. 11, #1, Winter 1994, pp. 40–47.

Taylor, Kimberly A. "Marketing Yourself in the Competitive Job Market: An Innovative Course Preparing Undergraduates for Marketing Careers." *Journal of Marketing Education,* v. 25, #2, August 2003, pp. 97–108.

"Teamwork Enhances Results, Job Satisfaction." *Alliant News,* v. 2, #16, November 16, 1993, p. 1.

Ward, Joe. "Ford's 'Mod Squad': Special Explorer Team's Self-Supervision Gives Labor Days a Different Look." *Louisville (KY) Courier-Journal,* Sept 4, 1994, pp. E1–E2.

Webb, Gisela. "Preparing Staff for Participative Management." *Wilson Library Bulletin,* May 1988, pp. 50–52.

Webster, Jonathan. "Teamwork: Understanding Multi-Professional Working." *Nursing Older People,* v. 14, #3, May 2002, pp. 14–19.

Yank, Glenn R., Jack W. Barber, David S. Hargrove, and Patricia D. Whitt. "The Mental Health Treatment Team as a Work Group: Team Dynamics and the Role of the Leader." *Psychiatry: Interpersonal and Biological Processes,* v. 55, #3, August 1992, pp. 250–65.

Zinn, Linda. "Teamwork: A Winning Approach to Wound Care." *Nursing Homes: Long Term Care Management,* v. 51, #6, June 2002, pp. 56–60.

Chapter 2

Barge, J. Kevin. "Leadership as Medium: A Leaderless Group Discussion Model." *Communication Quarterly,* v. 37, Fall 1989, pp. 237–47.

Berlo, David K. *The Process of Communication: An Introduction to Theory and Practice.* New York: Holt, Rinehart & Winston, 1960.

Buber, Martin. *Between Man and Man*. New York: Macmillan, 1947.

Buber, Martin. *I and Thou*, 2nd ed. Trans. Ronald Gregor Smith. New York: Scribners, 1958.

Buber, Martin. *The Knowledge of Man*. Trans. Maurice Friedman and Ronald Gregor Smith. New York: Harper and Row, 1965.

Columbia Accident Investigation Board. *Report*. Washington, DC: Government Printing Office, 2003.

Dance, Frank E. X. and Carl E. Larson. *Speech Communication: Concepts and Behavior*. New York: Holt, Rinehart and Winston, 1972.

Dulye, Linda M. "Toward Better Two-Way: Why Communications Process Improvement Represents the Right Response During Uncertain Times." *IEEE Transactions on Professional Communication*, v. 36, #1, March 1993, pp. 24–29.

Foss, Sonja K., Karen A. Foss, and Robert Trapp. *Contemporary Perspectives on Rhetoric*. Prospect Heights, IL: Waveland, 1985.

Gibb, Jack R. "Defensive Communication," *Journal of Communication*, v. 11, 1961, pp. 141–48.

Gronbeck, Bruce E. *The Articulate Person*, 2nd ed. Glenview, IL: Scott Foresman and Co., 1983.

Habermas, Jurgen. *Communication and the Evolution of Society*. Trans. Thomas McCarthy. Boston: Beacon, 1979.

Henkoff, Ronald. "Companies That Train Best." *Fortune*, March 22, 1993, pp. 62– 75.

Johannesen, Richard L. *Ethics in Human Communication*, 4th ed. Prospect Heights, IL: Waveland, 1996.

Knutson, Thomas J., Lawrence R. Wheeless, and Larry Divers. "Developing Teachable Small Group Communication Behaviors." *Communication Education*, v. 26, November 1977, pp. 333–37.

Leathers, Dale G. *Nonverbal Communication Systems*. Boston: Allyn & Bacon, 1976.

Lederman, Linda Costigan. "Suffering in Silence: The Effects of Fear of Talking on Small Group Participation." *Group and Organizational Studies*, v. 7, #3, September 1982, pp. 279–94.

McCroskey, J. C. and V. P. Richmond. "The Effects of Communication Apprehension on the Perception of Peers." *Western Journal of Speech Communication*, v. 40, 1976, pp. 14–21.

Panepinto, Joe. "Maximize Teamwork." *Computerworld*, March 21, 1994, v. 28, #12, p. 119.

Schramm, Wilbur. "How Communication Works." In *The Process and Effects of Communication*. Ed. Wilbur Schramm. Urbana, IL: Univ. Of Illinois Press, 1954, pp. 3–26.

Stinson, Sonya. "A Workplace Where Differences Are Second Nature." *The Black Collegian*, v. 25, #2, February 1995, pp. 56–60.

Sullivan, Anne McCrary. "Learning the Language of Response." Quoted in Peter Smagorinsky and Pamela K. Fly. "A New Perspective on Why Small Groups Do and Don't Work." *English Journal*, May 1994, pp. 54–63.

Sykes, Richard E. "Imagining What We Might Study if We Really Studied Small Groups from a Speech Perspective." *Communication Studies*, v. 41, #3, Fall 1990, pp. 200–11.

Toyota. "Hiring Process for Team Members." *Human Resources Department Employee Manual*. 1994.

———. "Human Resource Management in the Toyota Production System." *Human Resources Department Employee Manual*. 1994.

Von Bertalanffy, Ludwig. *General System Theory*. New York: George Braziller, 1968.

Chapter 3

Alderfer, C. P. "An Intergroup Perspective on Group Dynamics." In *Handbook of Organizational Behavior*. Ed. J. W. Lorch. Englewood Cliffs, NJ: Prentice Hall, 1987, pp. 190–222. Quoted in Richard Lichtenstein, Jeffrey A. Alexander, Kimberly Jinnett, and Esther Ullman. "Embedded Intergroup Relations in Interdisciplinary Teams." *Journal of Applied Behavioral Science*, v. 33, #4, December 1997, pp. 413–34.

Allen, Brenda J. "'Diversity' and Organizational Communication." *Journal of Applied Communication Research*, v. 23, May 1995, pp. 143–55.

Bailey, Antoinette M. "Thoughts on Building a House for Diversity." *Vital Speeches of the Day,* v. 66, #13, April 15, 2000, pp. 400–03.

Bantz, Charles R. "Cultural Diversity and Group Cross-Cultural Team Research." *Journal of Applied Communication Research,* v. 21, February 1993. In *CommSearch95.* CD-ROM. Speech Communication Association.

Borden, George A. *Cultural Orientation: An Approach to Understanding Intercultural Communication.* Englewood Cliffs, NJ: Prentice Hall, 1991.

Borisoff, D. and L. Merrill. *The Power to Communicate: Gender Differences as Barriers.* Prospect Heights, IL: Waveland Press, 1985.

Coppola, Susan, Cherie A. Rosemond, Nansi Greger-Holt, Florence G. Soltys, Laura C. Hanson, Melinda A. Snider, and Jan Busby-Whitehead. "Arena Assessment: Evolution of Teamwork for Frail Older Adults." *Topics in Geriatric Rehabilitation,* v. 17, #3, 2002, pp. 13–28.

Earley, P. C. "Social Loafing and Collectivism: A Comparison of the United States and the People's Republic of China." *Administrative Science Quarterly,* v. 34, 1989, pp. 565-81.

Ferran, Ernesto, J. "Workplace Cultural Diversity: A Manager's Journal." *Journal of Child and Family Studies,* v. 3, #1, 1994, pp. 1–5.

Figueroa, Manuel. "The Individual Is Important." *IEEE SPECTRUM.* June 1992, pp. 26–27.

Gayle, B. M., R. W. Priess, and M. Allen. "Gender Differences and the Use of Conflict Strategies." In *Differences That Make a Difference: Examining the Assumptions in Gender Research.* Eds. L. H. Turner and H. M. Sterk. Westport, CT: Bergin & Garvey, 1994, pp. 13–26.

Gearhart, S. M. "The Womanization of Rhetoric." *Women's Studies International Quarterly,* v. 2, 1979, pp. 195–201.

Gummer, Burton. "Notes from the Management Literature." *Administration in Social Work,* v. 18, #3, 1994, pp. 123–40.

Guzzo, R. A. "Group Decision Making and Group Effectiveness in Organizations." In *Designing Effective Work Groups.* Ed. P. S. Goodman. San Francisco: Jossey-Bass, 1986, pp. 34–71.

Harrison, Deborah. "Activities and Multiprofessional Teamwork on a Psychiatric Unit." *British Journal of Therapy and Rehabilitation,* v. 9, #2, February 2002, pp. 46–50.

Hart, Russell D. and David E. Williams. "Able-Bodied Instructors and Students with Physical Disabilities: A Relationship Handicapped by Communication." *Communication Education,* v. 44, April 1995, pp. 140–54.

Hayes, Cassandra. "The New Spin on Corporate Work Teams." *Black Enterprise,* June 1995, v. 25, #11, pp. 229–33.

Hoffman, R. and N. R. F. Maier. "Quality and Acceptance of Problem Solutions by Members of Homogeneous and Heterogeneous Groups." *Journal of Abnormal and Social Psychology,* v. 62, 1961, pp. 401–07.

Hofstede, G. *Culture's Consequences: International Differences in Work-Related Values.* Beverly Hills, CA: Sage, 1980.

———. *Cultures and Organizations: Software of the Mind.* London: McGraw Hill, 1991.

Janis, I. L. *Groupthink: Psychological Studies of Policy Decisions and Fiascoes.* Boston: Houghton Mifflin, 1982.

Johnson, Fern. "Feminist Theory, Cultural Diversity, and Women's Communication." *The Howard Journal of Communication,* v. 1, #2, Summer 1988, pp. 33– 41.

Kluge, Holger. "Reflections on Diversity: Cultural Assumptions." *Vital Speeches of the Day,* v. 63, #6, January 1, 1997, pp. 171–75.

Kohn, A. *No Contest: The Case Against Competition.* Boston: Houghton Mifflin, 1992.

———. *Punished By Rewards: The Trouble With Gold Stars, Incentive Plans, A's, Praise, and Other Bribes.* Boston: Houghton Mifflin, 1993.

Lederman, Linda Costigan. "Suffering in Silence: The Effects of Fear of Talking on Small Group Participants." *Group and Organizational Studies,* v. 7, #3, September 1982, pp. 279–94.

MacIntyre, A. *After Virtue: A Study in Moral Theory.* Notre Dame: Notre Dame Univ. Press, 1984.

Makower, Joel. "Managing Diversity in the Workplace." *Business and Society Review,* #92, Winter 1995, pp. 48–54.

McCroskey, J. "Oral Communication Apprehension: A Summary of Recent Theory and Research." *Human Communication Research*, v. 4, 1977, pp. v. 4, 78–96.

McEnrue, M. P. "Managing Diversity: Los Angeles Before and After the Riots." *Organizational Dynamics*, v. 21, #3, 1993, pp. 18–29.

McGee, M. C. and J. S. Nelson. "Narrative Reason in Public Argument." *Journal of Communication*, v. 35, 1985, pp. 139–55.

McNerny, Don. "The Bottom-line Value of Diversity." *HR Focus*, v. 71, #5, May 1994, pp. 22–23.

Meyers, Renee A. and Dale E. Brashers. "Expanding the Boundaries of Small Group Communication Research: Exploring a Feminist Perspective." *Communication Studies*, v. 45, Spring 1994, pp. 68–85.

Partlow, Jim and Don Wynes. "Teamwork Puts a Troubled Project Back on Track: A Case Study in Relationship Building." *Information Strategy: The Executive's Journal*, Winter 2002, pp. 12–15.

Rorty, Richard. *Philosophy and the Mirror of Nature*. Princeton: Princeton Univ. Press, 1979.

Siegel, Robert and Noah Adams. "Profile: Queens, New York." *All Things Considered*. National Public Radio. November 29, 1999.

Simons, Herbert W. "Introduction." In *Rhetoric in the Human Science*s. Ed. Herbert W. Simons. London: Sage, 1989.

Sosik, John J. and Dong I. Jung. "Work-Group Characteristics and Performance in Collectivistic and Individualistic Cultures." *Journal of Social Psychology*, v. 142, #1, February 2002, pp. 5–24. http://search.epnet.com/direct.asp?an= 6132862&db=aph.

Strenski, James B. "Stress Diversity in Employee Communications." *Public Relations Journal*, #7, August/September 1994, pp. 32–35.

Sunoo, Brenda Paik. "Amgen's Latest Discovery." *Personnel Journal*, v. 75, February 1996, #2, pp. 38–44.

Thomas, David A. and Robin J. Ely. "Making Differences Matter: A New Paradigm for Managing Diversity." *Harvard Business Review*, September/ October 1996, pp. 79–90.

Thomas, R. Roosevelt, Jr. "Organizational Development: Redefining Diversity." *HR Focus*, v. 73, #4, April 1996, pp. 6–7.

Webb, Gisela. "Preparing Staff for Participative Management." *Wilson Library Bulletin*, May 1988, pp. 50–52.

White, Daphne. "How to Manage a Multilingual Work Force." *Safety + Health*, January 1994, pp. 34–41.

Wyatt, N. "Organizing and Relating: Feminist Critique of Small Group Communication." In *Transforming Visions: Feminist Critiques in Communication Studies*. Eds. S. P. Bowen and N. Wyatt. Cresskill, NJ: Hampton Press, 1993, pp. 51–86.

Chapter 4

Alliant Health System. "Report to the Community." Advertising supplement to the *Louisville (KY) Courier Journal*, July 13, 1997.

Bales, Robert. *Personality and Interpersonal Behavior*. New York, NY: Holt, Rinehart, 1970.

Benhabib, Seyla. "Sexual Difference and Collective Identities: The New Global Constellation." *Signs*, v. 24, #2, Winter 1999, pp. 335–61.

Bormann, Ernest G. "Fantasy and Rhetorical Vision: The Rhetorical Criticism of Social Reality." *The Quarterly Journal of Speech*, v. 59, 1972, pp. 396–407.

Burningham, Caroline and Michael A. West. "Individual, Climate, and Group Interaction Processes as Predictors of Work Team Innovation." *Small Group Research*, v. 26, #1, February 1995, pp. 106–17.

Cochran, D. S. and F. R. David. "Communication Effectiveness of Organizational Mission Statements." *Journal of Applied Communication Research*, v. 14, #2, Fall 1986, pp. 108–118.

Cox, Sharon. "Career Scope South Central." *Nursing Management*, v. 34, #3, March 2003, p. 58.

Ferguson, K. E. *The Feminist Case Against Bureaucracy*. Philadelphia: Temple University Press, 1984.

Fisher, B. Aubrey. *Small Group Decision Making*, 2nd ed. New York: McGraw-Hill, 1980.

GEA Today, v. 4, #4, April 1994, p. 1.

Gibson, Cristina B. and Mary E. Zellmer-Bruhn. "Minding Your Metaphors: Applying the Concept of Teamwork Metaphors to the Management of Teams in Multicultural Contexts." *Organizational Dynamics*, v. 31, #2, Autumn 2002, pp. 101–17.

Graham, Charles R. "A Model of Norm Development for Computer-Mediated Teamwork." *Small Group Research*, v. 34, #3, June 2003, pp. 322–52.

Gunning, R. and D. Mueller. *How to Take the Fog Out of Writing*. Chicago: Dartnell, 1981. Quoted in Cochran and David, 1986, pp. 110.

Health System. "Cardiac Rehabilitation Team Mission; Employee Managed Team Certification Presentation; Elective Criteria Form #5." March 28, 1994.

Health System Rehabilitation Services Department. "Health System Clinical Quality Improvement Plan/Report." January–March 1993.

Janis, Irving L. *Victims of Groupthink*. Boston: Houghton Mifflin, 1972.

Johannesen, Richard L. *Ethics In Human Communication*, 4th ed. Prospect Heights, IL: Waveland, 1996.

Koch, Susan and Stanley Deetz. "Metaphor Analysis of Social Reality in Organizations." *Journal of Applied Communication Research*, v. 9, #1, Spring 1981, pp. 1–15.

Laurer, Charles S. "Teamwork Needs Cultivating." *Modern Healthcare*, v. 32, #38, September 23, 2002, pp. 1–2.

Lembke, Svan and Marie G. Wilson. "Putting the 'Team' into Teamwork: Alternative Theoretical Contributions for Contemporary Management Practice." *Human Relations*, v. 51, #7, July 1998, pp. 927–44.

Littlejohn, Stephen W. and David M. Jabusch. "Communication Competence: Model and Application." *Journal of Applied Communication Research*, v. 10, Spring 1982, pp. 29–37. Quoted in Johannesen, 1996, pp. 150–51.

———. *Persuasive Transactions*. Glenview, IL: Scott, Foresman, 1987. Quoted in Johannesen, 1996, pp. 150–51.

Locke, E. A., K. N. Shaw, L. M. Saari, and G. P. Latham. "Goal-setting and Task Performance: 1969–1980." *Psychological Bulletin*, v. 90, 1981, pp. 125– 52. Quoted in Martin Hoegl and K. Praveen Parboteeah. "Goal Setting and Team Performance in Innovative Projects: On the Moderating Role of Teamwork Quality." *Small Group Research*, v. 34, #1, February 2003, p. 6.

Maher, John R. and Darrell T. Piersol. "Perceived Clarity of Individual Job Objectives and of Group Mission as Correlates of Organizational Morale." *Journal of Communication*, v. 20, June 1970, pp. 125–33.

Mattson, Marifran and Patrice M. Buzzanell. "Traditional and Feminist Organizational Communication Ethical Analyses of Messages and Issues Surrounding an Actual Job Loss Case." *Journal of Applied Communication Research*, v. 27, 1999, pp. 49–72.

Meyers, Renee A. and Dale E. Brashers. "Expanding the Boundaries of Small Group Communication Research: Exploring a Feminist Perspective." *Communication Studies*, v. 45, Spring 1994, pp. 68–85.

Partlow, Jim and Don Wynes. "Teamwork Puts a Troubled Project Back on Track: A Case Study in Relationship Building." *Information Strategy: The Executive's Journal*. Winter 2002, pp. 12–15.

Putnam, Linda L. and Cynthia Stohl. "Bona Fide Groups: A Reconceptualization of Groups in Context." *Communication Studies*, v. 1, #3, Fall 1990, pp. 248–65.

Redding, W. C. "Ethics and the Study of Organizational Communication: When Will We Wake Up?" In *Responsible Communication: Ethical Issues in Business, Industry, and the Professions*. Eds. J. Á. Jaksa and M. S. Pritchard. Cresskill, NJ: Hampton, 1996, pp. 17–40.

Saturn Corporation. News Release. Spring Hill, TN, September 18, 1990.

Scheerhorn, D., P. Geist, and J. C. V. Teboul, "Beyond Decision Making in Decision-Making Groups: Implications for the Study of Group Communication." In *Group Communication in Context: Studies of Natural Groups*. Ed. L. R. Frey. Hillsdale, NJ: Erlbaum, 1994, pp. 247–62.

Shepherd, G. J. "Communication as Influence: Definitional Exclusion." *Communication Studies*, v. 43, 1992, pp. 203–19.

Stayer, Ralph. "How I Learned to Let My Workers Lead." *Harvard Business Review*, November/December 1990, pp. 66–83.

Stokes, Stewart L. "Moving Toward Self-Direction." *Information Systems Management,* v. 11, #1, Winter 1994, pp. 40–47.

Styhre, Alexander, Jonas Roth, and Anders Ingelgard. "Care of the Other: Knowledge-creation Through Care in Professional Teams." *Scandinavian Journal of Management,* v. 18, #4, December 2002, pp. 503–21.

Stys, Rick. HR Manager, Pet Products. Interview with author. July 12, 1994. Bowling Green, KY.

Sundstrom, E., K. P. De Meuse, and D. Futrell. "Work Teams: Application and Effectiveness." *American Psychologist,* v. 45, #2, 1990, pp. 120–33.

Tajfel, Henri. "Social Categorization, Social Identity and Social Comparison." In *Differentiation Between Social Groups: Studies in the Social Psychology of Intergroup Relations.* Ed. Henri Tajfel. London: Academic Press, 1978, pp. 61–76.

Tajfel, Henri, ed. *Social Identity and Intergroup Relations.* Cambridge: Cambridge Univ. Press, 1982.

Tajfel, Henri and J. C. Turner. "An Integrative Theory of Intergroup Conflict." In *The Social Psychology of Intergroup Relations,* 2nd ed. Eds. W. G. Austin and S. Worchel. Monterey, CA: Brooks/Cole, 1979, pp. 33–47.

———. "The Social Identity Theory of Intergroup Behavior." In *Psychology of Intergroup Relations,* 2nd ed. Eds. S. Worchel and W. G. Austin. Chicago, IL: Nelson-Hall, 1986, pp. 7–24.

Turner, J. C. "Towards a Cognitive Redefinition of the Social Group." In *Social Identity and Intergroup Relations.* Ed. Henri Tajfel. Cambridge: Cambridge Univ. Press, 1982, pp. 15–40.

———. *Rediscovering the Social Group: A Self-Categorization Theory.* Oxford: Basil Blackwell, 1987.

Wuthnow, Robert. "How Small Groups Are Transforming Our Lives." *Christianity Today,* February 7, 1994, pp. 20–24.

Chapter 5

Barker, Robert. "The Art of Brainstorming." *Business Week,* August 19–26, 2002, pp. 168–70.

Columbia Accident Investigation Board. *Report.* Washington, DC: Government Printing Office, 2003.

Ennis, R. H. "A Concept of Critical Thinking." *Harvard Educational Review,* v. 32, #2, 1962, pp. 81–111. Quoted in Smith, 1991, p. 49.

Ericson, Jon M., James J. Murphy, and Raymond B. Zeuschner. *The Debater's Guide.* Carbondale: Southern Illinois Univ. Press, 1987.

Gogoi, Pallavi. "Thinking Outside the Cereal Box." *Business Week,* July 28, 2003, pp. 74–76.

Guzzo, Richard A. "Group Decision Making and Group Effectiveness in Organizations." In *Designing Effective Work Groups.* Ed. Paul S. Goodman. San Francisco: Jossey-Bass, 1986, pp. 34–71.

Health System. "Employee Managed Teams Glossary." 1994.

Johnson, Craig E. and Michael Z. Hackman. *Creative Communication: Principles and Applications.* Prospect Heights, IL: Waveland, 1995.

Miller, W. *The Creative Edge: Fostering Innovation Where You Work.* Boston: Addison-Wesley, 1987. Quoted in Johnson and Hackman, 1995, p. 131.

Nucifora, Alf. "So You Want to Be Creative? Try Letting Go." *Business News New Jersey,* v. 15, #3, January 14, 2002, p. 18.

Osborn, Alex F. *Applied Imagination: Principles and Procedures of Creative Thinking.* New York: Charles Scribner's Sons, 1957.

Parnes, S. J., R. B. Noller, and A. M. Biondi. *Guide to Creative Action,* rev. ed. New York: Scribner, 1977. Quoted in Johnson and Hackman, 1995, pp. 134–137.

Paul, Richard W. "Dialogical Thinking: Critical Thought Essential to the Acquisition of Rational Knowledge and Passions." In *Teaching Thinking Skills: Theory and Practice.* Eds. Joan B. Baron and Robert J. Sternberg. New York: Freeman, 1987 pp. 127–48.

Smith, Carl B. *A Commitment to Critical Thinking.* Bloomington, IN: Grayson Bernard, 1991.

Steel Roll Mill Team Presentation. Tennessee. January 27, 1994. Springfield, TN.

Thompson, Leigh. "Improving the Creativity of Organizational Work Groups." *Academy of Management Executive,* v. 17, #3, February 2003, pp. 98–99.

Toulmin, Stephen. *The Uses of Argument*. Cambridge: Cambridge University Press, 1958.

Warnick, Barbara and Edward S. Inch. *Critical Thinking and Communication*. New York: Macmillan, 1989.

Whiting, C. S. *Creative Thinking*. New York: Van Nostrand Reinhold Co., 1958.

Wolfe, Charles. "Brain Data Lets Daviess Rethink Curriculum." *Louisville (KY) Courier-Journal*, June 14, 1998, pp. B1, B5.

Ziegelmueller, George, Jack Kay, and Charles Dause. *Argumentation: Inquiry and Advocacy*, 2nd ed. Englewood Cliffs, NJ: Prentice Hall, 1990.

Chapter 6

Bales, Robert F. *Interaction Process Analysis: A Method for the Study of Small Groups*. Reading, MA: Addison-Wesley, 1950.

Brilhart, John K. and Gloria J. Galanes. *Effective Group Discussion*. Madison, WI: Brown & Benchmark, 1995.

Burningham, Caroline and Michael A. West. "Individual, Climate, and Group Interaction Processes as Predictors of Work Team Innovation." *Small Group Research*, v. 26, #1, February 1995, pp. 106–17.

Buzzanell, P. M. "Gaining a Voice: Feminist Organizational Communication Theorizing." *Management Communication Quarterly*, v. 7, 1994, pp. 339–83. Quoted in Meyers and Brashers, 1994, p. 77.

Caws, Peter. "Committees and Consensus: How Many Heads Are Better Than One." *The Journal of Medicine and Philosophy*, v. 16, 1991, pp. 375–91.

Columbia Accident Investigation Board. *Report*. Washington, DC: Government Printing Office, 2003.

Dewey, John. *How We Think*. Boston: Heath, 1910

Glassman, Edward. "Self-Directed Team Building Without a Consultant." *Supervisory Management*, v. 37, #3, March 1992, pp. 6–7.

Gouran, Dennis, Candace Brown, and David R. Henry. "Behavioral Correlates of Perceptions of Quality in Decision-Making Discussions. *Communication Monographs*, v. 45, 1978, pp. 51–63.

Gouran, Dennis S. *Making Decisions in Groups: Choices and Consequences*. Prospect Heights, IL: Waveland, 1990. (Orig. pub., 1982.)

Guzzo, Richard A. "Group Decision Making and Group Effectiveness in Organizations." In *Designing Effective Work Groups*. Ed. Paul S. Goodman. San Francisco: Jossey-Bass, 1986, pp. 34–71.

Habermas, Jurgen. *Legitimation Crisis*. Trans. Thomas McCarthy. Boston: Beacon, 1975. Quoted in Caws, 1991, p. 380.

Hall, J. and M. Watson. "The Effects of a Normative Intervention on Group Performance and Member Reactions." *Human Relations*, v. 23, 1970, pp. 299–317. Quoted in Marshall Scott Poole and Gerardine DeSanctis. "Microlevel Structuration in Computer-Supported Group Decision Making." *Human Communication Research*, v. 19, #1, September 1992, p. 26.

Kanter, Rosabeth Moss. *Commitment and Community: Communes and Utopias in Sociological Perspective*. Cambridge, MA: Harvard Univ. Press, 1972. Quoted in Meyers and Brashers, 1994, p. 77.

Meyers, Renee A. and Dale E. Brashers. "Expanding the Boundaries of Small Group Communication Research: Exploring a Feminist Perspective." *Communication Studies*, v. 45, Spring 1994, pp. 68–85.

Moreno, J. "Ethics by Committee: The Moral Authority of Consensus," *Journal of Medicine and Philosophy*, v. 13, 1988, pp. 411–32. Quoted in Caws, 1991, pp. 380–85.

Ray, Sally. *Strategic Communication in Crisis Management: Lessons from the Airline Industry*. Westport, CT: Greenwood Press, 1999.

RCM Team. Interview with the author. 1994. Bowling Green, KY.

Simon, Herbert A. *The New Science of Management Decision*. Englewood Cliffs, NJ: Prentice-Hall, 1977. Quoted in Guzzo, 1986, p. 35.

Stewart, Thomas A. "GE Keeps Those Ideas Coming." *Fortune*. August 12, 1991, pp. 41–49.

Tjosvold, D. "Effect of Approach to Controversy on Supervisors' Incorporation of Subordinates' Information in Decision Making." *Journal of Applied Psychology*, v. 67, 1982, pp. 189–93. Quoted in Burningham and West, 1995, p. 108.

Chapter 7

Ambrose, Stephen E. *Citizen Soldiers*. New York: Simon & Schuster, 1997.

Bach, George R. "Marathon Group Dynamics I: Some Functions of the Professional Group Facilitator." *Psychological Reports*, v. 20, 1967, pp. 995–99. Quoted in Catherine R. Cowell. "Group Process as Metaphor." *Journal of Communication*, v. 22, June 1972.

Barnett, Demian, Charlene McKowen, and Gary Bloom. "A School Without a Principal." *Educational Leadership*, v. 55, #7, April 1998, pp. 48–49.

Barry, David. "Managing the Bossless Team: Lesson in Distributed Leadership." *Organizational Dynamics*, v. 20, #1, Summer 1991, pp. 31–46.

Bass, Bernard M. *Leadership and Performance Beyond Expectations*. New York: Free Press, 1985. Quoted in Zorn, 1991, pp. 179–80.

Bass, Bernard M. "From Transactional to Transformational Leadership: Learning to Share the Vision." *Organizational Dynamics*, v. 18, #3, 1990, pp. 19–31.

Benne, K. D. and P. Sheats. "Functional Roles and Group Members." *Journal of Social Issues*, v. 4, 1948, pp. 41–49.

Bennis, Warren and Burt Nanus. *Leaders: The Strategies for Taking Charge*. New York: Harper & Row, 1985.

Boussel, Patrice. *D-Day Beaches Revisited*. Garden City, NY: Doubleday, 1966.

Boyle, Richard J. "Wrestling with Jellyfish." *Harvard Business Review*, v. 70, #6, November/December 1992, p. 14.

Burns, James McGregor. *Leadership*. New York: Harper & Row, 1978. Quoted in Zorn, Theodore E. "Construct System Development, Transformational Leadership and Leadership Messages." *Southern Communication Journal*, v. 56, #3, Spring 1991, p. 179.

Clinton, Bill. "50th Anniversary of D-Day." *Vital Speeches of the Day*, v. 60, July 1, 1994, pp. 546–47.

CM1C Team. "Total Self Management Plan." Kentucky, August 19, 1993.

Columbia Accident Investigation Board. *Report*. Washington, DC: Government Printing Office, 2003.

Coon, Gene L. and Carey Wilbur. "Space Seed." *Star Trek*. Produced by Gene Roddenberry and Gene L. Coon. Desilu Productions, 1966.

Edwards, Mark R. "Symbiotic Leadership: A Creative Partnership for Managing Organizational Effectiveness." *Business Horizons*, v. 35, #3, May/June 1992, pp. 28–33.

Fiedler, Frederick E. *A Theory of Leadership Effectiveness*. New York: McGraw-Hill, 1967.

Fiedler, Frederick E., M. Chemers, and L. Mahar. *Improving Leadership Effectiveness*. New York: Wiley, 1976.

French, J. R. P. and B. Raven. "The Bases of Social Power." In *Studies in Social Power*. Ed. D. Cartwright. Ann Arbor, MI: Institute for Social Research, 1959, pp. 150–67. Quoted in Kevin J. Barge. *Leadership: Communication Skills for Organizations and Groups*. New York: St. Martin's Press, 1994, p. 175.

Gemmill, Gary. "The Mythology of the Leader Role in Small Groups." *Small Group Behavior*, v. 17, #1, February 1986, pp. 41–50.

Gouran, Dennis S. *Making Decisions in Groups: Choices and Consequences*. Prospect Heights, IL: Waveland, 1990. (Orig. pub. 1982.)

Hersey, P. and K. H. Blanchard. *Management of Organizational Behavior*, 4th ed. Englewood Cliffs, NJ: Prentice-Hall, 1982.

Hill, Timothy A. "An Experimental Study of the Relationship between Opinionated Leadership and Small Group Consensus." *Communication Monographs*, v. 43, August 1976, pp. 246–57.

Holifield, Mitchell. "The Servant's Attitude: An Ethical Code for Administrators." *Educational Planning*, v. 9, #3, 1993, pp. 35–41.

Holmes, Frankie. First Sergeant. Interview with author. March 28, 1994. Parris Island, SC.

Hospital Group Team Fair. Louisville, KY. March 1994.

Maccoby, Michael. *The Leader*. New York: Ballantine Books, 1981. Quoted in Manz and Sims, 1987, p. 106.

Manz, Charles C. and Henry P. Sims, Jr. "Leading Workers to Lead Themselves: The External Leadership of Self-Managing Work Teams." *Administrative Science Quarterly*, v. 32, 1987, pp. 106–28.

Nair, Keshavan. *A Higher Standard of Leadership: Lessons From the Life of Gandhi*. San Francisco: Berrett-Koehler, 1994.

Nucifora, Alf. "So You Want to be Creative? Try Letting Go." *Business News New Jersey*, v. 15, #3, January 14, 2002, p. 18.

Piller, Michael and Jeri Taylor. "Caretaker." *Star Trek: Voyager*. United Paramount Network (UPN), 1994.

Roby, Pamela Ann. "Creating a Just World: Leadership for the Twenty-First Century." *Social Problems*, v. 45, #1, February 1998, pp. 1–20.

Sashkin, Marshall and William C. Morris. *Organizational Behavior: Concepts and Experiences*. Reston, VA: Reston Publ., 1984.

Saturn Corporation. News Release. Spring Hill, TN, September 18, 1990, p. 1.

Sims, Henry P., Jr. and Peter Lorenzi. "Self-Managing Teams." *The New Leadership Paradigm: Social Learning and Cognition in Organizations*. Eds. Sims and Lorenzi. Newbury Park: Sage, 1992, pp. 199–216.

Stamberg, Susan. "Interview with Bournemouth Symphony Orchestra Conductor Marin Alsop, Power Part I." National Public Radio, *Morning Edition*. October 7, 2003.

———. "Interview with Retired Army General Hugh Shelton, Power Part II." National Public Radio, *Morning Edition*. October 14, 2003.

———. "Interview with Linguist Deborah Tannen, Power Part III." National Public Radio, *Morning Edition*. October 21, 2003.

Star Trek, Star Trek: The Next Generation, Star Trek: Deep Space Nine, Star Trek: Voyager. Beverly Hills, CA: Paramount Pictures.

Watwood, Barry. Personnel Star Point of CM1C Team. Interview with author. March 7, 1994. Aluminum Plant, Kentucky.

White, Ralph and Ronald Lippitt. "Leader Behavior and Member Reaction in Three 'Social Climates.'" In *Group Dynamics*. Eds. D. Cartwright and A. Zander. New York: Harper & Row, 1968, pp. 318–35.

Zawacki, Robert A. and Carol A. Norman. "Self-Directed Leadership." *Computerworld*. April 1, 1991, pp. 76–79.

Zorn, Theodore E. "Leadership in Times of Change." Public Lecture. Louisville and Bowling Green, KY. April 10–11, 2003.

Chapter 8

Anderson, Leann. "Gray Matters." *Entrepreneur*, v. 26, #6, June 1998, p. 117.

Clark, Thomas. "Teaching Students to Enhance the Ecology of Small Group Meetings." *Business Communication Quarterly*, v. 61, #4, December 1998, pp. 40–50.

Coppola, Susan, Cherie A. Rosemond, Nansi Greger-Holt, Florence G. Soltys, Laura C. Hanson, Melinda A. Snider, Jan Busby-Whitehead. "Arena Assessment: Evolution of Teamwork for Frail Older Adults." *Topics in Geriatric Rehabilitation*, v. 17, #3, 2002, pp. 13–28.

Cox, Sharon. "Career Scope South Central." *Nursing Management*, v. 34, #3, March 2003, p. 58.

Dennis, A. R. and J. S. Valacich. "Computer Brainstorms: More Heads Are Better Than One." *Journal of Applied Psychology*, v. 78, 1993, pp. 531–37.

Dewey, John. *How We Think*. Boston: Heath, 1910.

Dubrovsky, V. J., S. Kiesler, and B. N. Sethna. "The Equalization Phenomenon: Status Effects in Computer-Mediated and Face-to-Face Decision-Making Groups." *Human-Computer Interactions*, v. 6, #2, 1991, pp. 119–46. Quoted in Guzzo and Dickson, 1996, p. 322.

Ephross, Paul H. and Thomas V. Vassil. *Groups That Work: Structure and Process*. New York: Columbia Univ. Press, 1988.

Gallupe, R. Brent, Alan R. Dennis, William H. Cooper, Lana M. Valacich, and Jay R. Nunamaker, Jr. "Electronic Brainstorming and Group Size." *Academy of Management Journal*, v. 35, #2, June 1992, pp. 350–70.

Gouran, Dennis S. *Making Decisions in Groups: Choices and Consequences*. Prospect Heights, IL: Waveland, 1990. (Orig. pub. 1982.)

Guzzo, Richard A. and Marcus W. Dickson. "Teams in Organizations: Recent Research on Performance and Effectiveness." *Annual Review of Psychology*, v. 47, 1996, pp. 307–39.

Hollingshead, A. B. and J. E. McGrath. "Computer-Assisted Groups: A Critical Review of the Empirical Research." In *Team Effectiveness and Decision Making in Organizations*. Eds. R. A. Guzzo and E. Sales. San Francisco: Jossey-Bass, 1995. Quoted in Guzzo and Dickson, 1996, pp. 320–23.

Johnston, Rick. "Teamwork with a Technology Twist." *Association Management*, March, 2002, p. 35.

Joinson, Carla. "Managing Virtual Teams." *HR Magazine*, v. 47, #6, June 2002, pp. 68–74. http://www.ebscohost.com.

Katzenbach, Jon R. and Douglas K. Smith. *The Discipline of Teams*. John Wiley and Sons, 2001.

Kayser, T. A. *Mining Group Gold*. El Segundo, CA: Serif, 1990. Quoted in Clark, 1998, p. 41.

Kiesler, S. and L. Sproul. "Group Decision Making and Communication Technology." *Organizational Behavior Human Decision Process*, v. 52, #1, 1992, pp. 96–123. Quoted in Guzzo and Dickson, 1996, under "Communication Patterns."

Knack, Ruth. "Brainstorming by Byte: New Electronic Tools Take Collaborative Decision Making to Greater Heights." *Planning*, v. 60, #1, January 1994, pp. 19–23.

McLeod, P. L. "An Assessment of the Experimental Literature on Electronic Support of Group Work: Results of a Meta-Analysis." *Human-Computer Interaction*, v. 7, #3, 1992, pp. 257–80.

Schrage, M. *No More Teams!* New York: Currency/Doubleday, 1995. Quoted in Clark, 1998, pp. 44–45.

Straus, S. G. and J. E. McGrath. "Does the Medium Matter: The Interaction of Task Type and Technology on Group Performance and Members' Reactions." *Journal of Applied Psychology*, v. 79, 1994, pp. 87–97. Quoted in Guzzo and Dickson, 1996, under "Shortfalls of Computer-Mediated Group Work."

Thompson, Leigh and Leo F. Brajkovich. "Improving the Creativity of Organizational Work Groups." *Academy of Management Executive*, v. 17, #1, February 2003, pp. 96–112. http://search.epnet.com/zdirect.asp?an=9474814&db=buh.

Valacich, J. S., J. F. George, J. F. Nunamaker, and D. R. Vogel. "Physical Proximity Effects on Computer-Mediated Group Idea Generation." *Small Group Research*, v. 25, #1, 1994, pp. 83–104. Quoted in Guzzo and Dickson, 1996, under "Contextual Issues."

Chapter 9

Barker, James R. "Tightening the Iron Cage: Concertive Control in Self-managing Teams." *Administrative Science Quarterly*, v. 38, #3, September 1993, pp. 408–38.

Barker, James R. and George Cheney. "The Concept and the Practices of Discipline in Contemporary Organizational Life." *Communication Monographs*, v. 60, March 1994, pp. 19–43.

Bartkus, Kenneth R., Roy D. Howell, C. R. Parent, and Cathy Hartman. "Managerial Antecedents and Individual Consequences of Group Cohesiveness in Travel Service Selling." *Journal of Travel Research*, v. 35, #4, Spring 1997, pp. 56–64. http://search.epnet.com/direct.asp?an=9708106134&db=aph.

Bass, B. M., ed. *Stogdill's Handbook of Leadership: A Survey of Theory and Research*. New York: The Free Press, 1981.

Boyle, Richard J. "Wrestling With Jellyfish." *Harvard Business Review*, v. 70, #6, November/December 1992, p. 14.

Breidenstein-Cutspec, P. and E. M. Goering. "Acknowledging Cultural Diversity: Perceptions of Shyness Within the Black Culture." *The Howard Journal of Communications*, v. 1, 1988, pp. 75–87.

———. "Exploring Cultural Diversity: A Network Analysis of the Communicative Correlates of Shyness Within the Black Culture." *Communication Research Reports*, v. 6, #1, June 1989, pp. 37–46.

Burgoon, Michael, James P. Dillard, and Noel E. Doran. "Friendly or Unfriendly Persuasion: The Effects of Violations of Expectations by Males and Females." *Human Communication Research*, v. 10, #2, Winter 1983, pp. 283–94.

Burke, Kenneth. *A Grammar of Motives*. Englewood Cliffs, NJ: Prentice-Hall, 1945.

———. *A Rhetoric of Motives*. Englewood Cliffs, NJ: Prentice-Hall, 1950.

———. *Language as Symbolic Action*. Berkeley and Los Angeles: Univ. of California Press, 1966.

Chadwick, Alex. "Employees Make Success Story of Running Steel Plant." National Public Radio. *Morning Edition*. March 23, 1994.

Chute, Rebecca D. and Earl L. Wiener. "Cockpit-Cabin Communication: I. A Tale of Two Cultures." *The International Journal of Aviation Psychology*, v. 5, #3, 1995, pp. 257–76.

———. "Cockpit-Cabin Communication: II. Shall We Tell the Pilots?" *The International Journal of Aviation Psychology*, v. 6, #3, 1996, pp. 211–31.

Crozier, W. R. "Shyness as a Dimension of Personality." *British Journal of Social and Clinical Psychology*, v. 18, 1979, pp. 121–28.

Driskell, James E. and Eduardo Salas. "Group Decision Making Under Stress." *Journal of Applied Psychology*, v. 76, #3, 1991, pp. 473–78.

Dumaine, Brian. "The Trouble With Teams." *Fortune*, v. 130, #5, September 5, 1994, pp. 86–91.

Eakins, Barbara W. and R. Gene Eakins. *Sex Differences in Human Communication*. Boston: Houghton Mifflin, 1978.

Embry, Mike. "Center Opens a New Window on Automobile Production." *Louisville (KY) Courier-Journal*, June 22, 1994, pp. E1–E2.

Glanz, James and John Schwartz. "Dogged Engineer's Effort to Assess Shuttle Damage." *New York Times*, Sept. 26, 2003. http://www.nytimes.com.

Hawkins, Katherine W. and Robert Stewart. "Temporal Effects of Leadership Style on State Communication Anxiety in Small Task-Oriented Groups." *Communication Research Reports*, v. 7, #1, 1990, pp. 3–8.

———. "Effects of Communication Apprehension on Perceptions of Leadership and Intragroup Attraction in Small Task-Oriented Groups." *Southern Communication Journal*, v. 57, #1, Fall 1991, pp. 1–10.

Infante, Dominic A. "The Argumentative Student in the Speech Communication Classroom: An Investigation and Implications." *Communication Education*, v. 31, April 1982, pp. 141–48.

Infante, Dominic A., Andrew S. Rancer, and Deanna F. Womack. *Building Communication Theory*. Prospect Heights, IL: Waveland, 1990.

Jaffe, Eugene D. and Israel D. Nebenzahl. "Group Interaction and Business Game Performance." *Simulation and Gaming*, v. 21, #2, June 1990, pp. 133–46.

Janis, I. L. "Groupthink." *Psychology Today*, November 1971, pp. 43–46, 74–76.

———. *Victims of Groupthink*. Boston: Houghton Mifflin, 1972.

———. *Groupthink*, 2nd ed. Boston: Houghton Mifflin, 1982.

Janis, I. L. and L. Mann. *Decision Making: A Psychological Analysis of Conflict, Choice, and Commitment*. New York: Free Press, 1977.

Kelly, Lynne. "A Rose by Any Other Name Is Still a Rose: A Comparative Analysis of Reticence, Communication Apprehension, Unwillingness to Communicate, and Shyness." *Human Communication Research*, v. 8, #2, Winter 1982, pp. 99–113.

King, Walter, Thomas Murray, and Bruce Blocher. "Improving Intra-crew Communications." *Airliner*, October–December 1966, pp. 20–25.

Lederman, Linda Costigan. "Suffering in Silence: The Effects of Fear of Talking on Small Group Participation." *Group and Organizational Studies*, v. 7, #3, September 1982, pp. 279–94.

Luft, Joseph. *Group Processes: An Introduction to Group Dynamics*. Palo Alto, CA: Mayfield, 1970.

McCroskey, J. C. "The Effects of Communication Apprehension on Nonverbal Behavior." *Communication Quarterly*, v. 24, 1976, pp. 39–44.

———. "Validity of the PRCA as an Index of Oral Communication Apprehension." *Communication Monographs*, v. 45, 1978, pp. 192–203.

———. "Oral Communication Apprehension: A Reconceptualization." In *Communication Yearbook*, v. 6. Ed. M. Burgoon. Beverly Hills, CA: Sage, 1982, pp. 136–79.

———. "The Communication Apprehensive Perspective." In *Avoiding Communication: Shyness, Reticence, and Communication Apprehension*. Eds. J. A. Daly and J. C. McCroskey. Beverly Hills, CA: Sage, 1984, pp. 81–94.

McCroskey, J. C., J. A. Daly, V. P. Richmond, and B.G. Cox. "The Effects of Communication Apprehension on Interpersonal Attraction." *Human Communication Research*, v. 3, 1975, pp. 67–72.

McCroskey, J. C. and V. P. Richmond. "The Effects of Communication Apprehension on the Perception of Peers." *Western Journal of Speech Communication*, v. 40, 1976, pp. 14–21.

Meyers, Renee A. and Dale Brashers. "Expanding the Boundaries of Small Group Communication Research: Exploring a Feminist Perspective." *Communication Studies*, v. 45, Spring 1994, pp. 68–85.

Moshansky, V. P. *Commission of Inquiry into the Air Ontario Crash at Dryden, Ontario.* Toronto, Canada: Minister of Supply and Services, 1992.

Nicotera, Anne M. and Andrew S. Rancer. "The Influence of Sex on Self-Perceptions and Social Stereotyping of Aggressive Communication Predispositions." *Western Journal of Communication*, v. 58, Fall 1994, pp. 283–307.

Phillips, Gerald M. "Reticence: Pathology of the Normal Speaker." *Speech Monographs*, v. 35, 1968, pp. 39–49.

Song, Kyung M. "Alliant's Teams are Forging a World Without Bosses," *Louisville (KY) Courier-Journal*, July 20, 1994, p. 10B.

Stewart, Thomas A. "GE Keeps Those Ideas Coming." *Fortune*, Aug. 12, 1991, pp. 41–49.

Tompkins, Phillip K. and George Cheney, "Communication and Unobtrusive Control in Contemporary Organizations." In *Organizational Communication: Traditional Themes and New Directions.* Eds. Robert D. McPhee and Phillip K. Tompkins. Newbury Park: Sage, 1985, pp. 179–210.

Vallas, Steven P. "Why Teamwork Fails: Obstacles to Workplace Change in Four Manufacturing Plants." *American Sociological Review*, v. 68, #2, April 2003, pp. 223–50.

Verespej, Michael A. "When You Put the Team in Charge." *Industry Week*, December 3, 1990, pp. 30–32.

Watson, David and Ronald Friend. "Measurement of Social-Evaluative Anxiety." *Journal of Consulting and Clinical Psychology*, v. 33, #4, 1969, pp. 448–57.

Webb, Gisela. "Preparing Staff for Participative Management." *Wilson Library Bulletin*, May 1988, pp. 50–52.

Zimbardo, Philip G. *Shyness.* Reading, MA: Addison-Wesley, 1977.

Zimbardo, Philip G., Paul A. Pilkonis, and Robert M. Norwood. "The Social Disease Called Shyness." *Psychology Today*, v. 8, May 1975, pp. 68–72.

Chapter 10

Bales, Robert F. *Interaction Process Analysis: A Method for the Study of Small Groups.* Cambridge, MA: Addison-Wesley, 1950.

Bales, Robert F. and Fred L. Strodtbeck. "Phases in Group Problem-Solving." *Journal of Abnormal and Social Psychology*, v. 46, 1951, pp. 485–95.

Bell, Mae Arnold. "A Research Note: The Relationship of Conflict and Linguistic Diversity in Small Groups." *Central States Speech Journal*, v. 34, Summer 1983, pp. 128–33.

Bennis, Warren G. and Herbert A. Shepard. "A Theory of Group Development." *Human Relations*, v. 9, 1956, pp. 415–37.

———. "Group Observation." In *The Planning of Change.* Eds. Warren G. Bennis, Kenneth D. Benne, and Robert Chin. New York: Holt, Rinehart, and Winston, 1961, pp. 743–56.

Blake, Robert R. and Jane S. Mouton. "Managerial Facades." *Advanced Management Journal*, July 1966, p. 31.

———. "The Fifth Achievement." *Journal of Applied Behavioral Science*, v. 6, 1970, pp. 413–18.

———. *The Managerial Grid III.* Houston: Gulf, 1985.

Bormann, Ernest G. "Symbolic Convergence: Organizational Communication and Culture." In *Communication and Organization: An Interpretive Approach.* Eds. L. L. Putnam and M. E. Pacanowsky. Beverly Hills, CA: Sage, 1983. Quoted in Putnam, Van Hoeven, and Bullis, 1991, pp. 87–88.

———. "Symbolic Convergence Theory: A Communication Formulation." *Journal of Communication*, v. 35, #4, 1985, pp. 128–38. Quoted in Putnam, Van Hoeven, and Bullis, 1991, pp. 87–88.

———. "Symbolic Convergence Theory and Communication in Group Decision-making." In *Communication and Group Decision-making*. Eds. R. Y. Hirokawa and M. S. Poole. Newbury Park, CA: Sage, 1986.

Boulding, K. "Learning Peace." In *The Quest for Peace*. Ed. Raimo Vayrynen. London: Sage, 1987.

Bower, J. L. "Group Decision-Making: A Report of an Experimental Study." *Behavioral Science*, v. 10, 1965, pp. 277–89.

Bradac, James J., Roger J. Desmond, and Johnny I. Murdock. "Diversity and Density: Lexically Determined Evaluative and Informational Consequences of Linguistic Complexity." *Communication Monographs*, v. 44, 1977, pp. 273–83. Quoted in Bell, 1983, p. 132.

Conrad, Charles. *Strategic Organizational Communication*, 2nd ed. New York: Holt, Rinehart & Winston, 1990.

Coser, L. A. *Continuities in the Study of Social Conflict*. New York: Free Press, 1967.

Crum, T. F. *The Magic of Conflict: Turning a Life of Work into a Work of Art*. New York: Touchstone Books, 1987. Quoted in McCorkle and Mills, 1992, pp. 58–59.

Deutsch, M. "Conflicts: Productive and Destructive." In *Conflict Resolution through Communication*. Ed. F. E. Jandt. New York: Harper & Row, 1973, pp. 155–97.

Dunphy, Dexter C. *Social Change in Self-Analytic Groups*. Ph.D. Dissertation. Harvard Univ., 1964.

Ellis, Donald G. and B. Aubrey Fisher. "Phases of Conflict in Small Group Development." *Human Communication Research*, v. 1, 1975, pp. 195–212. Quoted in Fisher, 1980, p. 250.

Fink, C. "Some Conceptual Difficulties in the Theory of Social Conflict." *Journal of Conflict Resolution*, v. 12, 1968, pp. 412–60.

Fisher, B. Aubrey. "Decision Emergence: Phases in Group Decision Making." *Speech Monographs*, v. 37, 1970, pp. 53–66.

———. *Small Group Decision Making*, 2nd ed. New York: McGraw-Hill, 1980.

Guetzkow, Harold and John Gyr. "An Analysis of Conflict in Decision-Making Groups." *Human Relations*, v. 7, 1954, pp. 367–82. Quoted in Knutson and Kowitz, 1977, p. 55.

Hall, Jay and W. H. Watson. "The Effects of Normative Intervention on Group Decision-Making Performance." *Human Relations*, v. 23, 1970, pp. 299–317.

Heider, Fritz. *The Psychology of Interpersonal Relations*. New York: Wiley, 1958. Quoted in Sillars, 1980, p. 218.

Hocker, Joyce L. and William W. Wilmot. *Interpersonal Conflict*, 3rd ed. Dubuque, IA: William C. Brown, 1991.

Joinson, Carla. "Managing Virtual Teams." *HR Magazine*, v. 47, #6, June 2002, pp. 68–74. http://www.ebsco.com.

Keltner, J. W. *Mediation: Toward a Civilized System of Dispute Resolution*. Annandale, VA: Speech Comm. Assn., 1987.

Knutson, Thomas J. and Albert C. Kowitz. "Effects of Information Type and Level of Orientation on Consensus-Achievement in Substantive and Affective Small-Group Conflict." *Central States Speech Journal*, v. 28, Spring, 1977, pp. 54–63.

Littlejohn, Stephen W. *Theories of Human Communication*, 4th ed. Belmont, CA: Wadsworth, 1992.

Mack, R. M. and R. C. Snyder. "The Analysis of Social Conflict:Toward an Overview and Synthesis." In *Conflict Resolution through Communication*. Ed. F. E. Jandt. New York: Harper & Row, 1973, pp. 25–87.

McCorkle, Suzanne and Janet L. Mills. "Rowboat in a Hurricane: Metaphors of Interpersonal Conflict Management." *Communication Reports*, v. 5, Summer 1992, pp. 57–66.

Merton, Robert K. *Social Theory and Social Structure*. New York: Free Press, 1957. Quoted in Fisher, 1980, p. 247.

Osgood, Charles. "Some Effects of Motivation on Style of Encoding." In *Style in Language*. Ed. Thomas Sebeok. New York: John Wiley & Sons, 1960, pp. 293–306. Quoted in Bell, 1983, p. 128.

Prentice, Daniel S. "The Effects of Trust-Destroying Communication on Verbal Fluency in the Small Group." *Speech Monographs*, v. 42, November 1975, pp. 262–70.

Putnam, L. L. and M. S. Poole. "Conflict and Negotiation." In *Handbook of Organizational Communication*. Eds. F. M. Jablin, L. L. Putnam, K. H. Roberts, and L. W. Porter. Newbury Park, CA: Sage, 1987, pp. 549–99.

Putnam, L. L., S. A. Van Hoeven, and C. A. Bullis. "The Role of Rituals and Fantasy Themes in Teachers' Bargaining." *Western Journal of Speech Communication*, v. 55, 1991, pp. 85–103.

Saturn Corporation. News Release. Spring Hill, TN, September 18, 1990.

Schmidt, S. M. and T. A. Kochan. "Conflict: Toward Conceptual Clarity." *Administrative Science Quarterly*, v. 17, 1972, pp. 359–70.

Shulman, Seth. "Thinking Like a Virus." *Technology Review*, v. 106, #6, July 2002, p. 74.

Sillars, Alan L. "The Sequential and Distributional Structure of Conflict Interaction as a Function of Attributions Concerning the Locus of Responsibility and Stability of Conflict." *Communication Yearbook*. v. 4. Ed. D. Nimmo. New Brunswick, NJ: Transaction Books, 1980, pp. 217–36.

Sillars, Alan L. *Manual for Coding Interpersonal Conflict.* Unpublished Manuscript. Department of Communication, Univ. of Montana. 1986.

Simons, H. "Persuasion in Social Conflicts: A Critique of Prevailing Conceptions and a Framework for Future Research." *Speech Monographs*, v. 39, 1972, pp. 227–47.

Stokes, Stewart L., Jr. "Moving Toward Self-Direction." *Information Systems Management*, v. 11, #1, Winter 1994, pp. 40–47.

Tannen, Deborah. "How to Turn Debate into Dialogues." *USA Weekend*, February 27–March 1, 1998, pp. 4–5.

Thomas, Kenneth. "Conflict and Conflict Management." In *Handbook of Industrial and Organizational Psychology*. Ed. Marvin Dunnett. Chicago: Rand-McNally, 1976, pp. 889–935.

Tjosvold, Dean, Chun Hui, Daniel Z. Ding, and Junchen Hu. "Conflict Values and Team Relationships: Conflict's Contribution to Team Effectiveness and Citizenship in China." *Journal of Organizational Behavior*, v. 24, #1, February 2003, pp. 69–89.

Tuckman, Bruce W. "Developmental Sequences in Small Groups." *Psychological Bulletin*, v. 63, 1965, pp. 384–99.

Weaver, Richard L., II. *Understanding Business Communication.* Englewood Cliffs, NJ: Prentice-Hall, 1984.

Zimbardo, Philip G., George F. Mahl, and James W. Barnard. "The Measurement of Speech Disturbance in Anxious Children." *Journal of Speech and Hearing Disorders*, v. 28, 1963, pp. 362–70.

Chapter 11

Aristotle. *The Rhetoric of Aristotle.* Trans. Lane Cooper. Englewood Cliffs, NJ: Prentice-Hall, 1960.

Campbell, Karlyn Kohrs. *The Rhetorical Act.* Belmont, CA: Wadsworth, 1982.

DeVito, Joseph A. *The Interpersonal Communication Book*, 5th ed. New York: Harper & Row, 1989.

Dewey, John. *How We Think.* Boston: Heath, 1910.

Hamilton, Cheryl and Cordell Parker. *Communicating for Results*, 6th ed. Belmont, CA: Wadsworth, 2001.

Hovland, C. and W. Weiss. "The Influence of Source Credibility on Communication Effectiveness." *Public Opinion Quarterly*, v. 15, 1951, pp. 635–50.

Maslow, Abraham. *Motivation and Personality.* New York: Harper & Brothers, 1954.

Monroe, Alan H. and Douglas Ehninger. *Principles of Speech Communication*, 7th ed. Glenview, IL: Scott Foresman & Co., 1975.

Partlow, Jim and Don Wynes. "Teamwork Puts a Troubled Project Back on Track: A Case Study in Relationship Building." *Information Strategy: The Executive's Journal*, Winter 2002, pp. 12–15.

Sitzmann, Marion. *Successful Business Writing.* Skokie, IL: National Textbook Company, 1983.

Smith, Raymond G. "Source Credibility Context Effects." *Speech Monographs*, v. 40, 1973, pp. 303–309.

Thomas, David A. and Maridell Fryar. *Business Communication Today.* Lincolnwood, IL: National Textbook Company, 1984.

Whitehead, Jack R. "Factors of Source Credibility." *Quarterly Journal of Speech*, v. 54, 1968, pp. 61–63.

Wilcox, Roger P. *Communication at Work: Writing and Speaking*, 3rd ed. Boston: Houghton Mifflin, 1987.

Chapter 12

Avery, Christopher M. "Individual-Based Teamwork." *T + D*, v. 56, #1, January 2002, pp. 47–50.

Barker, James R., Craig W. Melville, and Michael E. Pacanowsky. "Self-Directed Teams at Xel: Changes in Communication Practices During a Program of Cultural Transformation." *Journal of Applied Communication Research*, November 1993, pp. 297–312.

Cohen, Susan G. and Diane E. Bailey. "What Makes Teams Work: Group Effectiveness Research from the Shop Floor to the Executive Suite." *Journal of Management*, v. 23, #3, May/June 1997, pp. 239–91.

Coppola, Susan, Cherie A. Rosemond, Nansi Greger-Holt, Florence G. Soltys, Laura C. Hanson, Melinda A. Snider, and Jan Busby-Whitehead. "Arena Assessment: Evolution of Teamwork for Frail Older Adults." *Topics in Geriatric Rehabilitation*, v. 17, #3, 2002, pp. 13–28.

Dewey, John. *How We Think*. Boston: Heath, 1910.

Glover, Carol. "Variations on a Team." *People Management*, v. 8, #3, February 7, 2002, pp. 36–40.

Gouran, Dennis S. *Making Decisions in Groups, Choices and Consequences*. Prospect Heights, IL: Waveland, 1990. (Orig. pub. 1982.)

Guzzo, Richard A. and Marcus W. Dickson. "Teams in Organizations: Recent Research on Performance and Effectiveness." *Annual Review of Psychology*, v. 47, 1996, pp. 307–39.

Goodman, Paul S., Elizabeth C. Ravlin, and Marshall Schminki. "Understanding Groups in Organizations." *Research in Organizational Behavior*, v. 9, pp. 121–73.

Hackman, J. Richard, ed. *Groups That Work and Those That Don't*. San Francisco: Jossey-Bass, 1990.

Hawkins, Katherine W. and Bryant P. Fillion. "Perceived Communication Skill Needs for Work Groups." *Communication Research Reports*, v. 16, #2, Spring 1999, pp. 167–74.

Kiffin-Petersen, Sandra A. and John L. Cordery. "Trust, Individualism and Job Characteristics as Predictors of Employee Preference for Teamwork." *International Journal of Human Resource Management*, v. 14, #1, February 2003, pp. 93–117.

Larson, Carl E. and Frank M. J. LaFasto. *TeamWork: What Must Go Right; What Can Go Wrong*. Newbury Park, CA: Sage, 1989.

Mahoney, Ann I. "Senge, Covey, and Peters on Leadership Lessons." *Association Management*, v. 49, #1, January 1997, pp. 62–67.

Mattson, M., T. V. Mumford, and G. S. Sintay. "Taking Teams to Task: A Normative Model for Designing or Recalibrating Work Teams." In *Academy of Management Best Paper Proceedings*, Ed. S. J. Havlovic. 1999.

Parker, Glenn M. *Team Players and Teamwork*. San Francisco: Jossey-Bass, 1990.

Pescosolido, Anthony T. "Group Efficacy and Group Effectiveness." *Small Group Research*, v. 34, #1, February 2003, pp. 20–42.

Stevens, Michael J. and Michael A. Campion. "Staffing Work Teams: Development and Validation of a Selection Test for Teamwork Settings." *Journal of Management*, v. 25, #2, 1999, pp. 207–29.

Varney, Glenn H. *Building Productive Teams*. San Francisco: Jossey-Bass, 1989.

Index